Not by might.

A *Gospel Herald* sampler with profiles of the editors
and selected writings from 1908 to 1983

Not by might.

Daniel Hertzler, Editor

HERALD PRESS
Scottdale, Pennsylvania
Kitchener, Ontario
1983

Library of Congress Cataloging in Publication Data
Main entry under title:

Not by might.

   1. Mennonites—Doctrinal and controversial works—
Addresses, essays, lectures.   I. Hertzler, Daniel.
II. Gospel herald (Scottdale, Pa.)
BX8122.N67   1983   230'.9773   83-10831
ISBN 0-8361-3342-0 (pbk.)

Contents

Foreword 9

THE PATRIARCH *(1908-1943) by Daniel Hertzler* 13

1908—Salutatory, by Daniel Kauffman; Wasted Money, by
    Mary Ebersole; Insurance, by Amos Gingerich 20, 21
1909—Wayside Sketches in the Southland, by C. K. Hostetler 21
1910—In What Fundamentals Do Mennonites Agree? by Daniel
    Kauffman; The Present Interest, by Daniel Kauffman 23, 24
1911—Another Argument, by Daniel Kauffman;
    Prayer, by N. E. Byers 25
1912—Are You Going to School Next Year? by J. S. Hartzler;
    Keep Your Balance, by Daniel Kauffman 27, 28
1913—The General Mennonite Convention at Berne, Indiana, by
    Daniel Kauffman; Reading Her Own Obituary,
    by A. Metzler 28, 30
1914—Fifty Years Ago, by John F. Funk; The Above Letter . . ., by
    Aaron Loucks; Inseparable Twins, by Daniel Kauffman;
    The Worker's Equipment, by Geo. R. Brunk 30, 31, 32
1915—J. S. Coffman as a Personal Worker, by R. J. Heartwole
    Our School of Agriculture, by J. E. Hartzler 32, 33
1916—Funeral Customs, by Daniel Kauffman; K. Odisho, by
    J. A. Ressler; We Are One, by Daniel Kauffman 34, 35
1917—Are Mennonites Slackers? by J. E. Hartzler 36
1918—Mennonite Relief Service, by Clara Eby Steiner;
    A Conundrum Passed On, by Daniel Kauffman 37, 38
1919—Smokes, by Daniel Kauffman; Is Feet Washing an
    Ordinance for Bums? by S. S. Hammers 39
1920—The Gospel Herald, by Daniel Kauffman; First Foreign
    Missionary, by Clara E. Steiner; The Candy Habit,
    by Daniel Kauffman 40, 41
1921—Did You Ever? by Ella Zook; Moving Pictures and
    Morals, by J. A. Ressler 41, 42
1922—A Day at Our Publishing House, by W. W. Hege;
    Our Editorial Work; Then and Now, by J. N. Durr 43, 44
1923—Warren G. Harding, by Daniel Kauffman; The Quarter Fund,
    by J. E. Martin; Radio, by John W. Hess 45, 46
1924—Factionalism, by Daniel Kauffman; Why Not More
    Mennonites? by Daniel Kauffman 47

1925—Four Hundred Years, by J. A. Ressler 48
1926—A Farewell Meeting, by Willis K. Lederach; Adios, by T. K.
    Hershey; Editor's Comments, by Daniel Kauffman; Suggestions
    for the Next General Conference, by J. A. Ressler 50, 51
1927—What South America Thinks of the United States, by
    J. W. Shank; Going to the General Conference,
    by J. A. Ressler 52, 53
1928—Thoughts on the Recent Election, by Daniel Kauffman;
    The Name of Our New Minister in India, by J. A. Ressler 54, 55
1929—A Shorter Bible? by Martha Stoltzfus; Liberalism's Bid
    for the Mennonite Church, by Daniel Kauffman 56, 57
1930—Indian Music, by J. D. Graber; A Comparison, by
    Daniel Kauffman 57, 59
1931—I Have Been Wondering, by Lina Z. Ressler;
    Flag Salute in Virginia, by Henry M. Shenk 59, 61
1932—An Ideal Meeting House, by J. A. Ressler;
    How Brethren Dress, by Amanda and Luella Miller 61, 62
1933—There Are Four, by Daniel Kauffman; Nick Names,
    by Jacob H. Mellinger; Fifty Years Ago, and Now,
    by Daniel Kauffman 63, 64
1934—A Monster Is Here, by J. S. Hartzler; Christmas—As Most of Us
    Don't See It, by Luther Shetler 65, 66
1935—Recurrence of Old Fads, by S. H. Brunk; A Legend About
    Menno Simons, by John Horsch; "Moderation Leagues,"
    by Daniel Kauffman 66, 67
1936—Social Security, by Daniel Kauffman; Lo, the Poor
    Farmer, by Daniel Kauffman 69, 70
1937—The Struggle in Spain, by Daniel Kauffman;
    Bump the Seventy-Year-Olds Aside, by D. D. Miller 70, 71
1938—Forty-Eight Years in the Mennonite Church, by Daniel Kauffman;
    Marks of an Ideal Church Paper, by Daniel Kauffman 72, 73
1939—Insurance, by Daniel Kauffman; Question Drawer, answered
    by C. K. Lehman; A Question of Human Rights,
    by Daniel Kauffman 74, 75
1940—Let Us Suppose, by Daniel Kauffman;
    The 1940 World's Fair, by George R. Smoker 75, 76
1941—Christian Snake Stories, by H. N. Troyer; Prophecy,
    by George R. Smoker 77, 78
1942—What Will You Do About No Tires and Gas Rationing?
    by C. F. Yake; What Does the World Think of Mennonites?
    by Beulah W. Weber 79, 80
1943—Reflections After the 1943 Evangelistic Meetings at Goshen
    College, by C. F. Derstine; Mennonite Men in the Army?
    by H. S. Bender; "Fare Ye Well," by Daniel Kauffman 81, 83, 84

THE PROFESSOR *(1944-1962) by Daniel Hertzler* 87

1944—Nonconformity, by Paul Erb; Parental
    Delinquency, by Paul Erb 92
1945—The Christian-Scholar, by Paul Erb; An Unusual
    Incident, by George J. Lapp 93, 94
1946—Looking Toward Death, by Paul Erb;
    Concerning Chenaniah, by Milford R. Hertzler 95, 96
1947—House Wrecking, by Paul Erb; Using Criticism, by Paul Erb 97, 98
1948—Fogy, by M. T. Brackbill 98
1949—What's Your Hurry? by Paul Erb; The Shepherd Psalm,
    by Edna Beiler; Toggenburg Goats and New Hampshire
    Chickens, by Ford Berg 100, 101
1950—The House by the Side of the Road, by Paul and Alta Erb;
    The Korean War, by Paul Erb 101, 103
1951—On Marriage Customs, by John A. Hostetler; Not
    by Might, by Paul Erb 104, 105
1952—Interracial Marriage, by Paul Erb 106
1953—Listening to Others, by Paul Erb; Word of You, by Helen Alderfer;
    When the State Is God, by John Howard Yoder 107, 108
1954—Of Ranchers, Thieves, and the Graveyard Shift, by
    Theodore Wentland; Christian Humanism, by Paul Erb 109, 111
1955—From Skepticism to Christ, by Harold Fly; The Hydrogen Bomb
    and Our Peace Testimony, by Sanford G. Shetler 112, 113
1956—Can You Become a Bible Scholar? by Alta Yoder Bauman 114
1957—A Loaf of Bread, by Rosanna Yoder Hostetler; What Address?
    by Paul Erb 116
1958—In Conclusion, by Glen M. Sell; The New Lunacy,
    by Paul Erb 117, 118
1959—Feed the Flock of God, by Chester S. Martin; If They
    Strike You, by J. Paul Sauder 119, 120
1960—Questions of Social Concern for Christians, by Guy F.
    Hershberger; That Pocketbook Nerve, by Boyd Nelson 121, 122
1961—I Chose to Be a Preacher, by Richard J. Yordy; Seething
    with Apathy, by Paul Erb; We Can't Go Back, Paul Erb 123, 125, 126

THE PREACHER *(1962-1973) by John M. Drescher* 129

1962—The Value of Involvement, by Elizabeth Showalter; Missions,
    but . . . by John M. Drescher; Never Go Back,
    by Lorie C. Gooding 133, 134
1963—At Such a Time, by John M. Drescher; On Clocks
    and Worship, by Charles B. Longenecker; Matthew 6:25-33,
    by Robert J. Baker 135, 136
1964—Fruitful Leisure, by John M. Drescher; Challenging God,

by John M. Drescher 136, 137

1965—The Prayers of Luke Warm, by John M. Drescher; Dear God,
by Luke Warm; Wind of Winter, by Lorie C. Gooding 138

1966—What Does the Church Say? by Nelson E. Kauffman 139

1967—In the 200 Block, by J. Paul Sauder; Truth or Treason?
by Robert Hartzler 140, 142

1968—Master Missionary: Milton Vogt, by Paul G. Kniss 142

1969—The Rich Experience, by Robert J. Baker 145

1970—Women, Equality, and the Church, by Dorothy Swartzentruber;
Tongues—Sign of the Spirit? by John M. Drescher.................147, 148

1971—Seth's Korner, by Brother Seth; The Morning Sermon,
by Ellrose Zook 149, 150

1972—Delivered by God: Brazil's German Mennonites, by
R. Herbert Minnich 150

1973—Bombing, Law and Order, and the Press, by John M. Drescher;
Responses by Howard J. Zehr, Mrs. Ralph Ulrich, John K.
Stoner, B. F. Weber; Surprised Both Ways, by John M. Drescher;
Hooked on Hair, by John M. Drescher 152, 153, 154

THE PRESENT STAFF (1973-) by Dave Graybill 157

1974—Send Us an Apostle, by James M. Lapp; To Aaron
Decter and Max Schenk, by Daniel Hertzler 161, 162

1975—On Passing the Age of 50, by Daniel Hertzler;
Not Liberated and I Love It, by Cena King 164, 165

1976—To Hans Herr, by Daniel Hertzler; What Makes Church
News? by David E. Hostetler.................................166, 167

1977—The Mennonite Dream, by David Augsburger........................168

1978—We Decided to Forgive Them, by Simon Schrock; The
Man Who Started Packing, by Daniel Hertzler 170, 172

1979—A Love-Hate Affair with the Automobile, by Daniel Hertzler;
It Does Matter How You Earn and Spend Your Money, by
José M. Ortiz 173, 174

1980—The Radicals, by J. Daniel Hess;
Foolishness? by David E. Hostetler............................175, 176

1981—Don't Ever Give to Beggars, by Jonathan G. Yoder; My Personal
Journey Through the Mennonite Church, by Anne Allen 177, 178

1982—The Day I Went Public with My Faith, by Martin W. Lehman;
To the Old Mennonites from a New One, by Timothy E. Rapson 180, 182

1983—GH—75 in 83, by Daniel Hertzler; To Live by Love, Not Die
by Fear, by Lynn A. Miller 184, 185

Afterword 187
Partial List of Authors 188
The Editor 191

Foreword

Editors, like Paul's Athenians in Acts 17 are typically concerned "to tell, or to hear some new thing." Accordingly, editors are continually looking ahead. When an issue of our publication appears, we stop to consider it, but at the same time three or four or more issues may already be in various stages of planning or process. We have to look ahead or we will get run over, as it were, by the movement of history.

But once in awhile it is appropriate to look back and the passing of a significant milestone seems as good a time as any. So as *Gospel Herald* approached the age of 75, we gave thought to how to celebrate this anniversary.

Two ideas came to mind and both are being followed. The first was to publish a special 75th anniversary issue of the *Gospel Herald*. This appeared on April 5, 1983. The second idea was to prepare a 75th anniversary volume and this is it. (Typical Mennonite supererogation, no doubt, but so it is.)

It was decided that the book would contain two things: (1) profiles on the editors and (2) selections of published materials from the past. This is what we have. I wrote the chapters on the first two editors with the help of two researchers. John Drescher was invited to write a comment on his own experience as editor and Dave Graybill has reported on the current staff.

The process of selecting material from each year for reprint was a little more complex. First I surveyed the back volumes year by year and noted those items which seemed to have more than average significance. This first survey took from one to two hours per yearly volume and yielded as many as 30 or more editorials or articles for a given year. Next I went through again and pared down the list to about 15 per year. These were shared with a panel of judges who were asked to select up to five per year. After this was done I made final selections, using the votes of the judges, but also in some cases ignoring them.

The basic criterion in making the final selections was perceived "significance." It is my judgment that each of these editorials or articles in some respect speaks for the Mennonite Church in a specific era.

It is not intended that these materials should be fully representative. This is impossible for such brief selections. Rather it is hoped that they may give a sense of flavor, a few quick snapshots of life and convictions at these times. (The headings, spelling, capitalization, and punctuation of the original articles are largely retained as they originally appeared.) Because one of our implicit criteria in making the selections was colorful writing, we passed over many items which were important in their time and even have historical significance, but which really do not seem very interesting after the passage of time. Another constriction in the selection process was a bias toward short articles. Some worthwhile longer items were simply passed over because of their length.

In attempting to carry through a project of this kind one is always reminded of how much help is required to accomplish the task. At this point it seems appropriate to acknowledge the help of the following: Dennis Hertzler and John Sharp as researchers; Helen Alderfer, Ben Cutrell, David E. Hostetler, Richard A. Kauffman, and J. Lorne Peachey who assisted in the selection of material for inclusion; Joyce Millslagle and Elva Yoder who carried out the reproduction of materials from the past issues.

The title for this book comes from Zechariah 4:6b: "Not by might, nor by power, but by my spirit, saith the Lord of hosts." It came to me first as a commentary on the frailty of the Mennonite Church—who are we among so many?—and the comparative frailty of writing and printing as a way of making a difference. But it occurred to me also that Daniel Kauffman and those who worked with him and followed him would have considered this an appropriate theme in line with our Mennonite emphasis on peace.

Then I discovered that Paul Erb had editorialized on this text on March 13, 1951, in which he included a few references to movements which came from small or obscure beginnings: "The Great Messiah was a peasant of Galilee. An obscure monk at Wittenberg sounded the note of the Reformation. A persecuted little group of Anabaptists brought into being the modern world separation of church and state. The Publishing House in which we write this editorial has grown in a few years from an attic press in a house down the street." This editorial is included in the material from 1951.

To allow for the inclusion of more items I have shortened some of the selections. As an editor I regularly shorten articles and even cut my editorials. In this case, of course, I have shortened already published items. So in some cases you will find that the selection in the book is shorter than the original article. (Omissions are usually indicated with ellipses.)

Editorials in the *Herald* were generally unsigned in the early days. It can be assumed that most were written by Daniel Kauffman, but some may have been done at times by associates. Occasionally an editorial writer is identified by an initial and eventually Paul Erb and then John Drescher followed this practice. The current editors include their names. This may be a sign of vanity, but at least it should be a help to historians in the future.

So here you have it. I hope this book will give you a sense of a church that has taken itself seriously and still does, even though there have been changes in cultural practices that would make it difficult for Daniel Kauffman to feel at home today.

It is still our hope that as Daniel Kauffman wrote in the first issue, "God may own and bless the work to his glory."

—Daniel Hertzler
March 2, 1983

1908-1943

THE PATRIARCH

The photo was taken by David S. Harnly as arranged by Ellrose Zook who recalls, "I discovered we had no good picture of Daniel Kauffman ... DK and I had a very good rapport and I did some helpful things for him and his family while he was sick. So one day I approached him and he finally consented."

1908-1943

Daniel Kauffman

The Patriarch

He came into the Mt. Zion Mennonite Church one night in October 1890, a widower in his mid-twenties. According to his own testimony, Daniel Kauffman was converted in a revival meeting held in Versailles, Missouri, by Mennonite revivalist and editor John S. Coffman. It was the last night of the three-week meetings, the last verse of the last song.

Daniel Kauffman had grown up in the home of a Mennonite bishop, but had turned away from the church. He moved into politics, and was now the superintendent of schools in Morgan County, Missouri. It is understood that he was on the way to bigger things. In November 1890 he was defeated at the polls in a contest for circuit clerk and recorder of Morgan County. In the same month he was baptized into the Mennonite Church. For him it was a parting of the ways. Within two years he was a minister, in another four he was a bishop, and in less than a decade he had published a book. In 15 years he was editor of *Gospel Witness*, a weekly journal begun as a direct competitor to *Herald of Truth*, the unofficial magazine which had served the Mennonite Church for 40 years. In another three years the two were merged into *Gospel Herald* and Daniel Kauffman was the editor, a post he would hold for more than 35 years.

What manner of man was this Daniel Kauffman? There is a persistent myth that he was an autocrat, ruling the Mennonite Church from his seat in the editor's chair and his influence on 22 committees. The myth is no doubt supported by the classic "old curmudgeon" photo of him which is generally brought forth when a photo is needed. The evidence from my brief investigation does not support the myth. The Daniel Kauffman found in the sources is a man of consensus, a man who labored to bring divergent parties together. He is almost universally remembered as a nice man. °

Ruth Ressler, whose father J. A. Ressler was a longtime associate editor with Kauffman, recalled that "Uncle Dan was jovial and kindly. He loved children. Children loved him, and he could take any baby in the congregation after church. He had an infectious chuckle that broke down formality."

A. J. Metzler, whose career at Mennonite Publishing House overlapped with Kauffman for nearly a decade, said, "He was the most humble and objective man that it was ever my privilege to work with. He could get a nasty letter from someone today and tomorrow if that man's name came up he would be the first to vote for him." J. C. Wenger remembers him as "judicious, kind, gracious, and optimistic."

Kauffman's lack of pretention was further documented by Homer North, former pastor of the North Main Street Mennonite Church in Nappanee, Indiana, who remembered following a car into the grounds of the Mennonite General Conference at Turner, Oregon, in 1937: "The car was loaded. And I could see Brother Kauffman in the trunk with the lid open and he was going to the conference that way."

But Daniel Kauffman lived with purpose. This purpose is summed up in his recollection of the night when he was converted: "I came forward and gave my hand to the evangelist and my heart to the Lord. I had counted the cost and decided to live for eternity and not for the glory of this world." In addition he decided after some struggle to join the Mennonite Church because "I could not get away from the thought that the unpopular ordinances and restrictions (which most churches either reject or ignore) have a place in the Word of God, and that having yielded myself to Him I cannot do otherwise than to yield myself in full obedience to 'all things whatsoever' our Lord commanded His people to do" (*Fifty Years in the Mennonite Church*, p. 3).

If humility and politeness were his lifestyle, they were not ends in themselves. As one reviews his correspondence and published material, one observes that the purpose guided all he did and that his devotion to his convictions maintained an even keel throughout. He was destined to serve in a creative but troubled period of the Mennonite Church and at times he found himself in the center between strong-minded opponents on the left and right.

Daniel Kauffman's approach to truth has been characterized as "nonhistorical." A glance at his first book, *Manual of Bible Doctrines*, published by John Funk's Mennonite Publishing Company in 1898 tends to support this observation. The topics are developed as one can imagine a schoolteacher might teach a course in health: simply and directly. There appears to be little concern for the backgrounds of the Bible texts. Kauffman, like many other Mennonite leaders of this era, began his adult life as a

---

°In preparation for this chapter, I have reviewed the Kauffman correspondence in the Mennonite Archives; a biography, *The Life and Times of Daniel Kauffman*, written by his daughter Alice K. Gingerich; and a research paper, "Let Us Go On: Daniel Kauffman's Struggle to Maintain Unity in the Mennonite Church," by John F. Lapp, which is filed in the Mennonite Historical Library at Goshen College. I have also contacted a number of persons who knew him personally.

schoolteacher. The evidence from his reception in the church and the sale of his books is that Daniel Kauffman knew how to communicate.

As I reflected on the issues discussed in the correspondence file, I got the impression that the years of Daniel Kauffman's editorship might be measured off by decades. The first, from 1908 to 1918, I would label the decade of consensus. The second, from 1918 to 1928, appears to have been a troubled period. The third, from 1928 to 1938 seems more peaceful, a plateau period when the editor was still active, but denominational leadership was shared more and more with emerging younger men.

After 1938 it appears he required considerable editorial assistance and during a major part of his last year, he edited from his daughter Alice Gingerich's home in Parnell, Iowa. He was replaced as editor and designated as editor emeritus with the first issue of 1944, but died before it reached him.

Between 1908 when the *Gospel Herald* began and the date of his death on January 6, 1944, the membership of the Mennonite Church had increased from roughly 30,000 to nearly 60,000. Surely he had something to do with it.

The beginning of the *Herald* in 1908 was tied up with a flurry of activity involving the organization of Mennonite Publication Board and negotiation for a group of publications owned by John F. Funk's Mennonite Publishing Company in Elkhart, Indiana. The name *Gospel Herald* came from the first word of *Gospel Witness,* which Kauffman had edited for three years, and *Herald of Truth,* which Funk had edited for more than 40 years. According to the Publication Board minutes, the name was chosen almost by default. "The Committee for selecting a name for the new church paper reported in favor of *Gospel Herald.* But under present conditions it was not fully decided that this name could be accepted by the Board; but for convenience sake it was allowed to stand on condition that no better name can be found by the time the first number of the paper is issued."

There is little correspondence in the Kauffman file for this first decade which related to the *Gospel Herald.* But Kauffman was chairman of the Publishing Committee which approved books for publication and this activity suggests the extent of this early frail concensus. J. E. Hartzler, who was to become president of Goshen College in 1913, a Mennonite minister and evangelist who had studied at Union Seminary in New York, and who was later to lose his place in the group, was a member of the fraternity in those early days.

Hartzler offered a book manuscript "Paths to Perdition" for publication and it made the rounds. In March 1910, D. H. Bender wrote, "I believe his position is safe, but his language is not beyond question. This can be handled by careful editing." Lewis J. Heatwole gave it my "hearty recommendation." D. J. Johns had the impression "the book should have a wide circulation." I. R. Detwiler considered the book "very good for its kind." S. G. Shetler predicted "that it will be a very good book for our people as well as others." But George R. Brunk held that "there is much good in it—some unwise and considerable that I look on as being dangerous." *Paths to Perdition* was published by Mennonite Publishing House in 1910 with an introduction written by Daniel Kauffman.

A major project during the period was the publishing of a book of doctrine. Kauffman's earlier *Manual of Bible Doctrines* was written, he had stated in the preface, because "When I started out in the Christian service, I tried to secure a book of this kind, and found, after diligent research, that it was not to be had." On page 272 (the last) he wrote, "The reader will observe that many of the doctrines presented here are treated somewhat briefly."

The next book was to correct this problem. It ran to 701 pages and although Kauffman was the editor, it was directed by a 10-member committee appointed by Mennonite General Conference. Some 15 writers contributed to the volume.

But all was not completely at ease in this Eden. The signs of trouble to come were in the wind. J. E. Hartzler could not support the emphasis on distinctive clothing which Kauffman espoused. On January 18, 1912, he wrote, "The more I study over the matter of attempting to adopt some uniform by which we as Mennonites may hold our identity the less I favor it. Modesty of apparel is the only scriptural rule." Whether or not Kauffman replied is not clear from the file, but on September 10, 1915, he wrote to J. S. Hartzler (no relation to J. E.) who was a Bible teacher at Goshen College and treasurer of Mennonite Board of Education: "During the past year I have refused sanction to a number of anti-Goshen College plans, until the confidence of some of my nearest friends has been shaken."

In 1918 the Goshen Hartzlers both lost their positions. J. E. had published a cheerful sounding article in the *Herald* on November 29, 1917, in which he acknowledged that "the problems arising in the educational work of the church, as in mission work, have been many and more or less perplexing. . . .

"Our two great problems are religious and financial. If our committees and all concerned can work constructively in these two fields, we can certainly accomplish the purpose for which the institution was founded. We appreciate the efforts and work of our brethren. Our church is standing on the threshold of a great opportunity" (p. 642).

Only a little more than three months later, an editorial note in the March 7, 1918, issue reported cryptically that George J. Lapp was appointed president of Goshen College and S. F. Ebersole treasurer of the Board of Education. Also that a committee was appointed to 'draft a new Constitution and By-Laws on a conservative basis."

Now the Goshen troubles began in earnest. J. E. Hartzler departed for the General Conference Mennonite Church, a haven for a number of Mennonite leaders from this era who found themselves out of favor with their own denomination. He was eventually to become a teacher at Hartford (Conn.) Theological Seminary. J. S. Hartzler came to Scottdale for a time.

George R. Brunk put out a letter to J. B. Smith, A. D. Wenger, and Daniel Kauffman in which he worried about continual liberal influence at Goshen and the problem of Scottdale becoming "Goshenized." He concluded that "I honor Bro. K for the able work he has done for the church. I love him . . . but I can no longer cooperate with him in his weak and ineffectual policies. . . ."

For the next several years Goshen went through presidents at the rate of about one a year and finally Kauffman was persuaded to become president with the 1922-23 school year. He continued as editor of the *Herald* and evidently wrote the editorials, but it is likely that most of the publication's work was done by other staff members. His work as president was not effective and the college was closed at the end of the 1923 school year. John F. Lapp observes that he was neither trained for nor familiar with this kind of work and was not able to rally the faculty and students or to raise funds.

There were other troubles in the twenties. At the beginning of the decade there were accusations that Mennonite relief workers in France were not conducting themselves in a proper manner and Kauffman as a member of the administrative committee needed to try to answer. In 1924, a rival magazine appeared, *The Christian Exponent*, fueled in part by concerns of the young relief workers and of persons who had been forced out or withdrew from Goshen College. Indeed Vernon Smucker, editor of *The Christian Monitor*, a monthly publication of Mennonite Publishing House, resigned to become the first editor.

Two other publications appeared at the end of this second decade. One was *The Mennonite Quarterly Review*, a scholarly historical journal edited by H. S. Bender, an able and ambitious young faculty member at the reopened Goshen College. The other was the *Sword and Trumpet* edited by George R. Brunk, and, according to the introduction, "born . . . of the conscientious convictions that there is a need and call for a Mennonite paper **specializing** against the religious drift in general and the evils which promote it in particular."

But there were compensations, too, among them the opportunity to edit yet one more doctrine book, *Doctrines of the Bible*, published in 1928. It has sold close to 30,000 copies and is available yet today from Herald Press. Paul Bender remembers that it "was considered definitive for Mennonite doctrine at that time and for some time following." Like the 1914 book, it was done by authorization of Mennonite General Conference. It was not considered a revision, although Kauffman acknowledged in the introduction that he had made extensive use of material from the earlier book. Some of the same writers appeared, but not, we observe, J. E. Hartzler who had written a whole section in the 1914 book.

There was also the 400th anniversary of Anabaptism, but Kauffman seems not to have taken much note of it, at least in the pages of *Gospel Herald*. However, the *Herald* was not completely bereft of Mennonite history, for John Horsch was a Mennonite scholar who wrote regularly for the *Herald*. Also there is a brief report in a 1925 issue of the *Herald* from J. A. Ressler who was at that time a missionary to India. He told of how he and his wife had a picnic with some General Conference Mennonite missionaries as a celebration of the anniversary.

As a percentage of the membership, the circulation of the *Gospel Herald* peaked at 35 percent in 1923, then began to decline. Today it is 21 percent of the North American membership, the same as it was in 1935.

In 1930 John F. Funk died at the age of 95 and Daniel Kauffman turned 65, an age when many today might expect to slow down. But not Daniel Kauffman. In 1931, he preached his second conference sermon for the biennial Mennonite General Conference, held that year at Archbold, Ohio.

His text was Hebrews 6:1, "Let us go on," and he applied it on several levels: to the General Conference, to the church, to individuals. His fourth and final point was "what it means to go on" and here he made six observations. The fifth was "It means a blessed fellowship." He acknowledged that members of the Mennonite Church were tempted to quarrel with each other when they should be fighting a common foe and listed some of the areas of potential disagreement. But he challenged this assembly with these words: "In the fellowship of God and of saints, united in THE faith and Spirit, let us labor together in love, let our prayers and our tears flow together, let our prayers ascend to the end that not one among us may be lost, praying and hoping and working to the end that full Gospel standards may be maintained in all of our conferences, and that this blessed fellowship may be maintained to the end of the age."

But in this period too there was controversy. An example is an exchange generated over the reprint of an article "The Situation in American Mennonitism" from *Sword and Trumpet*. It was written by Noah Mack of Lancaster County, Pennsylvania, and published by recommendation of an official group in the East. Silvanus Yoder of Goshen, Indiana, complained in a letter of January 1, 1931, "The outstanding impression which I received as I read it was the idea that Goshen College was arrayed with the enemies of God in plotting the church's overthrow. To me this appears as a most crucial stab."

Kauffman replied on January 3 that the article had not been inserted hastily and that it was a broader critique than Yoder held. He indicated that he would likely publish an article on the other side and consider the affair ended.

The thirties brought the Great Depression when according to an oral tradition, craft and clerical workers at Mennonite Publishing House worked less than full time in order to share the work. What editors did about this is not reported, but since they were evidently all traveling churchmen, they may well have simply taken more speaking engagements. Kauffman continued throughout the thirties as a strong committee member. It was as if it did not seem right to attempt to operate a major denominational committee without him. Lapp observes that he had almost to resort to subterfuge to get some relief.

Toward the end of the decade, he had the service of an office editor, George R. Smoker, who remembers him for his concern about consistency even to fine details such as choosing "Mennonite" postage stamps and avoiding the patronage of a public eating place that served alcoholic beverages. Smoker also takes credit for introducing a column of letters to the editor, labeled "Open Forum," while Kauffman was ill and out of the office. It made him get well pretty fast, recalls Smoker. Indeed, this column seems to have appeared only twice: July 31 and August 21, 1941.

Though most of my contacts were positive in their evaluation of Kauffman, J. J. Hostetler injected a minor note. He reports that "my first official contact was in 1938 while visiting Mennonite Publishing House on some church business activities. He

[Kauffman] seemed to have been a little irritated over the fact that I had a crease in my hat. Following that visit he editorialized in the *Gospel Herald* that clothing should conform to the body and if you have a dent in your head then by all means you would have a dent in your hat." The editorial appeared on October 13, 1938, p. 601.

The most thoughtful and comprehensive evaluation of Kauffman was given by his successor, Paul Erb. "I hate to think what could have happened to the Mennonite Church in those years if he or some other strong man hadn't come along," said Erb. "There were plenty of smaller men who could have driven the church into some very extreme positions.

"His books, particularly *Doctrines of the Bible*, became the standard of the church for many years. Lots of young preachers prepared doctrinal sermons by reading Daniel Kauffman. And he said it pretty well although he was not a profound theologian. He was not a profound man. He was a practical man, but he had a thought through position. He was in a sense the most literary man that we've ever had. He was always getting something down in print and he felt he had to do this. He was not a stylist. His was a prosaic, workhorse style, but it's very fortunate we had that kind of man who would write even though he wrote too much.*

"He was also an organization man. The General Conference came to be what it was for many years through his leadership. The statistics will show how often he was moderator and how often he preached the conference sermon. [According to *Mennonite Yearbook*, he was moderator four times and preached the conference sermon twice.] He was the easy and natural choice for any organizational leadership."

His grandson Daniel remembers his funeral in 1944. "I had never seen so many ministers and churchmen together at one time. It was the first time I was aware that my grandfather was an influential person in the church. His words, his stories, his letters all began to fall into place for me."

Ellrose Zook, whose service at Mennonite Publishing House overlapped with Kauffman's for more than a dozen years, believes we should assess his contribution in "the time frame" in which he lived. George Smoker concludes that Kauffman was "God's man for the Mennonite Church in his time. We shall not see his likes again."

The selections from his editorials and from feature articles which follow in this first section of reprinted materials will illustrate the breadth of his interests as an editorial writer and the nature of the issues which surfaced in the *Gospel Herald* during the more than 35 years when he was editor.

—*Daniel Hertzler*

---

*At the beginning of his autobiography, *Fifty Years in the Mennonite Church* (1941), there is a list of 20 books which he either wrote, edited, or coauthored.

1908

The first editorial and two of many practical, specific warnings against taking for granted what other people do.

Salutatory

First, a greeting of love to all in the name of Jesus. In sending forth the first number of the Gospel Herald we do so with the prayer that God may own and bless the work to His glory. Long may it live as a witness of the truth, a defender of the faith, a servant of the church, and a messenger of good-will to all people.

It shall be the aim of the Gospel Herald to defend and promulgate the doctrines of the Bible and of the Mennonite Church; to labor for the promotion of love, unity, peace, piety and purity in the home and in the church; to encourage the spreading of the Gospel by means of pure literature, mission work, and evangelistic efforts; to serve as a medium through which the whole brotherhood may keep informed as to the condition, work and progress of the church; to stand by and encourage all efforts put forth for the upbuilding of the cause and the salvation of the lost, whether such efforts are by individuals or institutions.

The Gospel Herald being devoted exclusively to the cause of Christ, no paid advertisements will be admitted to its columns. With the good-will and loyal support of our brethren we hope soon to see the paper self-sustaining.

We invite your careful consideration of the contents and scope of the paper. If you are in harmony with the principles for which it stands, we will appreciate your hearty cooperation.

Wishing you the choicest blessings of God, and with a fervent prayer for divine guidance, we send forth, in the name of Christ and the church, this first issue of the Gospel Herald.

—*Daniel Kauffman*

Wasted Money

by Mary Ebersole

"And whatsoever ye do, do it heartily, as to the Lord, and not unto men."—Col. 3:23.

We, as a Mennonite people, are professing to be a plain people, but I see we are getting far from being plain, far from doing all things to the glory of God. Our people are conforming to this world more and more, wasting a great amount of God's money, which might be given to save souls who are on the downward road to destruction. God is grieved to see His children spend money for things that are absolutely unnecessary. We can live neat and comfortable without being conformed to this world. We are to be a peculiar people and to keep ourselves unspotted from the world.

Dear brothers and sisters, are we free from these spots of the world? Would we wear neckties if the world didn't? Would we have a lot of fancy rings about our horses if the world didn't? Would our brethren wear such stylish hats if the world didn't? Would our sisters carry watches if the world didn't? Would we have lace curtains and musical instruments in our houses if the world didn't? Would we have our pictures taken if the world didn't? Could we keep warm without collarettes if the world did? We might mention a hundred more things, but this is enough to test ourselves whether we would do as we are doing if the world wouldn't.

Some people say it would be all right to take our pictures if we do not do it too often. Would those same people think it would be all right to take a drink of liquor if we wouldn't drink too often? Where would we draw the line? How often can we take pictures and not do wrong? How many dollars can we waste until it becomes sin to us? "Whether therefore ye eat, or drink, or whatsoever ye do, do all to the glory of God." Do we take our pictures heartily as unto the Lord and not unto men?

Some say there is nothing the matter with knowing the time, therefore it is all right for the sisters to carry watches. Any unnecessary thing is wrong, whether it is made of wood or of gold. How can we waste our money for unnecessary things when there are poor heathens who are suffering? Would we treat our own children that way? Then why not help other children to glory?

Protection, Kans.

Insurance

by Amos Gingerich

Insurance has become a common thing among the brotherhood in some places that it seems almost useless to say anything against it. We also hear very little said against it. Some ministers have their property insured and many that have not hardly dare raise a voice against it. Our church houses are sometimes insured. A person that does not insure is apt to be looked upon as ignorant, negligent, close or foolish....

Below we give a few reasons why we do not insure our property, with the hope that it might be helpful to someone who may be considering this problem.

1. We believe in one, loving, all-wise, and all-powerful God, the real Creator and owner of all visible things, without whom not even a sparrow shall fall to the ground (Matt. 10:29).

2. All that we have the Lord has given to us to use for a short time to His glory. When we realize that He can take it away any time at His will it helps us to feel our dependence upon Him more....

3. We want to use these things only to the best advantage for us and our fellowmen. When we realize our dependence upon our Heavenly Father, we will be more grateful for what He has given us, more careful and prayerful in the use of the same and more liberal in giving a portion of it for the advancement of His cause as He leads.

4. We know that our God is able to control the wind, the fire, the lightning, the heat, the moisture, the frost, the hail, the flood, everything. Then if He withholds the heat and moisture necessary for the earth to produce, or, if He allows something to destroy it before it is harvested, or after it is garnered, when we have done what we could to care for and

protect that which He has intrusted to us, then we want to humbly submit to Him because He knows what is best for us.

5. Insuring property is neither caring for nor protecting that property. Oftentimes it proves to be the very reverse. Thousands of dollars worth of property are destroyed annually which would not be destroyed if insurance had never been known....

6. If we insured our house, we would want the barn insured also, having house and barn insured we would not feel safe without carrying insurance on the contents, then the stock, the crops, etc. We would hardly know when to stop....

7. We believe life insurance wrong—it leads to great evil, perhaps, more directly than property insurance. But when we have our house, barn, crop, and stock insured, why not insure ourselves? There may be some reason but almost every argument in favor of one may be used in favor of the other....

8. We believe insurance has a tendency to make people worldly and forgetful of their God. There would be less extravagance and waste of money on buildings among our people if there were no insurance.

Kalona, Iowa.

1909

Wayside Sketches in the Southland

by C. K. Hostetler

The race problem will never be solved completely. When one side of it gets quiet, another issue steps forth and awaits adjustment. It is not the same problem that it was in 1865. A new generation is trying to settle it in its own new way. No oil of legislation can prevent social and economic friction. Precedents and established customs do not hold. Brute force, as a last resource, is the poorest weapon of all.

People who live in the North can not get a correct view of it, much less offer a practical remedy.

George William Curtis, in a recent article in the Chicago Record Herald, gave a very clear statement of conditions in the Southland and some very good reasons why the South has not developed more rapidly. In my estimation he did not place enough emphasis on the fact that two races have wasted enough energy in elbowing each other, to develop the agricultural resources of the South.

There is no place in the Southland where the colored man and the white man can meet, talk things over, and reach an understanding. The school, the church, social customs, the civil courts, all stand against recognizing any common ground anywhere on the face of the earth, and cases are recorded where the bones of a colored man were not allowed to rest in a white man's cemetery but were disinterred and removed to a burial ground for colored people.

The better class of negroes, under the leadership of men like Booker T. Washington, are making a heroic effort to elevate their race. Wonderful strides are being made, and more wonderful ones will be necessary in the future to accomplish what ought to be done. Their schools are making a splendid showing. Their annual graduating exercises are a great treat, and show rare talent. They have many warm friends among the whites, and some beautiful bouquets are handed across the color line, but they are the exception.

A few days ago I attended a mass meeting which was held in Birmingham in the interests of negro education. Among the speakers on the program were college presidents, federal judges, bank presidents, bishops and missionaries. The speakers were representative men of both races. The talks were helpful, practical, splendid. I have never heard any that were better anywhere. The music was furnished by choruses of colored students. They sang beautifully. The purpose of this meeting was to afford an opportunity for both races to meet and discuss a question of vital interest to both.

It was admirably planned. But it would not work. The speakers were there and delivered their messages. The colored people were there, but only a few white people came. The meeting was held in a large opera house. The first floor was reserved for white people and the two galleries for negroes. At the hour for opening the two galleries were packed and over one thousand colored people were crowded around the entrance. By actual count there were twenty-eight white people on the first floor. There was room for about a thousand. The program was delayed a half hour. A few more straggled in.

The crowd on the outside grew larger. Everybody got nervous. Finally the ushers went to every white man and woman on the first floor and asked each one personally whether they would object to moving up to the front seats and allowing the crowd waiting on the outside to occupy the vacant space. All were agreed and moved to the front. I drew a breath of relief. What a happy solution to a vexing problem! But hold! Several white people in the rear refused to move. There were cotton basket hats with long plumes that demanded recognition. They sat on the place where the trouble lay.

Special committees went back and gesticulated and expostulated. It was no use. The big hats and their owners sat still. The curtain rose and the program began forty-five minutes late. The police scattered the crowd at the entrance. A few dozen white people occupied the entire first floor. Fifteen hundred colored people went sadly homeward. They had hoped to hear the speaking and singing. They represented the best class of colored people and were hungry for something more than bread alone. It was denied them. The color line was drawn against them.

The daily papers next day said not one word about this unusual occurrence. They gave an exhaustive report of the meeting, told of the good speakers on the program, what they said and of the appreciative listeners, but nothing about the big crowd of colored people that was turned away. Or the vacant space on the first floor. The effect of the beautiful things said by the speakers was marred by the unsolved race problem. The bouquets faded before the meeting was over.

I have learned also that it is an easy matter to be misunderstood if you have a disposition to show any friendliness toward the colored people. One colored man whom I befriended came to me and brought me $17.00 in silver and asked me to keep it for him. I felt honored on account of the confidence he placed in me.

However, I learned from a detective that the money had been stolen by a colored woman, and that I was simply used as a rail in the "fence" that secreted it. A little later this same man came to me with a paper and asked for my signature. Two colored women accompanied him and begged me to sign it. I read it carefully, then refused. It was a bond for $200.00 for their appearance at court to answer to the charge of grand larceny.

Such instances might be multiplied, but this will suffice to show that it is easy to make mistakes in the solution of this problem, and then we do like we used to do when we were boys in school—when we see the figures are wrong, we rub them out and begin all over again.

Birmingham, Ala.

1910

In What Fundamentals Do Mennonites Agree?

We shall begin the consideration of this article with an attempt to define the words "fundamental" and "Mennonites."

By fundamentals we mean the doctrines essential to the existence of a church or creed, the foundation principles of the faith.

The word Mennonite is a derivation from the name Menno Simons. Though Menno was not the founder of the church, and the brethren in his day considered the name a reproach rather than an honor, it has since that time been accepted by the Church, and we are today known by that name. (Here it might be well to add that there is nothing in a denominational name, further than to distinguish one denomination from other bodies.)

At the present time there are Mennonites in Europe and America and a few in other lands; but we shall confine ourselves principally to the Mennonites of America, as we are more familiar with their doctrine and life than with those of other countries.

The first permanent colony of Mennonites in America was the settlement at Germantown, Pa., in 1683. Early in the next century another colony settled in what is now Lancaster Co., Pa. From these two centers there went out colonists to other places, new colonies were formed, until now there are thirteen Mennonite conferences which trace their organization back to Lancaster and Germantown. Later immigrations from Europe swelled the membership in the various settlements.

The beginning of the nineteenth century saw practically but two bodies in America known by the name Mennonite. These were the Mennonites, already mentioned, and the Amish Mennonites, followers of Jacob Ammon, a noted Mennonite bishop of Switzerland, the leader of one branch in a division which occurred a few years after the first Mennonite settlers reached America.

About the year 1811 a number of brethren withdrew from the Church in Lancaster county, Pa., and organized what they termed the "Reformed Mennonite Church." This was under the leadership of John Herr, and from his name the body became known as the "Herrites." The census of 1906 credits them with 2079 members.

The next schism of importance took place in the Franconia Conference about the year 1847, when J. H. Oberholtzer and a number of his co-workers withdrew from the conference and organized one of their own. Some years afterwards he united forces with a number of congregations in the West and they organized what has since become known as "The General Conference of Mennonites of North America." This organization has since been joined by most of the Swiss Mennonites in

America, later by many of the Russian emigrants to America, and is now the second largest body of Mennonites in America, having an accredited membership of 11,661.

Among the Amish Mennonites there have also been a number of divisions within the past century. Three of their conferences are now in practical accord with the thirteen conferences named above, making sixteen working in substantial harmony. Others refuse to give sanction to these conferences because they are too aggressive, and still others because they are not aggressive enough. Among the Mennonites there have been a number of later divisions, until the census bulletin of 1906 has the Mennonites and Amish Mennonites in the United States classed under fourteen heads, having a combined membership of 54,798. For an estimate of the total number of Mennonites in America, add several thousand because the more conservative among them have conscientious scruples against being numbered, hence it is not likely that the enumerators counted nearly all of them. Those living in Canada would bring the total up to about 65,000 or 70,000.

As we look at these fourteen bodies (which ought to be one body) we are made conscious of the fact that somebody disagreed, and that the scriptural admonition, "Be of one mind," has not been literally kept. But it is not the purpose of this article to fix blame, nor to dwell upon the merits or demerits of the disagreements; but rather to call attention to some points of agreement. It has well been said that if we tried as hard to find points on which we agreed as we have to show wherein we disagreed there might not be so many sad stories of division and subdivision among us.

Practically all Mennonites in America agree in the doctrine of the Trinity, in the divinity of Christ and the inspiration of the Bible; in the fall of man through Adam and restoration through Jesus Christ; in their opposition to war, swearing of oaths and secret societies; in the separation of Church and state, in obedience to the government and in living God-fearing lives. All agree that baptism should be administered to believers only, and nearly all believe that it should be administered by pouring. Many of the principles for which our forefathers were so cruelly persecuted are still cherished by most people known by the name Mennonite, but in some points many have drifted.

Notwithstanding the many differences which severed our people into so many bodies, there is still a bond of love between most of them, which bond has made many of them hope for the time when there will be but one Mennonite Church in America. God alone knows whether this hope will ever be realized. There are obstacles in the way which most dreamers overlook; but faith can remove mountains. When we see how far apart the Mennonites and Amish Mennonites were a half century ago and how near most of them are together now, it gives us hope that time, prayers and an overruling Providence may bring about more things of a similar nature. At any rate, let us work on, hope on, pray on.
—*Daniel Kauffman*

The Present Interest

The present interest in the high cost of living may result in something good or evil, depending upon how the people take it. If it will be a means of opening our eyes to our own extravagance and disregard for the interests of the kingdom of God upon earth; if it means that the people of America, seeing these things, will sober up in their mad rush for wealth and splendor and take a backward step in the direction of economy, simplicity and righteousness, we thank God that the interest has been awakened. If it means an industrial war in which the spirit of selfishness and retaliation will become more marked than it is at present, we tremble at results.

We Americans are somewhat peculiarly constituted. If prices on things that we buy are very high, we talk about trusts, graft, extortion, boycotting, etc., etc., etc. If prices are high on things we have to sell we talk about prosperity. In our scramble for high prices on things we have to sell and low prices on things we think we must buy, we forget about the Golden

Rule, forget about the Bible admonition, "in honor preferring one another," forget that our mission in life is not to get all we can out of the world but to put all we can into it.

In this day of industrial excitement let us not allow ourselves to be drawn into the maelstrom of discontent. "For I have learned in whatsoever state I am, therewith to be content." "Every one that striveth for the mastery is temperate in all things." "In patience possess ye your souls." "Set your affections on things above, not on things on the earth." "The weapons of our warfare are not carnal, but mighty through God." The cure for present-day ills lies not in boycotting, retaliation, threats, prosecutions, stirring up discontent and class hatred, but in righteousness, simplicity, economy, peace, faith, hope, meekness, prayer and an unselfish effort to advance the interests of fellowmen. Let us exercise ourselves along these lines.

—*Daniel Kauffman*

1911

An editorial against capital punishment, and an article on prayer by the president of Goshen College.

Another Argument

Another argument against capital punishment is furnished by the recent pardon of an Oklahoma convict by President Taft. The man had been convicted of murder in the first degree and sentenced to be hanged. This was afterwards commuted to life-imprisonment. After twenty-seven years of prison life the man was found to be innocent and was therefore pardoned. But what if the original had been carried out? It is not reasonable to suppose that this was the only instance of the kind, but we believe that many an innocent man has been hanged as a murderer. This world is too full of uncertainties, and human life is too sacred, for any one but God to pass the death sentence. "Vengeance is mine, I will repay, saith the Lord." There are many reasons for obeying the divine edict, "Thou shalt not kill."

—*Daniel Kauffman*

Prayer

by N. E. Byers

There are so many doctrines and theories, problems and practices included in our religion that one is in danger at times of losing sight of the simple, central, vital elements of the Christian life. Reduced to its simplest terms, religion is the true fellowship of man with God and this is promoted by prayer. It is important therefore, above all things, that we understand prayer and emphasize it in our daily lives.

The two essential conditions for prayer are: (1) a definite sense of the presence of a wise, loving, all-powerful, personal God, and (2) an honest purpose to live in harmony with His will. I believe that many honest souls fail in their prayer life because of the difficulty of realizing the presence of God. Some hesitate because they can not get a satisfactory picture or mental image of His form, others are skeptical because they can not comprehend His nature and attributes. Now what is needed is not the imagination of the artist nor the explanation of the theologian, but a practical experience of His spiritual presence. We have evidence in the Bible and in the lives of Christians as to His existence and nature and our souls cry out to Him and He responds. Now we begin to know Him in a concrete, practical, vital manner as a spiritual, personal Being. If we hold to this experienced God we can well dispense with images and explanations, for practical religious purposes. We must pray to God as we know Him in our own experiences.

But there are many more, no doubt, that are definitely conscious of a prayer hearing and answering God—they believe in Him and tremble—but they are not on speaking terms with Him. The consciousness of sin and the unwillingness to forsake it make it impossible for them to address Him, in faith, for the least of blessings. God hears the cry of the sinner, but not until he is willing to come to Him and submit himself to his Father's will.

The real prayer is the attitude of the heart toward God. "If ye abide in me, and my words abide in you,"—this is the condition in which we "pray without ceasing." Our whole attitude may be constantly that of dependence and trust, gratitude and praise, and of strong purpose in line with His will. This is more important than the words we use at special times. And yet it is important that at special and regular times we give our whole attention to Him and for the sake of concentration and definiteness of thought put our heart's desire into words.

The object of prayer is not so much to change God's purposes and plans as it is to make it possible for Him to accomplish His work through us. He always purposes that which is best and is "more willing to give than we are to receive," but not until we come to Him in the prayer, unuttered or expressed, "not my will but thine be done," can He give us what we need. As soon as we are willing, the answer is sure to come.

But at times it seems desirable that the regular order of nature should be interfered with for a special purpose. Can God oppose nature? No, God's regular habits of doing things constitute nature and so if for sufficient reason He desires on occasions to change His regular way of doing as a free, willing being He can so change. However we do not believe that He will do this often enough to seriously interfere with the uniformity of nature.

He no doubt does on occasions in extreme situations, in answer to petitions, send rain, furnish food, heal diseases, and put sermons into men's minds, but His regular ways of working, in all these cases, can easily be learned by men and usually it is His desire that we intelligently co-operate with Him and thus in answer to work as well as faith we receive as great blessings and get the benefit of the work as well. The best of men will turn a deaf ear to the requests for free gifts who refuses to do his share of work. Would it be strange if God would do likewise?

At times we desire that men's wills be changed for their own or others' welfare. Can God do this? God does not bless men against their will but He, through the convicting power of the Spirit, can influence men to willingly change their will. With our sympathetic co-operation He often guides men from above their freedom and yet they are free, willing beings and act in line with their own choices.

I have tried to discuss a few of the problems that may arise with reference to prayer, but I wish to say again, that what we need is not so much the explanation as the practice of prayer. Exercise faith and love and in humble submission come to Him with all your needs and praises and the answer will be sure to come in a way to forever convince that He hears and answers prayer.

Goshen, Ind.

N. E. Byers, president of Goshen College. The object of prayer is not so much to change God's purposes and plans as it is to accomplish his work through us.

1912

Perspectives on how to keep the faith with regard to clothing worn in Mennonite schools and on the 1912 election.

Are You Going to School Next Year?

by J. S. Hartzler

From present prospects there will be from 300 to 350 young people attending our Church schools within the next year. By far the greater number of these will come from Mennonite homes and will in most cases themselves be members of that faith. They will come from many different places in which order and discipline are almost as varied as the congregations from which they come.

As in a congregation, so in a school, any one who will act with proper decorum will be allowed to attend, and the schools, as separate from the Church, can not make rules governing the dress of the student so long as common decency is observed. For many it is their first experience away from home and home restraints and frequently they want to get away from church restraints as well. They prefer to leave their church letter where it is and so the church connected with the school has no jurisdiction over them. Many have never been taught why the Church opposes certain forms and fashions, but simply know that certain things have been demanded and obedience is expected to follow. What is likely to follow?

There are students who for the entire time at school have scarcely more than a passing grade in their recitations and very frequently are obliged to take the second examination before they are allowed to pass. They are not worried about this nearly so much as when they see that others have more on their person or are decked out in the later styles while they themselves are clad in more simple forms. I have repeatedly seen students both at Goshen College and Hesston Academy who held their membership in the home church, whose appearance was such that the congregation at the school would have considered them under censure had their letters been transferred, and had their conduct been the same at home as it was at school in some cases it would have meant a forfeiture of their membership.

But this is not always the fault of the student. After having talked several times with a young sister about her dress, I said, "Now sister, tell me the truth, are not your parents helping you in these violations and do they not send you things to wear that you and they know that you would not dare wear at home and should not wear here?" Tears came to the poor girl's eyes and she said between her sobs, "Yes, that is the truth, I am sorry to say." She and her parents were members of a very plain church, but they wanted to do that which would please their daughter. This placed the girl in a bad light with her fellow-students. Parents, you can do much that will count for "weal or woe" in these matters. Will you do your part? Will you see that your sons and daughters are supplied with such clothes as will harmonize with their profession? Dress is not Christianity, but it is a strong index of the condition of the heart that prompts the act.

Even pastors can do much by having a confidential talk with the student before he leaves home. A few words of encouragement and an advice to take a church letter along will often do much good. Write to the pastor of the congregation at the school and ask whether the letter has been handed in.

Much can be done to stem the tide of worldliness in the schools but it will require co-operation. Look after it now. Do not sit idly by and see what will be done and then find fault because you do not find just what you would like to see. Mothers, fathers, students, pastors and teachers all have a responsibility in this matter. "Am I performing mine?"

Goshen, Ind.

Keep Your Balance

We desire at this time to speak a word with reference to the presidential campaign that is rapidly approaching the red hot stage. The present indications are that this campaign will be noted for its unusual bitterness, to say nothing else about it. Already they are flinging mud in the fiercest kind of a fashion. Charges of corruption are bandied back and forth to an extent that if the laws of the country were enforced our country would need more jails and penitentiaries to accommodate all who are guilty either of corruption or of slander. Both of the leading political parties are divided into factions and numerous third parties are making frantic efforts to get a listening ear from the public. This is just the beginning of the struggle. What will happen before the November elections no one can foretell.

We call attention to these things that our people may not be drawn into these struggles. There is danger that amid the noise and din of carnal conflict even those who recognize that as citizens of the Kingdom their business is to work for the glory of God and the salvation of souls may lose sight of their calling and be drawn into struggles that are not for their own or anybody else's good. Lend no encouragement to writers and speakers whose business is to appeal to the passions and prejudices of men. Remember your high and holy calling, and under no circumstances allow yourself to be drawn into a frame of mind in which you will be tempted to bring railing accusations against fellow men. Keep cool, and advise everybody else to do the same. Pray for your rulers, be subject to the powers that be, remember your allegiance to Him who said, "My kingdom is not of this world."

—*Daniel Kauffman*

1913

The General Mennonite Convention at Berne, Indiana

The meeting held at Berne, Ind., on Tuesday and Wednesday, Aug. 19 and 20, 1913, was perhaps the most general of all Mennonite meetings ever held in America. Of the visitors present 148 reported, representing nine different Mennonite bodies.

We shall try to give as accurately as possible, a brief account of how this meeting came to be held.

For a number of years there has been a conviction on the part of some, that members of various Mennonite bodies should get better acquainted with one another, since it was believed that if this were done, it would be found that the differences holding them apart are not so great as some might imagine. To carry this thought into action, upon the suggestion of Bro. N. E. Byers of Goshen, Ind., the editor of "The Mennonite," published in Berne, Ind., appointed a committee consisting of a member each from as many Mennonite bodies as he could get men to agree to serve. This committee issued a call for the meeting which has just been held.

It will be remembered that at the time this call was issued, the editor of the Gospel Herald strongly dissented from the idea, for the double reason that not nearly all branches of Mennonites were represented on the committee and that the differences between the bodies which were represented are too vital to make that kind of meeting practical. Then, when the union school proposition came up we again sounded our note of protest.

I attended the meeting at Berne, however, in the first place because I was advised to do so by nearly all brethren whom I consulted on the matter. The reason why the brethren urged me to attend was that as editor of the Gospel

Herald, I would be in a position to report the situation more accurately and fairly if I attended than I could if I were to depend on hearsay for my information. In the second place there was the conviction that we would be better understood if we met face to face and stated our position. Now, after having attended the meeting, we can say that our former convictions are unchanged, and we are led to again state our convictions, by the grace of God. Having seen and heard, we shall endeavor to report as faithfully as we can. . . .

The following is the list of subjects:

The Blessings of Christian Unity. D. Brenneman.

Menno Simons as a Reformer. C. Van der Smissen.

Review of the History of American Mennonites. C. H. Smith.

What Contributions have Mennonites to make to American Christianity? J. W. Kliewer.

In What Fundamentals do Mennonites Agree? D. Kauffman.

The Bible Doctrine of Nonresistance. P. C. Hiebert.

What Think Ye of Christ? E. Troyer.

The discussions, as a rule, were spirited, and good interest and good feeling prevailed. Among miscellaneous business transacted was the passing of a resolution calling for another meeting in three years and a resolution calling for the publication of the papers read before the meeting. The majority of those present felt that the meeting was profitable to them, and showed their conviction in the call for another meeting.

Why, then, should any one disapprove of a meeting of this kind?

Before we attempt to answer, let us be sure that we understand the situation.

It may be well to state that there was no sentiment evident in favor of organic union among Mennonite bodies. That is entirely out of the question, because the differences are too great; hence nobody favors it. The fears expressed by some that an attempt would be made to consolidate all kinds of Mennonites into one body, regardless of differences, are unfounded. All that is attempted at this time is simply to get members of different bodies better acquainted with one another. Co-operation along lines in which all agree is also sought. This, as near as we can judge, is the object of these union meetings.

Before we begin to state objections, we also desire to say that none of these objections are founded upon lack of friendship for the Mennonite bodies, or a lack of desire for a union with them. Our prayers shall continue to ascend that our Savior's prayer for the unity of believers may yet be fulfilled among all who are named Mennonites. There should be no hatred or ill will toward any of them. Our older people doubtless remember the time when there was a more radical difference between the Mennonites and the Amish Mennonites than there now is between some of the bodies represented at the Berne meeting.

But there is another thing which is far more important than friendship or good will. We refer to the "ancient landmarks" with Scripture foundations. As a church we have been consistent in standing for nonconformity, nonresistance in its fullest sense, the devotional covering, washing of the saints' feet. We weaken our power of discipline and the force of our teaching whenever we favor alliances with other churches which refuse to stand with us on these Bible doctrines. Sociability is an excellent thing, but when its cultivation is sought through the holding of some precious Gospel doctrine in the background, we feel that it is the wrong kind of sociability to foster. As a rule, this kind of meetings fosters the spirit of compromise through the emphasis of "unity" at the expense of things which are essential to be united upon.

We have said before, and we repeat it, that a federation of bodies that are so far apart that organic union is not to be thought of, hinders rather than helps the cause of union upon a solid Gospel basis. Unless we are so near together that we preach practically the same thing and have practically the same rules and regulations, any attempt at federation means a compromise which neither we nor the cause of Christ can afford to make.

We referred to the coming together of the Mennonites and Amish Mennonites. This merging is a natural thing because they believe alike and "keep house" in practically the same way. They grew together. Being neighbors they compared notes, exchanged thoughts, learned from each other, and when they were near enough one that it was thought profitable, they united their efforts in a common cause. . . .

What, then, should be our attitude toward these union meetings which have been proposed? I answer for myself only. It is my candid conviction that we should hold aloof from them until it is clearly evident that there is a unity in the faith as well as a unity in friendship.

—*Daniel Kauffman, Scottdale, Pa.*

Reading Her Own Obituary

by A. Metzler

When the interurban car from the South arrived at the depot in West Liberty, Ohio, July 2, the undertaker was waiting there with his hearse to convey the corpse of Mrs. Geo. W. Carr to the home of her grief-stricken mother, who had received a telegram that her daughter died in Jacksonville, Fla., and her remains would arrive on that car. To the great surprise of the waiting spectators Mrs. Carr stepped off the car, greeted her mourning friends and walked into her mother's home, where the necessary preparations had been made to hold her funeral the next day. Some telegraph operator apparently had made a sad blunder in transmitting the message sent by her husband notifying her mother of her coming. The announcement of her death and funeral had appeared in the papers on the day of her arrival in apparent good health. The shock of her mother, in seeing her supposed dead daughter walk into her home was even greater than that caused by the announcement of her death, and Mrs. Carr can read her own obituary.

West Liberty, Ohio

1914

A greeting from the patron saint of Mennonite publishing, a statement of the editor's position, and a ten-point statement on what it takes to work for God.

Fifty Years Ago

by John F. Funk

The December days of 1863, fifty years ago, were busy days for the writer, in his home in Chicago, Ill. He was doing what he could to help the cause of Christ and the Mennonite Church in promulgating the teachings and doctrines of the Gospel. By the aid and counsel of a few devoted friends, he had formulated the plans for the publication of a Mennonite Church paper, and during these December days of 1863, aside from the duties of the business in which he was engaged, every moment was industriously devoted to collecting and preparing articles for the new paper to be launched into being, and on the first day of January, 1864, that proverbially cold New Year's day, the first number of the "Herald of Truth" had been printed and was ready to be sent to the friends of the undertaking, though there was not a single name on the subscription book, and not a dollar in the treasury.

But the Lord blessed the work and from it came good results. Under the management of the founder of the first Church paper of our branch of the Mennonite people, the work was maintained and prospered until the year 1908, when all the periodicals of the Mennonite Publishing Co., were sold to the Mennonite Publication Board, and the work is continued at Scottdale, Pa., under the firm name of the "Mennonite Publishing House," and now, after fifty years, on this New Year's day of 1914, the first editor of the first English Mennonite paper, is permitted in these lines, to send a brotherly New Year's greeting to all the readers of our Church papers.

May the loving kindness and the tender mercies of our heavenly Father rest and abide on all who love and serve the Lord in sincerity and truth.

Elkhart, Ind., Jan. 1, 1914.

The above letter from one who has borne the heat and burden of the day will be read with great interest. Those of us who are of the younger generation can hardly realize the enormity of the undertaking our brother writes about and what it meant fifty years ago. It is with a deep sense of gratitude toward our heavenly Father that we enter upon this fifty-first year of the publication of our Church paper. When we remember that the beginning of publication work was not attended with the organized forces of the Church as it now is, we realize all the more the greatness of the early efforts in this work.

Only a few of our district conferences were organized before this time and the Church was in a transition stage. The English language was coming into use. The spirit of progress was taking hold of some of our brethren. Active Sunday school work and evangelistic efforts followed closely in the wake of the establishing of the Church paper.

How much we owe to these early efforts in setting in motion the forces that are now active, and organizing them into working bodies, only eternity can reveal. This much is certain, that through the Church paper there is an avenue for communication and teaching that has meant much for the present prosperity and enlargement of the Church.

May our prayers to God and our consecrated efforts in His service be used in carrying forward the work He has left us to accomplish is our earnest wish and desire.

The sentiments expressed by our brother have the right ring. If those sentiments are accepted, lived, and exemplified they will have a powerful influence for good among our people.

—A.L. (Evidently Aaron Loucks, first general manager of Mennonite Publishing House).

John F. Funk, publisher of Herald of Truth, *a predecessor of the* Gospel Herald.

Inseparable Twins

That is the way we look upon conservatism and progressivism. They can not be separated without doing great damage. Especially is this true in religion. Remove the first, and the body flies off into liberalism and infidelity. Remove the second, and the body becomes stagnant and lifeless. To conserve the Christian faith and the Christian Church, it is necessary that the body of Christ be kept as an aggressive force for God.

As for progression, it depends altogether upon whether the progress is made in the direction of God and Godliness or in the opposite direction, as to whether it is conservative or destructive.

If you are wise, and true to God, you may properly be called an aggresso-conservative. It is as wrong to call deadness conservatism as it is to conclude that only drifting into worldliness is progression. The highest form of both conservatism and progression is that presented in II Pet. 3:18.

—*Daniel Kauffman*

The Worker's Equipment

by Geo. R. Brunk

1. It is desirable to have a liberal supply of good common sense, and if there be a dash here and there in uncommon sense, all the better.

However, third class mentality with first class religious equipment is better than first rate intellectuality and third rate spirituality. The Bible does not demand a "big gun" but a sound one. II Tim. 1:7.

2. As much learning as can be made practical in work for God and can be absorbed without inflation.

Bloating is about as likely to occur when people are carelessly schooled as when cattle are carelessly pastured.

We must neither deny the usefulness of human learning along right lines nor exalt it to an equality with the spiritual gifts and graces of God. To drink at the fountain of human learning merely for self gratification is as unjustifiable as any other form of selfishness. Little learning and little grace makes a drone. Much learning and little grace makes a cymbal tinkler. Little learning and much grace makes a Simon Peter. Much learning and much grace makes a Paul.

3. There must be a skyblue conversion that can look into the eyes of men and say, "I know that my Redeemer liveth."

4. There must be a consecration that will not shrink from anything that God may ask, whether it be to forsake pet sins and worldly vanities, or father, mother, brother, sister, wife or child.

5. A humility that bends low before God but at the same time can rebuke kings.

6. A loyalty that will make no provision for the flesh (like Naaman, who asked pardon in advance for inconsistencies he expected to engage in). II Kings 5:18.

7. The Holy Spirit anointing that gives boldness and sets the life on fire. Acts 18:24-28; 4:31.

8. Learned in the Scripture so as to be able to instruct the ignorant, comfort the troubled, make sinners tremble, and stop the mouths of the vain and unruly. Why should a worker not know the location and effect of texts as well as a druggist does his drugs?

9. A faith that does not stagger at the so called "impossibilities" of the Bible.

10. Persistency and watchfulness that will keep at the work for souls and keep in the love of God.

Denbigh, Va.

Amen. May it be the prayerful, sincere, unwavering aim of every Christian worker to be the happy possessor of these equipments.—Ed.

1915

Personal evangelism and Mennonite education: two ongoing themes in the *Gospel Herald*.

J. S. Coffman as a Personal Worker

by R. J. Heatwole

He believed that "a word fitly spoken is like apples of gold in pictures of silver." He once said of himself, "I am not what I once was, I am not what I ought to be, but by the grace of God I am what I am." He was a very sociable man. He could be familiar with a stranger quickly. He knew that "a man that hath friends must shew himself friendly"; and, furthermore, that "there is a friend that sticketh closer than a brother." That Friend, Jesus, when on earth, was very friendly to young and old, saint or sinner. Bro. Coffman certainly followed His example.

We know his life work was to help Christianize the world, by having series of meetings in the United States and Canada. Each evening, after services, he could be seen in the congregation shaking hands with every one as fast as he could approach them, with Christian courtesy, calling each one by name. Even if he had met them but once before, all were met as old-time friends, saying something seasoned with pleasantness to each one, and naming something that each one understood, even if it were not for the general public to understand and profit by.

"John, did you get that bridle on the wild horse yesterday?" "Well, Mary, it was quite unpleasant to be caught in the rain the other day." "Glad for your recollection of that song tonight, Susie, it was very suitable." "I wish you six boys would sit forward among the singers tomorrow night, and use your melodious voices to help sing the songs of Zion." "Rebecca, I saw those trickling tears tonight; I think you were almost persuaded, but don't forget the fact that 'almost' is lost. Now is the accepted time." By such expressions he succeeded in enlisting the interest and good will of others, thus starting a course that led to their conversion.

We conclude, as Paul said of the Thessalonian brethren, so Bro. Coffman at the reckoning day can enjoy the same; namely, "For what is our hope, or joy, or crown of rejoicing?" said Paul, "are not even ye, in the presence of our Lord Jesus Christ at his coming?" Those to whom they have been so pleasingly personal and friendly they will know, and to them they will be "a crown of rejoicing."

Brandon, Colo.

Our School of Agriculture

by J. E. Hartzler

During the past year many of our brethren have been interested in the establishment of a school of agriculture under the direct control of the Church. Many have given their encouragement in a very definite way. The financial support which has come from a large number of our people has been very encouraging. The attitude taken by the constituency bespeaks a happy future for the work.

It is the purpose of this article to give a statement of the progress and purpose of the agricultural work with special reference to the farm. It is only right that those who have so loyally supported the movement should hear occasionally what progress is being made. I shall be very brief.

Sixty acres of land, six good horses, eight head of grade holstein cows, five head of young stock, and seventy-five chickens constitute the starting capital on the new dairy farm. A sixty-acre tract of land has also been leased for one year. This will make 120 acres of excellent farming land. Work began March 1 with Mahlon Hartzler as superintendent of the farm. The leading crops for the year will be corn, oats, wheat, and soy beans. The entire farm will be covered with lime just as rapidly as possible. An honest effort will be made to raise clover and alfalfa.

The leading efforts on the farm will be in the development of a good herd of dairy cows. Grade stock will be gradually disposed of and registered stock will be made a specialty.

The International Harvester Company is supplying us with all farm machinery. It is a favor which the college appreciated very much to be able to get all our machinery from the above named company at 50 per cent discount from the regular price. This also means that the company holds the right to replace any machine or parts of any machine by way of improvement without any additional cost to us.

The purpose of all this effort is to set up and

maintain a model farm; one which shall serve for observation and practice in the agricultural department of the college, and to serve a financial benefit to the college. The teaching of agriculture shall not be a matter of theory only, but one of practice. The farming must be scientific and up-to-date and at the same time must be on an economic basis. The purpose shall not be so much to experiment as to work out the theories and experiments presented by the State Experiment stations.

Every prayer you offer, every word of sympathy you express, and every dollar you send for this work will be accepted and appropriated in the fear of God. Our work, our fields, our doors, our books, our all are open for your inspection at any time.

Goshen, Ind.

1916

Sometimes in the practice of charity, it is necessary to separate the truly needy from the truly phony.

Funeral Customs

Our readers have doubtless been impressed with the unusual number of death notices published in these columns during the past few months. There has been an unusual amount of sickness during the winter and many have been called home .... Naturally, in laying away our dead, there is more or less formality in the ceremonies. Local conditions give rise to customs and these are not always the same in all communities. These peculiar customs sometimes cut across the line and invade a territory affecting Christian principles, and there is where Christian people should be watchful.

For instance, there is a destructive extravagance in many places which is hard on poor people, to say nothing of wasting money and cultivating pride, both of which are unscriptural. We believe that all people should have decent burial, but needless expense is not decency.

The extravagant use of flowers at funerals is almost universally condemned. But many who are against the use of many flowers insist on a few, thus staying at the foundation upon which the many flowers folly was built. Make use of your flowers while your friends are living. Display is never in order, especially not at funerals.

Choir singing at funerals is a growing custom. We have often wondered why. Is it because the rest are so overwhelmed with grief that only a few can master their emotions and sing? We know of no more opportune time to worship the Lord in song and impress the stony heart with the music of heaven than at times when all hearts are melted or softened with grief.

In some places it is the custom for relatives not to kneel in prayer. Especially in congregations where kneeling is the custom during prayer, is this peculiar stiff-kneed funeral custom hard to explain.

At other places where in ordinary worship the devotional covering is visible on the heads of the sisters it is strangely absent or covered up during funeral services. This raises one of two questions: (1) Is a funeral service a service for worship or simply a formal memorial service? (2) If a religious service, why is not the covering taught in I Cor. 11:2-16 as needful there as in any other religious service?

Please do not accuse us of faultfinding, even though we may have put the question mark after a number of doubtful customs. The point we wish to make at this time is that we do not allow custom to sway us to an extent that our actions run counter to Gospel teaching or to the best interests of the cause of Christ and the Church. After you have prayerfully considered the points raised you will have done what this editorial is intended to accomplish.

—*Daniel Kauffman*

K. Odisho

by J. A. Ressler

A few weeks ago there came to Scottdale a man giving the above name and representing that he was a refugee from Urumia, Persia, and had fled from there just before the opening of the great European war and the fearful massacres in Persia. He had a story about his family being in Kansas and had letters from various people well-known to our people that seemed to substantiate what he said. He was asking for financial help to either go back to his place in Persia at the close of the war or to purchase a vineyard in California—and in the mean time support himself and family.

From here Mr. Odisho went to Johnstown, where the writer met him and spent several hours in conversation with him. We regret the necessity for issuing this warning, but we feel that it is the only thing we can do and be in the line of duty.

Mr. Odisho represented that he had been in this country a little over two years, and that he came on the last ship from Hamburg before the opening of the war. He did not remember the name of the ship. From reliable sources we find that he has been in this country more than three years and that he had been in this country about ten years ago.

He represents that he learned a little English and German before leaving Persia and simply obtained more practice since coming to this country, and that he only learned to speak within a few months. From several sources we know that he had about as good a knowledge of English over a year ago as he has at present.

He represents that he is supporting his family from the funds that he collects mostly among our people. From a very trustworthy source in Kansas we learn that his oldest daughter, who is in a private home near Hillsboro, Kans., has not heard from her father for over a year and that his wife, who is being supported in Topeka, Kans., by a local charity, claims not to know of his whereabouts. While in Scottdale he claimed to be engaged in writing a letter to his wife!

He promised the writer at the Stahl Church, near Johnstown, Pa., to write and keep us informed as to his journeys. Although more than two weeks have elapsed, there has been not the slightest information from him. . . .

We would by no means discourage genuine charity, but if this man comes into any of our communities in the future, he should be shown this article and asked for an explanation. Genuine and worthy sufferers from Turkish atrocities do not come around asking private charity. They have invariably some well-established mission organization back of them. It is always safest in these days to give through organized means of charity. In this we have the example of Paul who took gifts to Jerusalem in a regular and systematic way. . . .

Scottdale, Pa.

We Are One

For several decades there has been a gradual flowing together of the two branches of our church known as "Mennonites" and "Amish Mennonites." We used to think there was a decided difference between the two; but when we got close enough together that we could compare notes we found that we believed the same things. . . . Here are four things with which we are profoundly impressed:

1. There is no longer a lining up on opposite sides of the issues which separated Jacob Ammon from his brethren.

2. There is not a single question or issue at stake in which the body of Mennonites is on one side and the body of Amish Mennonites is on the other side.

3. Upon questions concerning which there is a division of sentiment there are Mennonites and Amish Mennonites to be found on one side and Mennonites and Amish Mennonites on the other side.

4. In reading the conference disciplines of our various conferences the only way you can tell whether the conference is "Mennonite" or "Amish Mennonite" is by the name of the conference. Whatever may be said of the opinions of individuals, it is encouraging to

note the practical unanimity among our conferences on points of doctrine.

We are glad that steps have been taken in several of our conference districts to merge the two bodies into one, and our prayer is that this movement may continue until there will be a complete merging into one from one end of the Church to the other. May God hasten the day.

—*Daniel Kauffman*

1917

One response to the war hysteria and the suffering brought on by World War I.

Are Mennonites Slackers?

by J. E. Hartzler

It is my privilege to spend a week with the churches of Illinois in the interests of school and missions. I think in my thirteen years of experience in the ministry I have not found so much real interest in school and missions. Especially is this true of the middle-aged men in the church. The men have come to the place where they are ready to do something. I have thus far visited the congregations at Sterling, Tiskilwa, Cullom, Metamora, and Roanoke. I shall yet visit Tremont, Deer Creek, and Washington. I regret that time and other duties will not permit me to visit the remaining churches of the state. I can not fully express the eagerness the churches are manifesting at this time in doing something for missions and war relief work.

To the present time the churches have not seen fit to purchase Liberty Loan Bonds. We can not consistently take part in the military service of the country and be true to the teachings of the Lord Jesus Christ. We can not send our boys to the trenches, the ammunition plants nor any other services which contributes directly to the killing of our fellowmen. The principle of non-resistance is fundamental in Christian faith and can not be denied by the church if we would live.

But we are called "slackers," because of religious convictions, we refuse to go to the trenches, buy Liberty Bonds, etc. Are Mennonites Slackers? That depends on circumstances.

We are slackers only to the extent that we fail or neglect to do and live the whole Gospel of Christ. No man is a slacker who lives true to Him who gave his life for our salvation. No man is a slacker who lives the principles of Jesus Christ in loving and serving our fellowman. The best, the most loyal and most valuable citizen under the American flag is the honest, sincere, and genuine Christian man who lives the teachings of Him who is the Prince of Peace.

We are slackers if we fail to do our duty to the poor, the suffering and destitute masses who are products of this great world war. Every man and woman in the Mennonite Church can render a greater and more noble service to God and to the human family than can the man who enlists in military service and dies on the firing line. It is not a difficult thing to die for a country; but it takes great faith and courage to live for God and our country.

There ought to be several hundred men in the church who would volunteer their service for one year or more to do war relief work. To do reconstruction work in Europe at the close of the war. In times of war it is needful to prepare for peace. There ought to be 500 men in the church who would write their personal check for $1,000.00 each toward a fund of one half million dollars for war relief and reconstruction. It can be done. These men and money should be placed in the hands of a commission appointed by the Church whose duty it should be to serve the Church as the official avenue through which we can do proper relief and reconstruction work. . . .

Brethren, whether the term "slacker" as applied to nonresistant people be just or unjust let us be up and doing. Let us not content ourselves in walking with the "be good" fellows who passed by the man who fell among thieves. Let us join hearts and hands with the "do good" man who came with oil and wine and carried the half dead man to the hotel and paid all his doctor bills. The good Samaritan was non-resistant but he did a service which the world shall never forget. No people on earth are in better position to do a similar service just now than are the Mennonites.

Goshen, Ind.

J. E. Hartzler: The good Samaritan was nonresistant but he did a service which the world shall never forget. No people are in a better position to do a similar service than the Mennonites.

1918

The Sisters' Share in the Mennonite Relief Service for War Sufferers

by Clara Eby Steiner

For more than twenty years some of our Mennonite women have been plying their needles month after month for the relief of the unfortunate ones and the needy and destitute. This work has grown until we now have in every conference district organized societies known as "Sewing Circles," "Sewing Classes," "Sewing Bees," "Ladies Aids," "Missionary Societies," "Junior Circles," "Children's Bands," etc. The amount of work that the sisters, who are laboring in these various organizations, have done during these years would surprise all of us could it be estimated.

Perhaps the greatest opportunity that has ever come to us is before us now, when we may, as a united body of women, work for the relief of suffering, caused by the horrors of war. We may be the means of bringing cheer and comfort to thousands who have lost everything through this war.

Some of our Sewing Circles were sewing, and others were contemplating doing so, and sending through the Red Cross when the Mennonite Relief Commission was organized. We believe we can at this time be of the best possible service by all working unitedly under the direction of our own Relief Commission. We notice that the Friends also recognize this fact when they say that "no church can scatter its efforts and accomplish any one thing." Millions of women are doing the usual Red Cross work, and it seems that Mennonite or our non-resistant women are peculiarly fitted to do their share in this civilian relief work. Not only are we fitted but we should perhaps consider it a duty and a privilege....

One sister wrote recently that the war is coming closer all the time. But, when we consider that our sons and brothers have so far only been compelled to go to camp, and will not be asked to give their life or to take life, we have great reason to be thankful for our faith and it is but fitting that we give expression to that faith that is within us, by helping those who have it not.

There is no doubt that the sisters will do their part. We were informed recently that Bro. Mumaw has received a number of inquiries from the women. One informant says, "So you see the women are interested not only in supporting missionaries but also in helping relief work in the war stricken regions. God bless the women of the Church."

We have had many new sewing circles organized through the efforts of our branch secretaries and more are to be organized soon. Will those who have made inquiries take note that they might begin by sewing in this relief work while they are looking for other needy fields?

Junior or Young Women's Circles have informed us that they intend to sew for Belgian babies.

Perhaps our young women could, in many of our churches, organize circles and thus have a share in this work. If our churches were as busy at organizing the women (young women and even children) as the Red Cross is, our sewing force could be more than doubled, yes, more than trebled. Any church wishing to organize a circle and wishing assistance may write to their branch secretary or to myself and we will gladly help you.

We have been in correspondence with the secretary of the Mennonite Relief Commission, Bro. Levi Mumaw, and he informs us that he is working on plans and having circulars printed and that as soon as the circular matter is off the press he will send us a good supply to send to our branch secretaries and sewing circles that may call for them and you may obtain these circulars from them, myself, or from Bro. Mumaw.

Columbus Grove, Ohio.

Clara Eby Steiner with granddaughter Alice Loewen, daughter Charity Hostetler and father Tobias Eby: If our churches were as busy as the Red Cross, our sewing force could be more than trebled.

A Conundrum Passed On

When Christian workers meet they often discuss their peculiar problems. Not many years ago a brother propounded this perplexing problem: Two brethren in the same church had some difficulties between them. Both were excellent, warm-hearted brethren. Speaking of one of these brethren, you would hear neighbors express themselves like this: "I never saw a better man. He is a good neighbor, a conscientious, obliging, Christian man." About the other, they would say: "If ever there was a Christian, this man is. He is devout, wholesouled, true to his convictions, a consecrated worker." Yet these two brethren were so dissatisfied with each other that they were after each other continually, kept the church in an uproar, and could scarcely live in the same church. Our brother wanted to know where the trouble was that two such good brethren could see so little good in each other. We couldn't tell him. Can you?

—Daniel Kauffman

1919

Smokes

We have noticed with sincere regret that during the past few years the tobacco habit has been on the increase.... The warning, "No smoking," conspicuously posted in many places, is becoming more and more ignored and America is rapidly becoming a home of tobacco-embalmed people. This condition is to be deplored, for a number of reasons.

1. It is inconsistent with the present cry of economy and conservation. With millions of people starving, why should America insist on blowing away in smoke billions of dollars which are worse than wasted? The tobacco bill of America would more than feed and clothe the starving people in Europe.

2. Since tobacco is entirely without food properties, and its medicinal qualities at least doubtful; since the nicotine habit stunts the growth of the body, blunts the moral sensibilities, and develops a sordid selfishness of which the user is not aware; since the great majority of tobacco users are diseased in some form or other, this waste is without excuse.

3. Tobacco enslaves its victims. Those who have the habit are not aware of this till they try to quit. Many a poor soul has smoked away his will power to the extent that when he would get rid of his master he is too weak to carry out his resolution.

4. The tobacco habit develops a disregard for the welfare of others. He who can, without remorse of conscience, send forth the fumes of nicotine which sicken those who are not already nicotinized, has developed a sordid indifference to the feelings of others which makes him incapable of having a proper regard for the welfare of others along any other line....

We appeal to the conscience of every tobacco user to throw off this yoke of slavery and use the money to better purposes. We appeal to those who are free from the blight of this habit to use their persuasive powers in working for the freedom of others, especially in saving the boys from the injurious effects of this baneful habit. We appeal to all who know the worth of prayer to bring the matter before the Throne to the end that God may awaken the public conscience to the ruinous work of this growing evil.   —*Daniel Kauffman*

Is Feet Washing an Ordinance for Bums?

by S. S. Hammers

Some years ago I dropped into a Presbyterian Sunday school and was invited into the Bible class. The minister of the church taught the class. The subject was Feet Washing. The lesson started with the usual questions and answers, when a member of the class asked, "Is feet washing an ordinance to be observed by the followers of Christ today?" "No," said the minister, "there is not the slightest indication that Jesus at this time appointed a ceremony to be performed in the Church. It is only a 'bum' ordinance. Once a year the Pope of Rome collects twelve 'bums' or tramps and washes their feet. We have no commandment that Christians should wash each other's feet."

We remarked that we believed it to be a Church ordinance. The minister remarked that the Brethren and the Mennonites and a few others practice feet washing as an ordinance. We then remarked that it was a fine thing that, if there were no others to follow Christ in His precepts and example, the bums, tramps, Brethren, Mennonites, and a few others were willing.

We hear Jesus say to His "bums," as this minister puts it, "If I then your Lord and Master have washed your feet, ye also ought to wash one another's feet." Now we ask, When were they to wash one another's feet if not intended as a Church ordinance? Christ said, 'I have given you an example, that ye should do as I have done to you." If feet washing was not intended as an ordinance, why did He give them the example?...   *Gettysburg, Pa.*

1920

The Gospel Herald

The Gospel Herald has, from time to time, received its just share of criticism. While most of the echoes we hear are in the form of favorable comment on the attitude we take on Bible doctrine and present-day issues, there are some notable exceptions to this. Some think we are too conservative, while others think we are entirely too lenient with liberalism. And the intensity with which these criticisms are sometimes brought, from both sides, makes one wonder how such exceedingly opposite and widely separated impressions can be gained from the same message.

Our policy has been this: We have kept in view the goal of the whole Church solidly planted upon a whole-Gospel platform, actively engaged in winning the greatest possible number of souls to this standard. Consistent with this view we have tried to be fair and considerate to all, conciliatory in tone, yet firm in our adherence to the true faith of the Gospel. It has fallen to our lot to stand in defense of some unpopular Bible doctrines, and from appearances we will have some more of that kind of work to do.

One of the criticisms which we hear quite frequently is that our teaching is largely of the negative character; that too much space has been occupied in denouncing evil, as compared with the space occupied in promoting the good. We are conscious of our short-comings, and are always glad when our friends remind us of our faults. It helps us to rectify them. But here is one fact that must not be overlooked: "The whole world lieth in wickedness." And from this evil world there come insidious influences that must be exposed and warned against, or well-meaning people will be overcome by them. We have testified in the past, and expect in the future to testify, against these influences in a most positive way.

One of these evil influences is "the sin which doth so easily beset us"; namely, the sin of unbelief. During the past few decades this sin has been laying hold of the churches in the form of "thinly veiled infidelity" variously known as "new theology," "new thought," "unitarianism," "higher criticism," "free thought," "socialism," etc., depending upon the peculiar brand of unbelief put forward. We expect to turn on the light until every man of faith is awake to this danger and will be outspoken against it.

In all that we say and do, we expect to heed the apostolic admonition of "speaking the truth in love" and will welcome any assistance you may be able to give us in the form of criticism, suggestions, advice, and prayers.

—*Daniel Kauffman*

First Foreign Missionary Assigned to Woman's Committee

by Clara E. Steiner

The first foreign missionary assigned to the Woman's Missionary Committee for support is Sister Mary Good. She is to sail for India about May 1st.

We know that the sewing circles and other sisters who have contributed to the fund for the sending and support of foreign missionaries will be interested to learn that our prayers along this line are being answered.

The fund was started in 1917 and our hopes were more than realized the first year so far as money was concerned. We, however, had no way of knowing how the war would affect missionary work and we simply were obliged to wait patiently until the Lord opened the way. Meanwhile, the money has been drawing interest and the fund has increased each year.

The object of raising this fund was not to support the missionaries already on the field and who were being supported by the Mission Board but to support additional missionaries and work—in other words, support workers and work that would not be supported except by more thoughtfulness and planning on our part—more self-denials and the giving of our abundance.

Last year, however, while we were waiting we were asked if we would support for a year Sister Helena Friesen, who is already in India for a second term. We promised to do so on condition that money for the purpose could be raised. The money came in. We have just pledged the support for another year on the same conditions. This means that, all going well, we will be supporting two missionaries in India, beginning May first. We praise the Lord for the privilege of serving Him in this manner. We are confident that we are able to support more missionaries and we trust that others may be sent in the near future.

With regular quarterly drafts upon our treasury it will be necessary for us to remember our foreign missionary fund with regular contributions. Since the need for relief work is constantly growing less we will be able to keep the treasury replenished. It should be a source of great joy that instead of giving so much money for physical needs brought about by the horrors of war, as has been given the past few years, we may give more directly to the cause of missions and the building of Christ's Kingdom of Peace.

Columbus Grove, Ohio.

The Candy Habit

This may not be an important subject, and we are sure that we will not bring in any radicalism in discussing it. Candy is not, like alcohol and tobacco, a poison in itself (unless some dopester puts it there) and it has some food properties that are helpful to the body. Yet there are a few facts about the candy habit that ought not to be lost sight of.

1. Candy has something in it that appeals to the "sweet tooth" and creates a progressive appetite for more of it.

2. The habit overloads the system with something it does not need, which makes it injurious to the health.

3. It is an expensive luxury which is hard to harmonize with I Cor. 10:31.

If your life is dedicated to the Lord, if you believe in spending your money for that which helps most in glorifying God and doing good to man, you will avoid the candy habit yourself and testify against it for the good of others.

—Daniel Kauffman

1921

Did You Ever?

by Ella Zook

When you were a child—did you ever walk about two miles to Sunday school on a cold December afternoon, when your toes were exposed to the biting cold? Did you ever?

I know a little five-year-old girl who used to come to the Mission in Kansas City that way.

Did you ever go to Sunday school barefoot because your parents were too poor to buy you a pair of shoes? There are a number of children who came to Sunday school at the Mission last summer just that way.

Did you ever go to Sunday school on a hot, sultry day, wearing your winter dress and winter hood because you had no other? I know a girl in Kansas City who came to the Mission last summer in that kind of an outfit.

Did you ever go to Sunday school with a promise of a whipping awaiting you when you got home as a reward if you dared to go?

I could tell you of such an unfortunate child in Kansas City who risked the whipping and came anyway. She seemed to enjoy the services too. Perhaps she thought that the promised whipping would at least have to be postponed until she got home.

Did you ever go to Sunday school some Sabbath afternoon having had no dinner and very little breakfast and all the while you could not help thinking how hungry you were and at the same time you remembered that there were only about two or three biscuits at home for supper and a half dozen others as hungry as yourself to be fed? Did you?

I could tell you of a family of children who came to the mission Sunday school hungry, more than once.

Since you are grown—Did you ever stay away from services because your husband was opposed to your going to church, and to keep him from storming around the house and pouring abuse upon your head you just stayed to "keep peace in the family?"

Let me tell you of a simplehearted little mother in Kansas City who must do that very often. But to go to her house and hear her as in her childlike, simple way, she prays to God to save her "poor, dear, sinful husband" (as she calls him) does a person as much good as reading a whole volume on the subject of "Missions." Perhaps more.

Did you ever stay away from communion services because the only pair of shoes you happened to possess were in the repair shop? I know a woman in Kansas City who had to do that the last time we had communion at the Mission. . . .

Did you ever have to stay at home from church because your husband objected to your going and had given you a "black" eye to make it real emphatic?

Once there was a young woman who was a regular attendant at the Sunday services at the Mission. She always brought her children along. One Sunday this fall she was missing from the ranks and the following week when one of the workers called upon her to learn the reason for her absence she found her with a bruised and blackened eye. But the woman was only waiting until her eye was healed and her appearance was again presentable so she could come back again.

Since we have never had to bear such inconveniences and abuses that many of our city sisters and brothers have to endure, we must decide that "there is someone that is worse off than we" and that surely "the lines have fallen unto us in pleasant places."

Did you ever think about it?

Kansas City, Kans.

Moving Pictures and Morals

by J. A. Ressler

You need not take prussic acid in order to find out its effects, neither need you attend the "movies" in order to know the poison they give out. The billboards and the newspapers tell the tale. Recent newspaper accounts tell of the successful efforts of a keeper of a "zoo" to put upon the film antics of animals in which human beings are imitated and in acts which would involve gross immorality. But the public pays for just this sort of thing.

Riding in the train the other evening we were engaged in conversation with a man of rather more than ordinary intelligence. He was not a prohibitionist, and was engaged in educational work. The subject was the relative influence of schools, the press, and the pulpit.

Our traveling companion then referred to the moving picture as having an influence in creating sentiment equal to, if not surpassing, any of the other forces mentioned. He himself frequently attends the picture shows. He said that many of the pictures are drinking scenes. One film he saw showed the whole process of making home brew.

Whatever may be said of the possibility of using the motion picture for good, the fact remains that as it is today, the "movie" is an outlaw. It is against the law to publish a recipe for making strong drink. But the screen shows it in a way to influence those most anxious for this sort of information. The increase of lawlessness is one of the things that all classes of right-thinking people are united in dreading as a menace to the institutions we hold most sacred.

Parents, the only safe place for your children at a "movie" is on the outside—and at a considerable distance. And it might be well to warn parents themselves to show a right example, for we were recently surprised to hear of a grandfather who attended these shows.—R. (Apparently this was J. A. Ressler, associate editor.)

1922

There are many things for which to be thankful in the present growth of the church. Nevertheless there seems to be a tendency to allow the spirit of hurry and restlessness to crowd out the deeper and more vital things.

A Day at Our Publishing House

by W. W. Hege

I arrived at Scottdale, Pa., at 8:30 in the evening of April 3, 1922, to attend the dedicatory services in the new Mennonite Publishing House the next day. I was met at the station by Bro. J. A. Ressler who is editor of several papers and also conducts successfully the correspondence between the little folks in the Words of Cheer; also Bro. John L. Horst, a native of our conference district, but who now operates a linotype machine. I was conveyed to Bro. C. F. Yake's home by auto, a favor which was very much appreciated after a tiresome journey of eleven hours by railroad across the Allegheny mountains. Bro. Yake is editor of the Youth's Christian Companion, a paper designed to furnish wholesome literature to those who are nearing or in the "teen age." The paper should have a wider circulation.

The new Publishing House is the largest building owned by the Mennonite Church. It is 80 x 110 feet, 3 stories high, above basement. The frame is of structural steel, the walls of tile, and the pillars, girders, and floors are very heavily reinforced with concrete. The construction of the entire building conforms to the recent code of state requirements. . . .

A visit to the Publishing House will convince any one that the Mennonite Church has great reason to rejoice because of the successful operation and management of her publishing interests. Bro. Aaron Loucks is the general manager, the spiritual welfare of the Church is carefully safeguarded, and the peculiar doctrines of the Bible upon which the Mennonite Church is founded are continually promulgated and emphasized. . . .

The co-operation and faithful service rendered by the workers and the harmony which exists among them is a feature which adds very much to the success of the work. Each morning the workers assemble in a room especially provided for the purpose, where the Scriptures are read and prayer is offered before any attempt is made to begin work.

The Mennonite Publishing House is the property of the Mennonite Church, and the house of God, just as much as our church houses are, and to the many thousands who do not have the opportunity to visit the home of our publishing interests, the very fountain head and source of our religious literature, we would say, your earnest prayers and support are continually needed that such messages and teaching may continue to go forth that will revive spirituality and cause a clinging to the indisputable facts and doctrines of the Bible.

Marion, Pa.

New construction at Mennonite Publishing House. The publishing house, says the author, is the property of the Mennonite Church, and the house of God, just as much as our church houses are.

Our Editorial Work

The editor having been elected president of Goshen College, a change will be necessary in the management of this office. Bro. J. L. Horst has been added to the editorial staff and he and Bro. A. B. Christophel will have charge of the office work after the editor moves to Goshen. The rest of the editorial roster remains the same until the Publication Board will see fit to make further changes.

Then and Now

by J. N. Durr

I was ordained a minister at Masontown, Pa., Feb. 5, 1872; as bishop Nov. 26, 1873. On Feb. 5, 1922, I was permitted to preach at my home church, Martinsburg, Pa., on the fiftieth anniversary of my ordination.

In the beginning of 1872 a series of meetings was held in the Masontown Church by Brethren J. F. Funk and Daniel Brenneman. At the close of the meetings, between forty-five and fifty converts were received. Two days later the writer and another young brother were ordained to the ministry.

Fifty years ago the Church was not so well organized as it is at the present time. Evangelistic work was merely begun. But this work continued to grow until the present time sees evangelistic efforts being made in almost every congregation as a regular feature of the church activities.

Evangelistic effort was mainly done on the responsibility of the individual, prompted by the Spirit. Instead of a call coming from a certain congregation, the Spirit laid it upon me to go to a certain congregation where it seemed that work was necessary. I would write to the place, telling them I was coming at a certain time. The congregation would arrange for the meetings. In this way a beginning was made in this conference district.

Means of communication and travel were not nearly so well established then as they are now. It was a long distance from Masontown to Johnstown, the trip usually occupying two days. . . .

Church buildings then did not have the comforts we are now accustomed to. Benches were usually without backs, yet the people were attentive and listened with deep interest to the Word that was preached to them. It is a question whether the comfortable benches we have at the present time do not cultivate sleepiness and inattention, especially when the house is so comfortably warmed by a furnace as most of our houses are now.

The singing was mostly in German fifty years ago, and the hymn was "lined," the congregation joined heartily in the singing after each two lines were read. English was introduced about this time and was used almost exclusively in a few of the congregations.

While this music was not ideal, it at least had the merit of being devotional. In this respect the singing then far surpassed much of the music that is practiced in the churches of the present day. It might be well to come back to more of the spiritual and devotional singing of those early days.

From the year 1880 to about 1893 the work at Scottdale, Pa., as well as the work at Rockton, Pa., was regularly in the writer's charge. There were no resident ministers in those places then.

There are many things for which to be thankful in the present growth and condition of the Church. Nevertheless there seems to be a tendency to allow the spirit of hurry and restlessness, not to say worldliness, of the present day to crowd out the interest in the deeper and more vital things that pertain to the spiritual life. . . .

My wish and prayer is for a deeper fellowship with God and a deeper work of grace in the hearts of all His professed followers.

Martinsburg, Pa.

1923

One of the nicest comments ever heard on behalf of Warren G. Harding.

Warren G. Harding

As we write this a special train is bearing the body of him who, until but a few days ago was the Chief Executive of his country, to the nation's capital. Crowds are gathering at the stations as the train rushes by, paying tribute to the man and honoring the position which he held. A nation is bowed in grief, and for the time being partisan rancor is hushed.

There are a few things which the death of President Harding brings to our minds. First among these is the difference between what men say of him now and what many of them said a month ago. Then he was the center of a political storm, and the hardest things that could be said of him were said with a relish. Now all this is hushed, and even his former critics are now talking about his kindness, his fitness for the place he held, his being the very man that was needed for troublesome reconstruction times. If the kind things said of him now could have been said while he was living, if the nation had been drawn to him then as it is now, it would not only have meant sunshine in his own life but would have been far better for the nation. Will the people of America think of this in connection with the new President?

The outstanding lesson to be learned from the life of Harding is the power of kindness. Whatever else men said of him, his generous heart won the affections of an unusually large number of people. Even his political enemies admired him because of his kindly disposition. Now that the man is gone his kindness stands out as the big asset in his life, and is universally recognized as a powerful factor in tiding the nation across the troublesome times of the past few years. Well may his countrymen forget his shortcomings and remember this outstanding quality as an element of towering strength.
    —*Daniel Kauffman*

The Quarter Fund

by J. E. Martin

Last spring quarters to the amount of $3.50 were distributed among those members of the Sunday school at Marion, Pa., who desired to invest them. Amount realized including the $3.50 was $40.25.

Following the regular Sunday school session on Dec. 10, each one investing quarters was asked to state, briefly his or her experience of the investment. Following we quote some of the expressions given:

"With my quarter I purchased 12 duck eggs, hatched 10, raised six, for which I got $5.20."

"Bought a rat trap with my quarter; my father gave me ten cents for each rat. I caught ten rats, so I have $1.00 besides the quarter. Would have caught more rats but some cats came to our place and caught them."

"Bought 15 eggs with my quarter; hatched 14 chicks. They grew nicely for a while then some rats killed nearly all of them, but I still realized $1.00 besides the quarter." (400 per cent on the investment if the rats did have a feast.—J. E. M.)

"I invested my quarter in seed potatoes. The season was dry and they didn't yield as well as expected. Sold what I raised for $1.00."

"We invested 4 quarters in 5 dozen eggs; hatched 41 chicks and raised 38. We sold 23 for $16 and still have 15 chickens."

Another also invested 4 quarters who turned in $15 plus the $1.00 invested. Much interest was manifested. The ministers, the local mission board member and the superintendent gave brief addresses along missionary lines.

The children were encouraged to keep on doing business for the Lord.
    Chambersburg, Pa.

Radio

by John W. Hess

Only in the last year are we confronted with questions relating to the radio and its effects on our homes.

Recently at a Bible conference this question came up in the question box, Is it right for members of the church to install radio outfits in their homes?

This question coming personally and publicly is an index that many anxious spiritual parents and children are considering the future outcome of this wonderful way of communication.

Many are interested, since so much has been written in the public press, and the natural makeup of man is to find out, or to have new things.

The aeroplane, at present in the minds of most of us, is too dangerous, also quite expensive, and therefore we have no special desire to ride in one, or own one.

The radio does not bring with it any special danger naturally, and is also coming in the reach of many in price, but we firmly believe it is bringing many dangers spiritually.

As in the coming of the printing press, telephone, autos, the radio is used for some useful things while in other things may bring a curse instead of a blessing.

The radio on the ships on the oceans is a great help in calling for help, or getting in touch with those whose lives are in danger.

In this late snow storm when the wires were about all down, the elevator men and the stock buyers would have been without markets, but for the radio.

God in His word says, "The children of this world are in their generation wiser than the children of light" (Luke 16:8). And since the trend of this age is fully in line with II Tim. 3:13, which says, "But evil men and seducers shall wax worse and worse, deceiving, and being deceived," this is a fast method for both to make use of.

Much of the religious program will no doubt more and more cater to the now popular teachings and to modern views of those who have forsaken the fundamental teachings of the Bible.

On this last Lord's day a man in our neighborhood claims to have listened to four sermons, making special mention of two, one being preached by a Christian Scientist, and the other by a Spiritualist. What else he heard (without going to church or obeying the command in Heb. 10:25, "Not forsaking the assembling of ourselves together") I do not know; but I know that I would not want to listen to the two named, and much less have my family of children hear them.

This is one more addition to the many things that keep people away from church. We have many vacant churches and many that the attendance should be larger. Even with better roads and much improved vehicles of travel our own churches in many places are dwindling down in attendance.

Many businessmen have installed the radio as a means of attraction, thru entertainment, which must be put on the program to draw certain classes of people. As to the bedtime stories for the little ones, I never heard any of these, but if they compare with many of them in our school books they will not take the place of the beautiful Bible stories, which are often repeated by the faithful Christian father and mother.

Are we willing to sacrifice the useful uses for the spiritual welfare of our children and the church? Would be glad to hear others express their convictions thru the Herald.

Manson, Iowa.

1924

Reflections on the small size of the church.

Factionalism

The partisan spirit thrives best in an atmosphere of jealousy and envy. Where people "love one another with a pure heart fervently" there is a constant drawing together rather than falling apart. But let certain individuals or groups become envious of each other, and everything will be welcomed to cast discredit on "the other side."

For illustration, let us suppose a congregation where members have been given to strife. It happens that on one side there are those given to smoking while on the other side there are some who insist on wearing jewelry. The temptation is for side number one to keep hammering away on the iniquity of wearing jewelry, while side number two harps continually on the awful sin of smoking. Thus the pot keeps calling the kettle black (and, as a rule, under such circumstances, both pot and kettle keep on getting blacker) until they come to blows. Neither side is reformed, but both sides are terribly deformed because they were more absorbed in the thought of discrediting and demolishing their opponents than in the efforts to win transgressors from the error of their way.

But our purpose is not so much to denounce factionalism as it is to point out a few things which may help us to steer clear of or overcome this awful plague.

1. When you hear something against yourself, make a prayerful study of yourself in the light of truth to see if there is any foundation to the report. If guilty, repent and reform; if not guilty, be man enough to live above the spirit of vengeance and retaliation.

2. If you are more tolerant with the sins of those who stand with you in the controversy than you are with the sins of those on "the other side," you should at once change your attitude and pray the Lord for a more Christlike spirit.

3. When you see the other side at its worst, it is possible that you may have but an exact photograph of yourself as others see you.

4. You can at all times afford to listen to the counsel of level-headed friends who have been far enough away from the seat of the conflict to keep the blood cool.

5. The surest way (and the only right way) to get rid of an enemy is to kill him with love.
—*Daniel Kauffman*

Why Not More Mennonites?

Notwithstanding our boasted progress, there are probably less Mennonites in America today than there were a century ago. In the days of Shem Zook he estimated that there were about 100,000 Mennonites in America, although those figures were disputed by some. Now there are about 80,000 Mennonites (all kinds) in America. When we think of the several million descendants of Mennonites in America, the question naturally arises, Why so few of them in the Mennonite Church? We feel our shortcomings in attempting to answer, but here are a few things for your consideration:

1. No church standing for a full-Gospel religion needs to dream of a very large membership, for there are not enough converted people in the world. It has always been that churches that stood for the true evangelical faith have been comparatively weak in numbers. The lure of the broad way is so strong that neither the Mennonite nor any other church that insists on keeping the narrow way can ever hope to be among the most populous churches.

Aside from this fact, however, there are a number of other reasons why our church is not any larger than it is. Before the present evangelistic wave swept over the Church the membership had dwindled down so that the census of 1890 placed the membership of the Mennonite Church in the United States at 17,000 and all branches of Mennonites at 43,000. The fact that the Church has about doubled in membership since that time indicates that aggressive work counts.

Again, the growth of the Church has been checked by indifference and worldliness. We will notice each of these briefly:

2. History has proven that when the body of members in any church were "white hot for God" there was a growth in membership, even in the face of opposition and persecution. But when indifference creeps into the lives of members, so that they neglect to live the prayer life, to read their Bibles diligently, to attend church services regularly or to take an active part when they are there, to obey the unpopular commandments of the Bible, to bring up their children in "the nurture and admonition of the Lord," you can expect results as described in the next paragraph.

3. It is while men sleep that the enemy sows his seeds. While the soul is wrapped in the sleep of spiritual indifference the heart furnishes an excellent seed-bed for the seeds of worldliness. And this is what has happened to too many sleepers. Some have become victims to this world's money, some to this world's fashions, some to this world's pleasures, some to this world's vain show, some to this world's lust for popularity and power, some to other worldly attractions. No man who has surrendered to either of these worldly attractions will peaceably submit to the discipline of any church that insists on holding its membership to the whole-Gospel faith. Members who resent church interference with their assumed liberty to walk "according to the course of this world" are a double injury to the Church: (1) they themselves are not right with God. (2) The influence on their families and others is against the Church.

Men tell us that strict discipline is what drives people out of the Church. That is true only when this discipline is either unscriptural or harshly administered without the spirit of the Gospel. Faithful discipline is always wholesome, even though it sometimes appears severe to those who look at it from the standpoint of human sympathy only. Laxness in discipline simply puts off the day of retribution and multiplies the losses and sorrows of the Church.

Not merely for the sake of getting numbers, but for the sake of saving souls, let every member awake to righteousness, shake off the load of indifference, and shine for God. When the whole Church is wakened up, the dead timber removed, the live branches purged, the whole body active, we may expect the joy of the Lord in its fulness to take possession of our souls, the work of division among us to be stopped, the light of the Gospel to shine in our own homes and communities, and many souls will be won for Christ and salvation and the Church.

—*Daniel Kauffman*

1925

On the 400th anniversary of Anabaptism, a picnic in India with Scripture reading, prayer, and song.

Four Hundred Years

by J. A. Ressler

According to the best available authorities it is now four hundred years since the first Mennonite congregation was organized in Zurich, Switzerland, and that organization has continuously been kept intact as a denomination until the present time. It is true that the name Mennonite was not applied to this people until some time after this, but the organization has remained the same.

Among Mennonite societies in Europe, and among some of the Mennonite branches in

America there has been some effort made to commemorate in a suitable way the four hundredth anniversary of the founding of the Church. In India there are three Mennonite branches at work. One is in South India, the Breudergemeinde from Russia, who had formerly worked in connection with the Baptists, another is the Mission of the General Conference of Mennonites of North America, working about two hundred miles northeast of Dhamtari, and the third is our American Mennonite Mission, centered about Dhamtari, Central Provinces.

When the matter of an Indian Mennonite commemoration of the four hundred years was mentioned, those who dealt with the matter felt that the gain from such a meeting would hardly justify the expense involved. The South India Mennonites would have had to make a long journey to come here and they did not feel able to invite our people to come to visit with them. So the matter was dropped.

However, a few days ago there happened to come into our Dhamtari community, all unpremeditated and without thought of any anniversary, three families of the General Conference missionaries. One family was traveling by train, the others by two autos. And the two "visitors" from America were on hand. And someone had a bright idea.

Over at Maramsilli, where the storage reservoir for the Great Mahanadi Canal is located, is a spot where nature and man's art have united to make one of the most beautiful places in the Central Provinces. The road from Dhamtari is beautiful. Why not take the visitors out there for an afternoon lunch and spend an hour in a meeting for mutual spiritual help and uplift?

And so it was arranged. All of the American Mennonite Mission families were there except two who were out on tour. The meeting was not planned for in advance, but it was a success, nevertheless. The meeting was opened by Scripture reading, prayer, and song. Missionary problems are much the same, and the temptations that come to converts are the same in most of the missions we come in contact with.

These facts were brought out in the talks that were given. The missionaries returned to their stations in the late afternoon feeling that the day had been well and profitably spent.

A feature of the return journey that was not on the schedule was a free entertainment given by a panther of immense size. This beautiful creature of the jungle was quietly seated by the side of the road as the cars came by. Not all of us saw him, but those who did declared he was a very fine specimen. When the young folks in the car saw him they called the attention of the Doctor to him. The car was quickly brought to a standstill, and the panther politely withdrew into the jungle!

Dhamtari, C.P., India. January 20, 1925.

Lina Z. Ressler in India with friends Ragua and Dolat. This article is an account of how one group celebrated the 400th anniversary of Anabaptism.

1926

A Farewell Meeting

by Willis K. Lederach

Hoboken, N.J., Pier 3
Feb. 13, 1926

Dear Readers of the Gospel Herald, Greetings of Love in Jesus' worthy name:—At ten this morning, the writer accompanied by Paul Histand, Arthur Kolb, Elmer Kolb, and Henry Ruth, all of the Franconia District, arrived in New York City to see Bro. and Sister Hershey leave. We were later joined by the following brethren and sisters: Jason H. Weaver, D. E. Weaver, and Joseph Weaver, all of Virginia, and Amos Hershey, Milfred Hertzler, Harry K. Hershey and wife, Elmer Lehman and wife, and Benj. Mellinger and wife, of Lancaster County.

About 11:30 some of the brethren went to the hotel to help carry the baggage to the boat. Upon the arrival of Bro. and Sister Hershey and son Lester, and Sister Elsie Shank who is returning to her parents, J. W. Shank's, in South America, each of us visitors was given a permit to board the boat, "The American Legion," which will be their temporary home for the next seventeen days.

After inspecting their quarters we united in a brief but impressive farewell service. We sang, "Nearer My God to Thee," after which we knelt before God in a special prayer in behalf of these dear ones. Realizing that seven years and about four thousand miles shall separate us, yet with joy could we sing "Blest Be the Tie That Binds," and "We'll Never Say Goodbye in Heaven."

After visiting the dining room and sitting room, we were obliged to return to the pier where we waited until about 1:45 p.m., when the last ties were loosed, and the stately ship was towed from the shore and glided out toward the great Atlantic. . . .

In His service, Willis K. Lederach.
Norristown, Pa.

Adios

by T. K. Hershey

Adios, or Good-bye, is our last word to the beloved Church of our choice. In a few minutes we leave for Argentina, S. A. Many and varied are the thoughts that have run through our minds these last moments of our stay in the Home Land. Looking back we thank God for the rich experiences during our furlough. If we have been a blessing to any, give God the praise and honor.

We return to Argentina because we believe God has called us there. We leave very reluctantly, our dear widowed mother, who is now in her 81st year, as well as our daughter Beatrice; but we believe that He who has called us will care for them.

We look forward with fond anticipation and believe God has some definite work in Argentina for us.

We want to thank the brotherhood for their hearty cooperation and desire to carry forward the work of the Mennonite church in South America as indicated by their hearty contributions and the many promises of united prayer. . . .

Wishing to all God's richest blessing, we say, "adios" (Good-bye). Pray for us.

T. K. Hershey about 1920 building a garage for the first "Mission Ford" in Argentina: "We return to Argentina because we believe God has called us there."

Editor's Comments

The above message speaks for itself. By the time this reaches the eye of the reader they will be well on their way to the land whither they are going to bear the message of the Gospel.

Bro. Hershey has demonstrated, as our missionaries at home on furlough usually do, that coming home to rest means a change of labors, rather than a cessation from all activities. In the year and ten months in which he and his family were in America he attended five district conferences, one meeting of Mennonite General Conference, and many missionary, educational, and other special meetings. He conducted five series of meetings, anointed with oil nine members who called "for the elders of the Church," visited one hundred seventy-one congregations, preached three hundred and fifteen sermons, and spoke words of encouragement to many Sunday schools and young people's meetings. He wrote a score or more of articles for publication, and through extensive solicitations secured about twenty thousand dollars in support of the work in Argentina. His travels took him through twenty-five states and several provinces. In addition to these activities he spent about two months in a Bible school in Philadelphia.

—*Daniel Kauffman*

Suggestions for the Next General Conference

by J. A. Ressler

The William Penn Highway runs right thru the Kishacoquillas Valley and thru the town of Belleville. This highway is less mountainous than many of the roads in Pennsylvania, yet its gentle windings and long slopes seem like gigantic mountains to those who have been used to the straight, long levels of the Middle West.

It will be well to caution persons driving automobiles for the first time in Pennsylvania that brakes should be in good order, and that the mechanical provision for using the engine as a brake and not depending on friction alone is often the means of saving repair bills and preventing accidents.

The mountain roads need not deter persons from using their autos for travel in Pennsylvania. Thousands travel by these mountain roads every day. But those who are not accustomed to the hills will do well to be cautious. Persons from the West, stopping at Scottdale, often ask whether the mountains east of here are worse than those over which they have come. We smile indulgently and tell them that they have not crossed any mountains yet—mountains of Pennsylvania and Maryland are east of Scottdale.

The legal speed limit in Pennsylvania is thirty miles an hour. Many persons travel faster than this, but it is well to remember that with the winding roads, where often the road ahead cannot be seen more than a hundred feet, it is not safe to travel at so great a speed as in more level country. It is well to respect the laws of the state in which we are traveling.

Commit your keeping into the hands of the Father, and exercise the judgment and caution with which He has endowed you, and He will take you safely thru.

Scottdale, Pa.

1927

A report on Argentine reaction to the U.S. execution of Sacco and Vanzetti.

What South America Thinks of the United States

by J. W. Shank

The tide of opinion against the United States has about reached its limit. Who would have thought it possible that within the short time of a few months such a hatred and explosion of vituperation could be developed here and expressed daily in the press and in public posters?

A short time ago there was a perfect storm about the Nicaragua affair. The newspapers cried down the United States for oppressing poor Nicaragua and refusing to listen to any cries of mercy.

At that time the feeling continued to get hotter until some conciliating action was taken that quieted the spirits of the impulsive Latin American.

Now the Sacco-Vanzetti case is upon us. If a comparison could be made, we would have to say that the feeling runs much higher and is much more wide-spread than in the Nicaragua case. There are certain "yellow" dailies published in Buenos Aires that are chiefly responsible for the present disturbance. These dailies are of the sensational type. They are always coming out with a hue and a cry against something or someone. Because of their sensational character the masses, who like stirring reading, buy them and become worked up over whatever is being heralded before the public.

These papers speak of Sacco and Vanzetti as innocent martyrs of the moneyed interests of the United States. Governor Fuller is painted as the blackest type of barbarian. The long delay in dealing with this criminal case is reported as a cat-and-mouse play, Governor Fuller being the brutal cat who delights to see the mice (Sacco and Vanzetti) suffer torment as long as possible.

Argentine has for some forty years already laid aside the capital punishment law. Thus the average Argentine thinks the United States still hangs to this relic of barbarism, and that Argentine is far ahead of her in having come to a humanitarian conception of how to deal with criminals.

It may be interesting for some to know just what the Argentine law provides for such criminal types as these in question. Here that type of criminal is sent to a desolate Island far toward the south pole. They say that those who go there suffer untold misery until death relieves them. A certain criminal had by some means escaped and returned to Argentine. As the authorities were taking him on board a ship to return him to that awful place he suddenly jumped into the sea and was drowned. He preferred death by suicide rather than to return.

To most North Americans this form of penalty would seem much more cruel than death by electrocution. But the Argentines do not look at the matter in that light. They consider the death penalty as the most barbarous that it is possible to inflict.

To-day, Aug. 22, there is a general strike of all laboring men in this country. Even the milk men have not made their usual rounds. Every day there are public meetings and demonstrations in general, in protest against the criminal Americans who are resisting with stony hearts the pleadings of the world in favor of the condemned. There are rumors of terrible revenge if the men are electrocuted.

The missionaries dare not say anything except to express our sentiment that we do not favor the death sentence in any case but rather life imprisonment, and that we think the men ought to be banished from the country and sent to the land that is making the greatest cry in their behalf. We would not venture to express an opinion as to the justice of the trials they have had.

The two events just referred to can not help but make our work much harder. It makes the people point the finger of scorn at North American Christianity. The people who come to our mission regularly do not take so radical an attitude. They can see by our teaching that we could not be classed as brutal barbarians. But those outside, who are ready to believe any lies about the missionaries and the mission, would be ready to assault the mission if they dared.

We believe that right must prevail somehow in the things in question. We will trust the Lord to see us safely through. We ask for your prayers that we may at all events be faithful to Him for whom we are working.

San Luis, Argentina.

Going to the General Conference at Belleville

by J. A. Ressler

The accompanying map was sent us by the General Conference Arrangement Committee of Belleville, Pa., with the suggestion that it be published in the Gospel Herald as a help in finding the place by auto.

Persons from the west who prefer to avoid city traffic can keep out of Pittsburgh in several ways, the two most practical of which are:—

1. Join the Lakes to Sea Highway at Meadeville or Franklin, Pa. (in the northwestern part of the state), and follow Route No. 5 to Belleville. Grades are easy through the mountains and the road is in good condition.

2. Find the best route from your place to Wheeling, West Virginia. Then take the following towns in order: Washington, Pa., West Newton, Greensburg, New Alexandria (on the Wm. Penn Highway), and follow Route No. 3 to Belleville. From Water Street, Pa., Routes 3 and 5 are the same.

Persons from the Shenandoah Valley region follow the route indicated on the small map

herewith printed, via McConnellsburg, Pa., Mount Union, Mill Creek, where Route No. 3 is picked up. Inquire at Mill Creek.

Persons from the east go to Lewistown, then Reedsville, Belleville.

Main highways in Pennsylvania have the route numbers painted on a "keystone" on poles by the roadside.

Many persons have trouble with brakes when they first try to drive in Pennsylvania. With Fords, use the three foot pedals alternately, never keeping the pressure on for more than thirty seconds at a time.

With three-speed cars learn to go down the first hills by putting the car in second and using the brakes only to snub the speed down to a safe place. Never keep the pressure on the foot brakes long at a time. Release at frequent intervals. If second gear is too fast for your nerves go into low. In all cases go down hill with the engine in gear and ignition on, gas shut off as much as possible.

Safety is far more important than speed.
Scottdale, Pa.

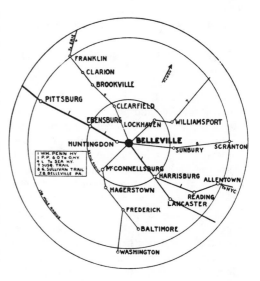

1928

No matter how elections go, let it not be forgotten that the forces of evil are still with us.

Thoughts on the Recent Election

During the past year the Presidential election in the United States attracted the attention of millions of people. That election having now passed into history, we may well ponder over results.

Whatever may be the viewpoint from which such events are regarded, impressions are made and lessons learned that can be meditated upon with profit. Some talk about the rise of independentism in politics and the consequent loss of prestige on the part of practical politicians, others moralize upon what this election will mean for the temperance cause, others are discussing the probable effect on Catholicism as a factor in politics, others have their eye centered on what the future has in store on the question of peace or war. What have you been thinking about?

1. For the first time in history a Quaker is elected President and an American Indian (quarter blood) Vice President. Ten years ago, had any one ventured the idea that an American Indian might come to his own and occupy the highest position within the gift of the American people, the answer immediately would have been, "Never in the world." But such is now among the possibilities. Should Herbert Hoover, after his inauguration, be removed through death or otherwise, the office would go to the Vice President, whose grandmother was a full-blood Indian. The question naturally arises, Will the President-elect prove true to the historic attitude of his church on the question of nonresistance, or will his political affiliations take precedence over his religious connections so that he will line up with the militarists? We are hoping and praying his attitude on the question of peace or war will give evidence that the faith of his fathers will not have been forgotten.

2. The country seems to be politically "dry." With an avowed champion of the "wets" going down under an avalanche of votes and a professed champion of the "drys" elected by an overwhelming majority, it seems clear that the majority of people are in favor of giving the cause of prohibition a further try-out. But it must not be forgotten that there were other issues at stake which appealed to the voters with sufficient force to enable Hoover to carry a number of "wet" strongholds, and that of all the leading contenders for the Republican nomination the one nominated was least objectionable to the "wets." His personal record being favorable, however, it is hoped that he will prove himself loyal to the temperance cause. But it will take years of strenuous education before the rank and file of the American people, especially the foreign element, will merit the name of being personally "dry."

3. Another fact has again been made evident; namely, when Church people become thoroughly aroused on any issue, the rest of the people usually respect their wishes and their judgment. That accounts for the election of Herbert Hoover, even though the church members of the Protestant persuasion in America are in the minority. The great reason why the world is not any more deeply impressed by the moral and spiritual issues pertaining to the cause of real Christianity is because the rank and file of professing Christians make such a feeble profession that it fails to impress seriously the unsaved world. The failure to "make disciples of all nations" must be laid to the door of indifference on the part of an apathetic Church.

4. Another item worthy of notice was the very large sums of money spent during the campaign. Officially the two major parties report a total expenditure of about nine million dollars. This does not include the millions spent by individuals in behalf of their favorite candidates whether state or national. With all

the professions made in favor of "clean elections" it is no very closely guarded secret that corruption had an important part in deciding results in certain places. On this issue there is seemingly no very great difference between the political parties . . . .

5. Moral questions are not as a rule decided by political contests. Had Alfred E. Smith been elected the nature of the conflict on some of the issues would have been somewhat different from what it will likely be since a Protestant and an avowed advocate of the Eighteenth Amendment was elected, but on all moral questions upon which people are taking opposite sides it will take more than elections to definitely settle them one way or the other. No matter how elections go, let it not be forgotten that the forces of evil will still be with us and must be converted to Christ before they are effectively overcome. The Bible tells us that in the last days "evil men and seducers shall wax worse and worse." We do our most effective work by wrestling before the Throne. Your personal life is the most important factor in the matter of promoting the cause of truth and righteousness.

6. Regardless of issues which the next few years may bring to the fore, there are several duties which are very clear. We owe to our rulers our loyalty and our prayers. "Let every soul be subject unto the higher powers." We are commanded to "obey magistrates," and to pray for our rulers. And while we should at all times have a submissive attitude toward those in authority, we should never lose sight of the fact that the Highest of all rulers is He from Whom all blessings flow and to Whom our supreme allegiance belongs. In times of war the attitude of nonresistant people is often misunderstood and misinterpreted, but we are quite sure that the more loyal we are to the standard of the Cross in times of peace the more readily our attitude will be comprehended and understood in times of war. With a steadfast prayer that God may overrule and direct in the affairs of nations, may our record as "strangers and pilgrims in the earth" be such as to prove a blessing to any country that gives us shelter.

—*Daniel Kauffman*

The Name of Our New Minister in India

by J. A. Ressler

I have just finished reading the manuscript for the Report of the American Mennonite Mission in India and I was struck, as I read, by the fact that the missionaries spell the name of the first ordained Indian minister in at least four different ways: Isabax, Isabux, Isa Baksh, and Isa Bax. I am not sure that there is not a possibility of finding one or two other spellings.

Some close observer will be sure to notice this and will ask which is right and why it is that the editor of the Supplement does not see to it that the name goes into the paper correctly spelled.

And when those letters of criticism and inquiry begin to come in this poor editor will be utterly helpless.

The first part of the name, Isa, is one of the Indian forms for the name Jesus. The second part, the one which is so variously spelled, means a gift. Hence the name of our minister means "The Gift of Jesus." A beautiful name. He used to have another name when I knew him in the Mission years ago, but let's forget about that other name.

"Bakhsh" is a Persian word incorporated into the Urdu, and means "giving," or "a gift." It should be printed with a dot under the "k," and this would give the "kh" the sound of German "ch" in "Buch." The "a" is sounded like "u" in "but," "B" is sounded as in English, and the "sh" also. Now try to pronounce the original of that second part of the name of our new preacher!

An Englishman (and some few Americans) can't say "Buch" no matter how they try, so they try a short cut in pronouncing the name for "a gift" by making the "khsh" equivalent to "x." That's how we got the name "Isabax," and you can divide it and say "Isa Bax" if you like, or spell it with some of the modifications of the original. But I for one absolutely refuse to decide which one spelling is right to the exclusion of all others.

1929

A Shorter Bible?

by Martha Stoltzfus

There is much talk among Christians and among Mennonites of the "Restoration of the Jew to Palestine," of the "Postponed Kingdom," of "Dispensationalism" and such subjects as grew out of the study of unfulfilled prophecy.

Several years ago we read repeated warnings in the Gospel Herald concerning a "Shorter Bible." I feel sure few Mennonites will be led astray by one who offers a shorter Bible and states what it is. But there are folks who have a very short Bible who have connived a subtle way of being relieved of parts of it and still not offend much!

They are the ones who believe the postponement theory. Of the worst of these it was said by a Mennonite Bible teacher that "it is Dispensationalism gone to seed." What can you expect? Plants eventually do go to seed if left to grow. All books available on these subjects which deal with them in any detailed way are by non-Mennonite authors, all of whom do not accept some one or other of the doctrines which our church holds as vital. In view of the general misinformation on these subjects, could not a number of Mennonite Bible students get busy studying the Bible on this line and lead us out of the slough? I realize that since I read some of the books on this subject, it will be impossible to reach any scriptural conclusions if we start with the thought that we must accept the theories of writers who are generally accepted as authorities.

Some of the things that have impressed me as being detrimental, a hindrance to Christian growth, is the mass of Bible supported (?) speculation concerning current political events. "In such an hour as ye think not," is the unalterable fact. Also the paving the way for folks to think there is some future dispensation for Jewish repentance and conversion.

The Bible teaches that Jew and Gentile are one in Christ and His Church. Why call this a Gentile dispensation as if to exclude the Jew?

The purpose of this article is to stir up thought and research as to which of these "theories" are the plants that go to seed and bear a "Shorter Bible" and like evils and therefore should be plucked up; and which of these plants bring forth seed to God's glory and should be cultivated.

Martinsburg, Pa.

Liberalism's Bid for the Mennonite Church

It has been several decades since it first became the writer's privilege to watch the progress of the Mennonite Church in America. During this time this church has a little more than doubled its membership—that is, increased from a little less than 20,000 to a little above 40,000 members. During this time also we have witnessed the beginning and progress of our missionary organizations, the building up of three church schools and several times that many short-term Bible schools, the consolidation and expansion of our publication interests, the organization and growth in power and influence of the Mennonite General Conference, and a number of other things through which the power and growth of the Church have been promulgated.

Naturally we may expect an aggressive church to be beset by counteracting influences. If the enemy of souls was bold enough to undertake to thwart the work of Christ through manifold temptations, we may expect him to employ similar tactics in attempting the overthrow of a Christ-honoring church. In this the Mennonite Church has been no exception. Radicalism, absorption in world affairs, indifference, personal ambition, fanaticism, factionalism, liberalism, and numerous other things have been the channels through which the enemy of souls has succeeded in overthrowing the faith and thwarting the efforts of many. Of these the last has probably been the most destructive.

Nations and churches have fallen, not so much because they have been overcome by superior numbers and powers, but because they have been undermined and weakened through subtle and deadly influences. Thus Rome (both civil and religious) which for a time swept everything before her was finally brought to the dust because through a number of centuries she was undermined by subtle influences which corrupted her until she was little better than or different from the paganism from which she had risen. The same is true (with varying details) of other churches which might be named. Aggressive churches have more to fear from the dazzling influences of prestige, popularity, and power than they have from the discouragements arising from adversity and opposition. As the curse of Catholicism has been a chained Bible which left the masses in ignorance, so the curse of Protestantism is a Bible stripped of its orthodoxy.

Liberalism's bid for any church is an effort to capture its young people, especially the most talented and wide-awake among the rising generation. In this there is a double advantage to be gained: (1) It is from this class that church leaders arise. (2) Oftentimes, when bright young people are captured for liberalism, their parents follow after. And such defections from the ranks of the faithful are most sweeping when the leaders in the apostasy succeed in discrediting faithful leaders in the eyes of the people.

Modernists take it as a matter of course that intelligence is on the side of liberalism, while ignorance and bigotry are the mainstays of orthodoxy. Their description of conservative churches (especially the most conspicuous leaders) abound in such epithets as "bigotry," "ignorance," "narrow," "bosses," "blind," "the hierarchy," "dogmatism," "400 years ago," "divine rights of bishops," "formalism," "out-of-date," "bondage," "ultra-conservatism," "blatherskite," "pin-headed," claiming for themselves superior light and liberty, and a breadth of reason to be found only among those who have renounced the slavery and bondage of the old-time orthodox religion.

And, couching their liberalism in the language of orthodoxy, they often succeed in misleading intelligent people who are short on experience, blinding their eyes to the well-established fact that the Bible and common sense are in perfect agreement, and that the world's ripest scholars and most fair-minded thinkers are on the side of orthodoxy....

At this time we desire to call the attention of our conferences to responsibilities devolving upon us and the opportunities lying before us. Within the next month nearly half of our conferences will hold their annual meetings. May we rise to our opportunities, and as a united, praying, faithful brotherhood go on record and give a faithful testimony against this modern octopus which threatens to destroy every church that adheres to the old-time Bible faith. May we do our full duty in stemming the tide of liberalism and saving the Church from its ravages.

—*Daniel Kauffman*

1930

Indian Music

by J. D. Graber

India is a land of music. I have no less an authority for this statement than H. A. Popley, for years a distinguished lyrical missionary in India. But one need not quote authorities if he keeps his ears open. The cart drivers, as they wend their way slowly along the roads at night, sing a great deal of the time, all sorts of nonsense rhymes, if not obscene songs or religious classics, perhaps to inform lurking robbers that they are fully awake. "Graveyard whistling" we would call it in American idiom.

The housewife and the daughter-in-law, as they sit grinding the flour, sing to one another the stories of the ancient heroes of India. The boatman as he plies his oar or punts his dugout canoe often sings a quaint and beautiful song whether it be in the backwaters of Travancore or in the great rivers of Bengal. In Darjeeling I have been attracted by what sounded like a chorus rehearsal and found it was the concert singing of about twenty men and women laborers who were pulling a heavy road roller up and down the steep mountain roads. Coolies pounding the metal into the road add color to their monotonous task by singing rhymes made up to the "phat! phat!" of the falling hammers. The western "Heave, ho!" when all hands take hold is much too prosaic for musical India. Here the muscles twitch in unison to the catchy rhythm of a strictly indigenous tune. In the Panjab the women hire drummers and singers to help them as they reap the grain.

And then for festivals, marriages and holidays! Musicians are hired by the wholesale and the shrieking of the home-made flute, with the vents punched in by guess, and the dreary drone of the tom-tom can be heard far into the night. Some of these musicians, if they were up on American sensational thrills and love of contests, could qualify for drumming Marathons. They beat their pigskins for eighteen hours a day, as long as the master of the feast continues to furnish the coin. I have seen them so exhausted that they reeled and tottered, but a drink of country liquor or a pinch of some stimulating drug helps keep up the monotonous rhythm.

But, I have written this about our local music. It is a common mistake among Europeans to suppose that Indian music is primitive and unscientific. America has its country jazz bands and its popular hits, but it would be as unfair to judge western music by them as to judge Indian music by the common barber's band. Experts say that it is also a common mistake to suppose that Indian melodies are so full of microtones that it is impossible to put their music into European notation. Mr. Popley says that India has, however, developed its music along somewhat different lines from that of the west. It is a system of melodies sung to a drone which is usually the tonic with or without the fifth.

The Indian Church in the Hindi speaking area does not have a good Hymnology. There have been Christian Bengali poets; Tilak wrote beautiful songs in Marathi; and some of the south Indian languages have a rich Christian lyrical treasure. We are still awaiting a real poet to express Christian devotion and aspiration in Hindi verse. Some songs are continually coming forward, however, and our hymn books grow with the years. There has appeared recently a new tune book in which several hundred of the most common Hindi Bhajans have been set to our musical notation. This book will do much to make for uniformity in the singing of these songs as well as affording a means of learning new ones. We have good translations of most of the standard western hymns. Their sentiment is certainly without fault, but the western tunes do not fit the Indian situation or temperament. Unless especially trained in western music the Indian does not sing in harmony so that our church singing is in unison, and when it is not in unison it is likewise not harmonious.

Dhamtari, C.P., India

J. D. Graber: It is a common mistake among Europeans to suppose that Indian music is primitive and unscientific.

A Comparison

One of the most widely advertised subjects for discussion at the present time is that of Prohibition. Brewers, distillers, moonshiners, bootleggers, money-grabbers, and wet politicians are in an unholy alliance and straining every nerve to break down respect for law, especially the Eighteenth Amendment, and have succeeded in getting some very well meaning people to thinking that there should be a radical change in temperance legislation. But what the nature of this change should be, no one seems to be ready to come out with an acceptable substitute. About as far as they are ready to go is to say that most anything would be better than prohibition, although none of them profess to favor the return of the open saloon. They did for awhile seem to think that some law patterned after the Canadian law of government regulation would be the thing to adopt, but since the official report from that government shows that under that law liquor consumption increased and the hoped-for improvements have thus far failed to materialize you hear less about making that the substitute for Prohibition. Temperance people are ready to listen to any one who has something better than statutory Prohibition, but so far none of these substitutes has been put forward seriously for consideration. If the foes of temperance can succeed in breaking down respect for law and inducing the American people to rise up en masse and vote this hated Prohibition out of existence they will have won their point. But what will America have in the place of it? The only alternatives in sight are anarchy and the licensed saloon—and few people profess to favor either of these.

A similar situation seems to face the Mennonite Church with reference to some of its distinctive doctrines. There are those who say the Mennonite Church is all wrong on the Dress Question, on its stand in opposition to Life Insurance, on its attitude toward War, on a number of other points in which it stands almost alone among churches. We have been listening for some one among the critics to bring forward some substitutes, that we might be able to compare them with what we already have. No thoughtful loyalist would object to considering any substitute that might be offered, or to accept anything that might stand the test of Scripture and be a real improvement over what we already have. The Mennonite Church has made changes in the past, and we believe stands ready to do so again; but we are loath to change until we can see clearly what we are changing to. Speaking of the Dress Question, shall we change from an attitude of scriptural regulations to that of fashion domination? "No!" comes the answer from nearly all members, critics among the rest. Then what shall we change to? No definite answer from any of the critics. Then take Life Insurance. Shall we change our attitude against Life Insurance to one favoring it? Some, but not many, are ready to answer yes to that question. If not ready to sanction it as a church, what shall be the substitute? A similar test might be made of any other tenet of our faith for which we have been criticized.

—*Daniel Kauffman*

1931

I Have Been Wondering

by Lina Z. Ressler

It is interesting to watch little minds as they unfold and ask questions. Children's minds, they are, and the questions are an evidence of growth.

Things come into more mature minds that remind us of these qualities. The other day when a nice, new car ran into our faithful little "Chevvy," piled a lot of window glass into the corner of the rear seat, and crushed my head right into the mass of broken glass, I was sufficiently shocked and hurt to stop my real or imaginary busy career and do some thinking—and, wondering.

The heavenly Father was good to me. I did not even have the pain of the shock then; the little car on the Baltimore Pike threw me into a mixture of glass and I was mercifully saved from any consciousness of how I came there or what happened. Neither did I know how anxiously my dazed companion pulled me out of the wreckage of glass and suit cases and clothing.

Kind hands helped us to reach the friendly refuge of a hospital with competent medical care. I was not comfortable, but I really did not care—much—I wondered if I was dying—if this was death it was all right—for I was trusting in the Father.

People seemed to be working over me frantically. I pulled hard and my eyelids opened slowly. Three pairs of hands moved quickly and skillfully over my head. I wondered what they were doing. Anyway, I could not help them, so I dropped off to sleep again.

        o   o   o

The prick of a needle in my cheek caused me to gain consciousness again—this time I got the glimpse of a pair of friendly brown eyes bending over me while two firm, soft hands were holding mine. I did not know why they should hold my hands. I could never raise them, but maybe they thought I might. Anyway, I did not care.

After a while I felt a razor shaving my scalp. I wondered what that was for. Again I tried to look. I saw the doctor and nurses working frantically, the doctor giving short, quick directions, the nurses carrying them out with white, set faces and tightly closed lips. How the white fingers flew as the stitches went in one by one! I remember now that they talk about "hospital training." The poise and cooperation of those awful, tense moments could not be acquired in a day.

I am glad we have hospitals. I am glad there are opportunities to cultivate the art of ministering to suffering human creatures. The effort to remain conscious was too severe. Without a bit of anaesthetic, local or general, I dropped off to sleep again and again. Nature's anaesthetic, loss of blood, smothered out the pain while the final stitches were being put in place. The jolt of the bandaging again roused

me and I was taken to a sunny room and a comfortable bed. White-capped nurses with swift, skillful fingers tucked me in. It all seemed so dim and unreal. I tried to think of dear ones far away, but they seemed like part of another world. I was glad for the warm touch of Uncle J. A.'s hands and then I went to sleep, grateful, quiet, happy in the Father's care.

Unusual, all of it. I wonder why such experiences come to us. We were in the line of duty, and felt confident of the Father's care. We wonder why the pathway led this way. Was there a lesson to learn? Was there a testimony to give in that far-away, out-of-the-way place? We wonder again and again why it all happened. Perhaps there was a lesson for us to learn. Perhaps we had not been appreciating hospitals and nurses as we should. How we praise God for their gentle ministry!

And then the pathway led among friends— friends of long ago, with loving sympathy and kindly ministrations—toward home. We are wondering still what it all means, as we shall likely wonder about many of our experiences until we reach the place where we shall know even as also we are known.

Scottdale, Pa.

Lina Z. Ressler: We wonder again and again why the accident happened. Perhaps there was a lesson for us to learn.

Flag Salute in Virginia

by Henry M. Shenk

Quite a stir has been going on here in eastern Virginia on the flag salute question since last fall when one of our boys who was attending school in Newport News could not comply with the requirement of saluting the flag, which was a part of the school exercises.

Because of the principle involved, and the hardships experienced by the child, in an attempt to relieve the situation Bro. Geo. R. Brunk appealed to the school board of the city, stating fully and clearly our positions on the question and asking to have the lad exempted from that part of the school exercises.

The Board went on record as granting the request; but when this was published in the newspapers, immediately there was a storm of protest by many so-called patriotic organizations and by many individuals in which there were stern criticisms of the church for its principles, and the school board for its action.

Bro. Brunk has been in the center of the controversy ever since and has made published defenses against attacks from individuals and organizations who either could not or else would not understand our position. The matter was carried to the state board of education by several organizations, whereupon Bro. Brunk appealed to state officials to also hear representatives of the Mennonites before taking action in the case. The state board granted this request and appointed a committee to give a hearing.

Bro. Brunk also placed the matter before the executive committee of the Virginia Conference with the result that a committee of three brethren was appointed to represent the Conference at the hearing by the state authorities. The brethren appointed were Geo. R. Brunk, S. H. Rhodes, and Chester K. Lehman. The date was set and the hearing was held at Richmond, Va., on Friday, April 3, 1931. It was made the occasion for a public meeting, and beside the committee of Mennonites there were delegations present from the American Legion, Junior Order of United American Mechanics, and the Ku Klux Klan who took part in the discussions and the questioning of our committee. The opposition and sentiment against the Mennonites was very strong from some quarters.

However the state officials were very considerate and courteous, and by the time the hearing was over, a general good feeling seemed to prevail. While no decision has been rendered as yet (April 13) by the state officials we have good hopes that no action will be taken which would cause our people to either violate our religious convictions or forfeit the benefit of the public schools.

Denbigh, Va.

1932

In spite of the depression a sense of humor in the form of irony has not fled the writers.

An Ideal Meeting House (A Parable)

by J. A. Ressler

As this piece of writing is a parable, it is not to be understood that the ideal is that of every one, nor that it is a proper ideal, nor that it is the ideal of the Being who is to be worshiped in the Meeting House, nor even of the writer himself. But, judging from the conduct that is seen in some places, it would seem that many people wish that Meeting Houses were built in the way here described.

This Ideal Meeting House should be built in the form of a horseshoe, with the entrance at the toe end, and the Pulpit at the part indicated by the joined heels of the shoe. The Chief Attraction of this form of Meeting

House would be a very long Back Seat, beginning near one side of the Pulpit, and running all the way around the curved part of the wall to near the Pulpit at the other side. There would, of course, be a break at the Entrance Door. This long Back Seat would have to be fastened securely to the wall lest anyone should come in late and creep behind it.

There should be provided in the Ideal Meeting House a few Front Seats near the Pulpit for those who still prefer them, and these should be curved so that all may see the Preacher directly before them.

There would thus be a large open space between the Back Seat and the Front Seats. In this space there would be room for many chairs with rubber tipped feet, so that they could be moved at any angle and to any position without noise. This would permit late comers to move to a place that is just right.

Among the advantages of the Long Back Seat would be that all who sit on it could see one another and the Preacher and those who come in at the door without danger of injury to their necks.

But there is one serious difficulty in the plan of the Long Back Seat. It would have only four Seat ends. And it appears in evidence that there are many who dearly love to sit at the End of the Seat and have four, five, or more people trample over them and their tender feet trying to get a Seat farther in.

To please the many Lovers of Seat Ends it would be necessary to build Meeting Houses much larger than those needed by our present plans. If the houses were only large enough all might enjoy the pleasure and distinction of sitting at the end of the seat.

I see a grave danger if either plan were to be seriously considered. If the Long Back Seat Party should insist on having all the Meeting Houses made in the shape of a horseshoe, and all the Lovers of Seat Ends should insist that the Meeting Houses all be made large enough to have an End Seat for every one, there might be a more serious division in the ranks of Church Goers than any that has yet broken out—for the two plans will not combine to advantage.

And here the parable ends.

The trouble is a real one, however, and I suggest that before it becomes more serious, we all, without any committee or resolutions of conferences, begin with one accord, to take such places in our houses of worship as are assigned us by the careful ushers. If there are no such persons present then let us quietly see what seats are vacant, occupy them, and worship God.

Scottdale, Pa.

How Brethren Dress

by Amanda and Luella Miller

We have often read articles concerning sisters' dress, which is perfectly all right; but we think the writers should also touch the other side, sometimes. Some brethren are known to dress as much like the world as some sisters do. When you see some brethren in town or other public places you can not tell by their appearance whether they are Catholics or Mennonites. When you see a sister on the street you can at least tell where she belongs.

Some brethren wear plain coats to a Mennonite church, but not to other places. And when they work in town, they have an extra suit, because they don't want people to see their plain coats. Some even wear neckties under their plain-cut coats. What if the sisters would wear hats to town and other places through the week and then wear bonnets to church? It is just as necessary for the brethren to wear their plaincoats as it is for sisters to wear their bonnets.

When it is style to wear caps, our brethren wear them; when it is style to wear hats, they wear them; and when it is style to go bareheaded, they do so. It is just as bad for the brethren to dress like the world as it is for the sisters to do so.

Prattsville, Mich.

1933

There Are Four

There are four things that are contributing their share of causes for the present world-wide financial depression, and each of these is rooted and grounded in selfishness. They are: organized capital, organized labor, communism, and prodigality (spending "money for that which is not bread.")

By organizing themselves into trusts and monopolies, capitalists have been able to maintain prices so that notwithstanding the exceedingly low prices of farm products and other commodities people are paying more than twice as much for public utilities and other things people are compelled to use than they did a generation ago.

Organized labor has been able, to a limited extent, to compel organized capital to compromise by maintaining high prices for certain kinds of skilled labor. But only a fractional part of labor gets the benefit of this compromise, and increased unemployment and pauper wages exist because of the combination between organized capital and organized labor.

We point to Russia as a frightful example of what communism means wherever it gets a foothold, but America is not free from this terrible blight.

If the billions of dollars spent annually for "the unnecessaries of life" were conserved for actual service in supplying food, clothes, and other necessities of life for those in need, it would mean a brighter, happier world than what we are witnessing.

As a remedy for the ills connected with present-day living problems, let us heed our Savior's advice: "Seek ye first the kingdom of God and his righteousness, and all these things shall be added unto you."

—*Daniel Kauffman*

Nick Names

by Jacob H. Mellinger

It has often been a matter of wonder to the writer why we use nicknames. A child is given a name soon after birth; and as it grows older, instead of being called by its given name, it is called by that name in a changed form, either as a term of endearment, or to shorten it, or possibly just from habit. Henry is called "Hen," Richard is called "Dick," Sarah is called "Sall," and so on. We have become so accustomed to this that we naturally fall into the habit of doing it, and do not think anything about it. But why do we do it? The fact that it is a habit is no good reason for continuing it. If it is a good habit, all right. But, if not, would it not be better to discontinue it?

We notice in our church papers that this is frequently done; that brethren are called by such names as "Abe" and "Ben" and "Christ," etc. And we are made to wonder if this is altogether the best way. Doesn't it lack just a little in Christian dignity? (If that is the proper term.) We do it from a feeling of friendliness and familiarity. But after all, wouldn't it sound a little better, and wouldn't it look a little better in print if a person's full Christian name were given? It would give us a shock if the inspired writer had referred to the patriarchs as "Abe" and "Ike" and "Jake" and "Joe" and "Ben" and "Mose." Or, if He had referred to Judge "Sam" and King "Dave" and "Sol," and the prophets "Lige" and "Jerry" and "Dan." We would resent hearing the mothers of John and Jesus referred to as "Liz" and "Moll," and we would hardly like to hear the apostles referred to as "Pete" and "Andy" and "Jack" and "Jim" and "Phil" and "Tom," and so on.

While the writer, like almost anyone else, sometimes uses nicknames and does not object being called by a nickname, yet the Scriptural and the Quaker way of calling a person by his or her full Christian name has always appealed to him. It might seem a little stilted, but wouldn't it seem a little more Christ-like, and would we not have a little more respect for ourselves if we were a little less free in our use of nicknames? Maybe this is the wrong view to take of this matter, and maybe the subject isn't worth writing about. But these thoughts are given in a brotherly way only as a suggestion. What do you think about it?

Soudersburg, Pa.

Fifty Years Ago, and Now

We sometimes hear people compare the conditions of the church to-day with what it was fifty years ago. On the one hand, the activities of the church now are compared with apparent activity then, and a picture is painted which makes it appear that the church in the last century was about dead but that an awakening in the seventies and eighties started it on the upward grade; and that our present "transition" period points to glorious times ahead. On the other hand, there are those who see in the church a drift worldward, and who fear that the time is not far distant when all distinction between the church and the world will be entirely wiped out.

There are some things that substantiate both of these visions. In the first place, we recognize what the Mennonite church lost during a large portion of the last century in not availing itself of a number of opportunities—the Sunday school, evening meetings, revival meetings, etc.—that have proven themselves actual church-builders during the past half century. We thank the Lord for men of vision a generation ago, and our daily prayer is that our efficient organization for aggressive and constructive Christian work may never become impaired through unscriptural alliances and methods.

On the other hand, in our launching out in aggressive work we have not kept ourselves wholly free from world standards. There are some who are not fully awake to the fact that there is a difference between religious activity and real spirituality; that it is possible to do "many wonderful works" and still a loving Savior must say, "I never knew you." With all our emphasis on Bible study, we do not witness very many people reading their Bibles as constantly and devotedly as some whom we knew fifty years ago. Neither is there the same clear and positive line of demarcation between the church and the world that there was in those days.

We might go on and enumerate other things that are either favorable or unfavorable to the present-day church as compared with the church of fifty years ago, but our purpose is not so much to moralize as to point out Christian duty and safety. Paul admonishes us to "Prove all things; hold fast that which is good." In comparing the church of to-day with the church of a half-century ago, let the Word of God be the standard by which we are to judge whether our changes are for the better or the worse. Here are the deciding questions: Are we more loyal to the standards of the Gospel than we used to be? Is our progress heavenward or worldward? Are we, both as individuals and as a church, becoming more devoted and reverent toward God and the Bible? Are we growing more humble, more completely separated from the world, more peaceful and less contentious, more conscientious as to how we spend the Lord's money, more burdened for the ingathering of the lost and the spiritual upbuilding of the saved? It is by these standards whereby we may judge as to which direction we are moving. Here is a fact that will help us keep right with God and man: They who are completely upon the altar of the Lord are also—so far as they have the light—completely "unspotted from the world."

Our path of safety lies along the line of clinging closely to the things wherein we are nearer the standards of the Gospel than we used to be, and retracing our steps in the things wherein we have drifted in the other direction.

—*Daniel Kauffman*

1934

A Monster Is Here

by J. S. Hartzler

We want to keep out of politics. "My kingdom is not of this world." "Your citizenship is in heaven" (R. V.). "Not of the world even as I am not of the world." These and many other Scriptures show us our place in the kingdom of God, and it is very proper that we should consider them. They have had an effect, but it was not always in the right direction. These references are not intended to make us inactive. We are apt to forget that we are to be "ambassadors for Christ"; that we are to "earnestly contend for the faith"; that we are to be "living epistles"; to "cry aloud and spare not." Measuring up to these, there will be a ring to our conversation and life that will show clearly where we stand. Passiveness is a prevailing sin which we consider but little to-day.

Strong drink is again here, supported by our government. The bootlegger was to be a thing of the past, but he is not. The old corner saloon was never to make its appearance again, and possibly will not. Why should it? The stuff can be gotten now with many of the objectionable things out of the way. The very names, saloon, bar-tender, etc., were considered of low degree, but to-day those that the world calls "refined society," can sit down to a nice, clean table—not in a saloon—but in a fine restaurant and get their drinks with little or no questioning. A young man and his lady friend are out rather late. Before going home, they want something to eat. He orders a mild drink which is brought to their table. She, and probably he too, feel conscience pricking them a little; but both must be "gallant," and since there can be no harm in one glass, they drink. O, the deception! The 60,000 who filled drunkards' graves each year in the United States alone in "Old saloon days," started the downward road with "only one glass." In those days comparatively few women drank, but now girls as well as boys will be trapped by present methods and laws. Will there be less drunkards in years to come than there were when liquor was handed out over the bar under the protection of the law? Verily, No. The number of recruits will have to be vastly greater, but the liquor element need have no alarm. The fine eating places with fine appearing young lady table waiters, and the general refinement which the liquor element is trying to associate with the "social glass"—these and a number of kindred things will deceive more people than that element was in any position to do before prohibition days....

What can be done to check this tide? Entering into politics will not help, and even if it had the semblance of doing some good, it is against our principles. What, O, what can the Church of to-day do in this matter? The very least that should be done is to institute a campaign of scientific and Biblical education. There will not be so much danger if people are properly taught, but they must know. "My people are destroyed for lack of knowledge."

Elkhart, Ind.

J. S. Hartzler: Strong drink is here again, supported by our government. The bootlegger was to be a thing of the past, but he is not.

Christmas—As Most of Us Don't See It

by Luther Shetler

She drew her ragged shawl more closely about her, for it was cold, cold. The wind drove the snow with ever-increasing fury through her threadbare clothing and numbed her body. It was Christmas eve, and the street was filled with people doing their last-minute shopping. Ahead the light from a shop window cast a cheerful glow out onto the street. She struggled to the window and leaned gratefully against it for a moment's respite from the driving fury of the wind. After all, she thought, she might just as well stand there awhile as to move on; for she had no place to go, because she was only—a beggar. The window was filled with Christmas gifts strewn with tinsel glittering brightly in the strong light as did the snowflakes outside as they were carried hither and thither in great swirls by the wind. As she looked upon this cheerful scene, she forgot her physical suffering for the moment and a smile replaced the look of weariness on her face as her mind wandered back to the many happy Christmases she had spent with her mother as a child. And then, as her mind came back to the present she wished she could go to be with her mother once more on this Christmas eve.

o o o

The streets were empty now, for it was late. The last hurrying gift-seeker had long since gone home to prepare for the joyous tomorrow soon to come. The wind had spent its fury and had given way to a still, deadly cold. The light in the shop-window was gone, leaving only the corner street light to cast a glow over the snow-covered streets. Around the corner the scene was still more desolate, revealing a windswept park dotted with bare-limbed trees under which were lonely and unprotected park benches. On one of these a figure huddled, shivering, futilely trying to keep out the merciless, penetrating cold. As time went on the figure grew quieter, until suddenly the bells in a nearby church commenced to chime the hour of midnight, the beginning of Christmas day. At the first stroke of the bells the figure raised its head and slowly the look of weariness and suffering was replaced by a transfixed smile of happiness. As the bells ceased toiling the figure lowered its head and deathly stillness reigned once more.

o o o

It was morning, Christmas morning; the Christmas spirit was in the air. The sun shone brightly, glistening on the hardened crust of snow. An early morning passerby came whistling through the park, full of Christmas joy. He saw the drab figure, huddled on the bench and, moved by pity at the sight of one so unfortunate as to have no home to go to, he came to offer such aid as wealth and a generous spirit could supply. He tapped her on the shoulder and, receiving no response, he shook her gently. When the figure still remained quiet, he suddenly realized what had happened. Yes, her dream had come true. She had gone home to be with her mother on Christmas day.

Goshen, Ind.

1935

Recurrence of Old Fads

by S. H. Brunk

The periodic recurrence of old things reminds us very forcefully of the truth of the wise man's assertion that, "There is nothing new under the sun"—meaning that which is really new, is of creation, which comes of a higher source. However, there is sufficient variety that something different can be brought to the stage, and taken up with the same interest as though it had never been heard of. It reminds us of the children at school; at one time it is marbles, then all must hunt up their old marbles—and if they must have new ones, they could not be persuaded that they can as well play with their top instead; but when the time comes to play with tops, then the marbles and other things are again lost.

The world's fashion designers need only bring to the public some fad from an earlier generation, pay some prominent personage to take it up, when their whole following must have that certain style at any cost. We think of the same thing when hearing our children read the same old stock humorisms that we read from the papers and passed around when we were children.

The particular fad which occasions these lines at this particular time is the recurrence of the old *chain letter* fad. How many of the older generation cannot remember times when the old chain letter game was being played. My own recollection is that of about a quarter century ago. At that time the form of the letter was, good luck to the receiver if they multiplied them and sent them on, and an evil omen if they dared break the chain. This was decried in the Church as being a waste of time and money beside fostering of heathenish superstition.

Last year the world took up the chain letter fad, and added a gambling feature, by promising large returns to the receiver upon condition that he enclose one dollar to one person only. Now we are amazed to see this same fad come into the Church, and passed along by those who should know better. Of course some one near the edge of the Church knew that this form of gambling with real money would not take so well in the Church and treacherously substituted some household commodity. . . .

Beside the evils of the old chain—that of a waste of postage and time this involves the same gambling feature of trying to get much for little. It should not require much reasoning power to decide that some one must lose in this game, as these quilt pieces cannot multiply in the mail.

We do have the promise of some of our labor increasing an hundredfold, but this is by Divine Blessing, and is not at the expense of another. Then who of God's children wishes the friendship of the world.

—*Fentress, Va.*

A Legend About Menno Simons

by John Horsch

A number of writers have related a supposed occurrence in Menno Simons' life: He was riding with others in a wagon, while attempting to escape a number of officers who were sent to arrest him. The officers overtook the wagon, and since they did not know him personally, asked, "Is Menno Simons in the wagon?" Thereupon Menno, turning to his fellow passengers, said, "It is asked if Menno Simons is in the wagon." A negative answer was given, and Menno replied to the officers, "The friends say that he is not."

Coming now to the question of the trustworthiness of this story, we notice that there are various renderings of it. Some have it that Menno was traveling on a stage coach and was sitting with the driver, others that he was standing on the stairs and that he asked, "Is Menno Simons sitting in the coach?"

Secondly the fact is noteworthy that in none of the various renderings of this story the place is indicated where this incident is supposed to have occurred, nor is it stated whither Menno was traveling at the time. Observe further that the passengers in the wagon, or coach, are assumed to have known Menno Simons personally, to be able to answer the question which is supposed to have been addressed to them. And, as the story runs, the officers also were evidently supposed to have assumed that the passengers knew the man they were seeking, and that they would answer the question truthfully. Strange it would apparently be that the officers, instead of searching the wagon to see whether the one whose personal description they undoubtedly would have carried with them, if they were sent to apprehend him, would simply ask the question whether Menno Simons was in the wagon.

It seems safe to say that only in the vicinity of Witmarsum, where Menno was born and where he had been a priest for over a decade, was he so generally known, that people in general could have been expected to know him. He had left those parts immediately after his conversion. Without question he was in greater danger of life where he was generally known, since a great reward was offered for his arrest, and among the general population of a village or town there probably were always those who were ready to betray him for a large sum of money.

None of Menno Simons' contemporaries nor any writer of the same century relates this story. The earliest writers tell such a story, not about Menno Simons but about another person, a Mennonite minister named Hans Busscher. The incident is represented to have taken place while Hans Busscher was traveling to Antwerp in a wagon, about a century after Menno's death. In any case there is no evidence of historical reliability. Concerning a man of keen conscientiousness, such as was Menno Simons, the story is unbelievable.

Scottdale, Pa.

"Moderation Leagues"

While the battle for the repeal of national prohibition was at its height, it was a common expression among the "wets" that "the saloon must never come back." We called attention, at that time, to the fact that it matters little whether the place where intoxicating liquors are sold is called a "saloon" or known by some other name. Now since the liquor evil has again been legalized, the system now in vogue is far more objectionable than the regulations in pre-prohibition days; for then, as a rule, only the abandoned sots and libertines patronized the saloons whereas now, since strong drink is kept on sale in restaurants, drug stores, filling stations, and even in private homes, people laying claims to respectability patronize them.

One of the latest devices that is proving a snare to many well-meaning people is the organization of what are known as "moderation leagues." The promoters of this move profess to abhor drunkenness and claim to be promoters of the cause of temperance. Their proposition is that people drink in moderation

and stop when they have enough. But they have a double purpose in such deception. First, they want to make drinking popular among respectable people, knowing full well that it is from the ranks of moderate drinkers that drunkards are manufactured. Through such deceptive devices many an innocent boy or girl is lured to some (thought-to-be) respectable restaurant or lunch counter for lunch or recreation, and while there is beguiled to take "just one glass" of beer or wine or "soft drink," not thinking that many who made that kind of a start thereby took their first steps on the road that leads to a drunkard's grave and a drunkard's hell!

Beware of so-called "moderation leagues" or kindred devices to beguile the unsuspecting youths in our land. We should practice total abstinence in two senses: (1) never touch a drop of intoxicating liquors whether known by the name of beer, whisky, alcohol, brandy, wine, hard cider, or anything intoxicating whether mild or strong; (2) never knowingly patronize any place of business that makes a practice of handling such intoxicating drinks.

—*Daniel Kauffman*

1936

Social Security

This word has become prominent in the minds of Americans during the past few months. During the past few weeks it has been brought still further into the limelight because of the preliminary steps being taken by the federal government looking to the enforcement of the Social Security Act passed by Congress and signed by President Roosevelt Aug. 14, 1935. The law itself is one of the results of the prevailing trend in the direction of socialism. As the machinery of the law is being brought into action, its defects are becoming more pronounced, and these may or may not be corrected by the Congress soon to begin its work. Perhaps the question uppermost in the minds of many of our readers with regard to this law, is, What should be our attitude toward it? It is this question that calls for this discussion.

1. We see nothing in the law that would justify any law-abiding man or woman to withstand it. Beginning with Jan. 1, 1937, all wage-earners (with certain exemptions) in the United States are required to pay a tax of one percent of their earnings into the federal treasury, which sum is to be matched by a like sum by the employers of labor. The rate is to be increased by one-half per cent tax each year until the total reaches three percent tax from each of these two classes, after which the tax is to remain stationary. These taxes are to become the source from which old age annuities are to be paid after people arrive at the age of 65. The states are by this law encouraged to provide for unemployment insurance, but this is to be borne by the states and not by the federal government. Whatever we may think of the wisdom or unwisdom of the provisions in this law, we see nothing in it that should stand in the way of any conscientious man paying the tax thus levied, the same as he pays all other taxes levied against him.

2. Our submission to any law should not depend upon whether we like it or not. The divine injunction is, "Let every soul be subject unto the higher powers." Only in case a law of man proves to be contrary to the higher law of God, should any one be moved to say, "We ought to obey God rather than men." Should that conflict not be in evidence, our duty is to comply with its provisions as they apply to us. Many unwise laws have been repealed. That responsibility rests with those vested with the responsibility of government. Our liking or disliking a law ought not to figure in the question as to whether we should obey or disobey it.

3. Another question that has occupied the minds of some is that of whether people who are opposed to life insurance should avail themselves of the benefits which this law offers the needy. This question is worth considering;

but at this time, when the law is yet in its primitive state and none of these benefits are to be paid over immediately, we believe it would be wise to await a conclusion until the final working out of the law is more clearly evident. As already stated, it is possible (even probable) that the law will be materially changed before its working out will assume final form, and then will be the time to determine finally what should be our attitude toward it. It may be that the basis of the law will prove to be similar to that of a savings bank, in which case there will be no question of the propriety of receiving what is offered you. Or it may prove to be similar to that of life insurance (including its gambling features) in which case we should have the same attitude toward it that we have toward life insurance. For the present we see little to do but to pay the required taxes, as provided for in the law as it exists now, and leave the problems of tomorrow for disposition when tomorrow comes.

—*Daniel Kauffman*

Daniel Kauffman with granddaughters Joyce and Erma: For the present we see little but to pay the required social security taxes and leave the problems of tomorrow until then.

Lo, the Poor Farmer

We have heard the farmer pitied in public and private for something more than half a century. Especially during the political campaigns preceding general elections one would think that the chief issue before the people is the sure relief of the downtrodden farmer. Strong resolutions are incorporated in the party platforms, stirring speeches are made recounting his woes, and bitter denunciations of the opposite party's insincerity and treachery are heard almost daily. After the elections, laws are passed, but lo; the poor farmer's problems remain unsolved. It will probably take several more political campaigns to reach the heart of his troubles.

Nor is the politician the only man who offers relief to the farmer. The insurance man offers his panaceas. Now if only the farmer will take out an insurance policy for himself and every member of his family, and in addition to that he will take out an accident policy every time he travels, carry property insurance, hail insurance, automobile insurance, unemployment inusrance, and several other kinds of insurance, he will be perfectly protected against every form of loss. Capital idea!—in the minds of some people. But one question remains: Where will he get hold of the money to pay all these fees or premiums?
—*Daniel Kauffman*

1937

The Struggle in Spain

At first sight, from this distance it looks like a civil war. There are dissatisfied elements in that unhappy country that were no longer content to live under the present government, and they rose up in rebellion against it.

As we watch the progress of this struggle we are impressed with the interest which other nations have been and are taking in this war. For this there must be a cause. As we hear others tell it, we hear two explanations:

1. On the one hand we are told that the loyalists are but the tools in the hands of the avowed enemies of the Christian religion; that a few years ago, through propaganda and rebellion they seized the reins of power in Catholic Spain; that Catholic priests and nuns, as well as other religionists, are being murdered by the wholesale; that those who are the real brains in this struggle are atheistic Communists, bent on the destruction of the Christian faith among the people; that through their arrogance conditions became so intolerable that the liberty-loving people rose up in rebellion, and that this accounts for the present effort to wrest the reins of government from the hands of the party in power.

2. On the other hand we are told that this is an underhanded effort on the part of the Catholic Church to regain its power in Spain; that but for this fact, together with the aid of the Fascist rulers, Mussolini and Hitler, the insurrection would have been put down long ago; that the present government is more tolerant toward the churches (including Catholics) than the Catholic regime ever was toward Protestants; that the party in power was put there by a vote of the people, and let alone, would do its best to secure the liberty and prosperity of the people.

These conflicting explanations let us into a deeper view of the issues at stake. Not all loyalists in Spain are Communists, neither are all insurgents Catholics or Fascists. It is natural, also, for each side to put the most favorable construction on its side of the conflict as they possibly can. While on both sides there are false claims and charges in evidence, there is some foundation for both the versions already noted.

To say nothing about the line-up among the Spanish people themselves, it is quite evident that the majority of those among the nations lined up on the side of the loyalists are either Communists or of liberal leanings, while those allied with the insurrectionists are either

Fascists or in sympathy with the Fascist governments. To be plain, Russia and France are on the side of the loyalists, while Italy and Germany are on the side of the rebels. Moreover, it is also noticeable that those who are liberally inclined, religiously, have more sympathy for the loyalists, and less sympathy for the rebels, than the militant fundamentalists have.

While militarists, as a rule, have more sympathy for the Fascist side than pacifists have, and, on the other hand, pacifists are more favorable to the Red side of this conflict than the militarists, nonresistant Christians see no reason why Christian people should take either the Communistic or the Fascist side in any of the conflicts in which these two aggressive present world movements are engaged. In the first place, the militaristic character of the Fascists (as typified by Mussolini and Hitler) is diametrically opposed to the peace principles of the Prince of Peace, and the record of the Communistic states like Russia and France is fully as objectionable from the peace standpoint.

Besides this, the fact that the leaders in the present world communistic movement are so decidedly atheistic (as evident in their record in Europe and America) it is unthinkable that any real Christian should waste any sympathy on that cause. . . .

The struggle in Spain is but one of the rumblings which should open the eyes of all people as to where this world is heading for. In Europe, in China, in America, and wherever there is a conflict between opposing classes, there you will find the Reds on one side and the sympathizers with the cause of Fascism on the other side.

This fact, instead of discouraging us from fighting "the good fight of faith" with weapons that are "not carnal," should serve as a challenge to us to redouble our efforts to bring the Gospel of Christ to a lost and dying world, to hold up Christ as the only hope for perishing humanity, to "lift up a standard for the people" that means life and not destruction.

—*Daniel Kauffman*

Bump the Seventy-Year-Olds Aside—Let's Go!

by D. D. Miller

But he forsook the counsel which the old men gave him, and took counsel with the young men that were brought up with him. II Chron. 10.

Thus did King Rehoboam whose father was classed among the wise, and whose age was at least great enough for him to be Rehoboam's father. Yet he rejected of the old men's counsel, so he could accept the young men's who had grown up with him and were "broader minded." We need not tell the reader how much the ten tribes loved Rehoboam right after this. . . .

Today, gradually, and yet almost suddenly, in national governmental affairs an attempt is being made to push the 70-year-olds out of the way. Why? The truth is, they have given good and safe counsel and it is no longer acceptable under the new and liberal policies of the present administration, which wishes for us to know that they are aware of the fact that we are no longer living in the "Horse and buggy days." That fact is not hard to see, but the cautious man, whether 25 or 75 years old need not look far nor think very deep to at least see some danger in a number of present-day workings.

Today, of all days, the 70-year-olds are possibly needed, although they may ere long have the opportunity to "voluntarily push out." The thought of the change suggests danger; the act itself may mean anything.

We have been told that we live in a day when "the son knows more than his father." We might add that "he (the son) has gone through three schools and two seminaries, and really has a chance to know." Further, "His training at 33 is so complete that there is no use for him to ask counsel from even any 75-year-old." So all there is left for this 33-year-old is to advise others; and since average people and aristocrats do not take advice from anyone there is nothing for this poor 33-year-old to do but look for a job, which is the best thing that can happen as long as he cannot take counsel from the aged.

We need the counsel of the aged to balance the forward movements of the younger. The counsel of the older is very often most valuable in supporting eternal principles which dare not be set aside without ruin. The counsel of the aged has often been a nightmare to challengers of the truth. The counsel of the aged has often "saved the day" by checking liberalism. And today, of all days, the good advice of those who have had experience by travelling the way before us is needed; and, mark the day if you choose, when this counsel is set aside, discarded, or even lightly considered, and you shall have marked the beginning of a dark future ahead.

God bless our aged and their brains, which are not excelled by either the present responsible or the coming responsible generation, for good. God be praised for a Church in which we find young, middle-aged, and old working together regardless of age or age-limits. And thus should it ever be. God used "old man Abraham." God used Paul at middle age. God used the children. Our future is foretold in the answer to the following question: What are we doing with the counsel the "old men" give us? And we believe this to be correct, nationally or spiritually.

Protection, Kans.

1938

Forty-Eight Years in the Mennonite Church

This is intended as the last of the series of editorials under this general head. Throughout the series I have felt myself cramped for want of space, which kept me from going into details which would have made these weekly messages more illuminating. The well-informed and thoughtful reader may ponder over these things with profit, and fill in the missing spots.

As we think of the record of the Church during the past half century, we find many things to challenge our interest; some to be regretted, some for which we glorify God. Here are a few things for which we praise the Lord:

1. Our total membership in America has about trebled during this time, not counting the thousands who have, during this time, answered the heavenly summons and gone home to glory.

2. Our Church-wide organizations—missionary, educational, publishing, charitable—have nearly all been originated and completed during this time.

3. We have organized and maintained the Mennonite General Conference, through which every enterprise in the Church has been greatly strengthened and extended.

4. We now have mission stations at home and abroad, in cities and rural districts, besides a number of charitable institutions which are doing an effective and commendable work.

5. We now have three regularly organized Church schools (colleges), besides several times that many special short-term winter Bible schools.

6. Since 1908 practically all of our Church publications are owned and controlled by the Mennonite Church, the publication work continually strengthened, the members of the Mennonite Publication Board being chosen by

the Mennonite General Conference and by district conferences, and our literature exerting an ever-widening sphere of influence.

7. There has been a merger between the most numerous bodies of Mennonites and Amish Mennonites in America, laboring harmoniously together in support of our various Church enterprises.

On the other hand, there are a number of things which we deplore and our prayers ascend continually to the end that these hindrances may yet be overcome and rectified. In this list we may mention the following:

1. During the past half century there have been at least four secessions from the mother Church, to say nothing about numerous minor schisms in local congregations.

2. Generally speaking, the discipline in the Church is not as nearly in accord with Gospel standards as it was a half century ago.

3. While in some respects there has been an improvement in the standards maintained by our ministry, in some instances there has been a recession, and the unity in methods and loyalty to the standards of the Gospel and of the Church is far from being perfect.

4. We see influences at work among us from which we pray to be delivered. Looking forward, we naturally ponder over the question as to what the future has in store for us. In taking up this phase of our meditations, we want to avoid both blind optimism and blue-eyed pessimism. Since God is always faithful and ready and able to do His part, the future of any church depends wholly upon its own attitude towards God and the world, its willingness or unwillingness to "wholly follow the Word."

—*Daniel Kauffman*

Marks of an Ideal Church Paper

Here are a few of the things that belong to an ideal Church periodical:

1. Christian loyalty. This includes loyalty to both God and the supporting church. Where it is impossible to be both, God must have the preference and an honest effort made to raise the standards of the church into an attitude of loyalty to God. But granting that the supporting church is loyal, the periodical should make it a point to promote the standards of the Gospel and of the Church; both in doctrine and life.

2. A discussion of living issues. In every age there have been, and are, living issues and problems confronting the Church. It should be the aim of every Church periodical to present an intelligent and Scriptural discussion of these issues; to the end that the membership may be kept informed and take a proper attitude toward them.

3. Church news. Every live member wants to know what is going on among the brotherhood in every community where the Church is represented. The live Church periodical is a medium through which this contact between members and Church at large may be kept up.

The conference, the congregation, the Church institution; marriages, deaths, special meetings, various kinds of Church activities, all should have a place in these Church news.

4. The missionary spirit. The last command of Christ before His departure for the realms of glory was that His people should carry the Gospel into all parts of the world. It is not enough that we confine our efforts to "the household of faith," even though that is of first importance (Gal. 6:10). The "other sheep" also need our attention. Church extension belongs to the policy of every live church, and the live Church periodical should lend its full weight in supporting and promulgating every enterprise in the Church.

From the time the Gospel Herald was founded, it has been the aim of this periodical to keep alive these four features in its weekly messages.

That this may be faithfully and efficiently done, we invite the prayers, support, and helpful suggestions on the part of all who are interested in the same cause.

—*Daniel Kauffman*

1939

The spirit of monopoly is not only destructive to human rights but is also the cause of much trouble and distress wherever it is found.

Insurance

One of the favorite arguments of the insurance agent is to convince people how much they save by investing in life insurance. Let him fix up his own story, and to most people it sounds very plausible. But after he is through, these facts remain:

1. Not over half (usually less than) the money paid in premiums gets back to the pockets of the policy-holders.

2. They who take out an insurance policy to enable them to borrow money, thereby pay a double tribute for the privilege: (1) interest on the money borrowed; (2) premiums on the insurance policy taken out.

3. To realize a big percentage on the investment—or, in other words, "to beat the company at the game"—it becomes necessary to die early.

4. While some, by dying early, leave a comfortable margin to those left behind, yet for the average investor it is a losing proposition.

5. It is a contribution to substantial manhood or womanhood for each individual to take charge of his or her own business and conduct it according to Christian principles.

6. We have the assurance from God that He will care for His own; also that "it is better to trust in the Lord than to put confidence in men."

—*Daniel Kauffman*

Question Drawer

If ye will inquire, inquire ye.—Isaiah 21:12.
But avoid foolish questions, and genealogies, and contentions, and strivings about the law; for they are unprofitable and vain.—Titus 3:9.

Where did four-part singing originate and what are the grounds that it is God-honoring?

For about a thousand years church music was entirely in unison. This limited the possibilities of musical expression. About the eleventh century a new principle, that of harmony, the combination of two or more parts, made its appearance, and since that time has revolutionized church music. It made possible almost unlimited scope and variety in rhythm and harmonic effects. It must be felt that since God ordained the law of harmony its use in church music can and should be to His praise. As far as the Mennonite Church is concerned, our oldest brethren and sisters still remember the time when our hymns were all in unison. Melody is beautiful, but harmony enriches melody; it perfects our praises in song.

How is it that our International Sunday school lessons are copyrighted by the International Council of Religious Education when the lessons are part of the Bible?

The copyrighted material is the lesson title, the Golden Text, the selection of the Scripture, and the daily readings. Of course the Bible is not copyrighted. The International Council of Religious Education makes the selections and consequently has the right to copyright its work.

Where does the expression, "Forgive us our trespasses," come from?

The word trespasses comes from Tyndale's translation, and has found its way into the prayer-books of some denominations. It has no foundation in the Greek language, for the original word carries with it the idea of something owed and not that of going beyond a boundary, as in Matt. 6:14.

—*C.K.L. (Evidently C. K. Lehman).*

A Question of Human Rights

In the prolonged struggle between the mine workers and mine operators in the soft coal regions of America, during part of which time almost a half million workers were out of employment and the industries of the country suffered to a greater or less extent, there is one phase of the struggle concerning which there was surprisingly little said. We refer to the right of every man or corporation of men to conduct their own business, unmolested by outside interference.

The mine owners being under the protection of the government, it is but right to expect that they conduct their business in accordance with the laws and regulations of the government that gives them protection. They, like all other individuals or firms under the government, should respect the rights of others, as well as to claim the proper rights for themselves. As for employers and employes, the only relations that exist between them is the contract between them. Should either of the parties to the contract violate this agreement, so that charges are brought against them by the other, the only authorized body to deal with the situation is that of the government (state or national) itself. Neither Labor nor Capital has any right to dictate to the other party as to what it must or must not do. And when coercive measures (especially deeds of violence) are resorted to in order to compel the other party to come to terms, this means fostering the spirit of monopoly which not only crushes our personal rights but is also destructive to orderly and free government. The world today is suffering because the rights of man are being trampled upon and the spirit of monopoly has taken its place. And whether this monopolistic power is in the hands of a national dictator, or a political clique, or a combination of financial barons, or a powerful labor union, the results will be similar.

If those seeking employment can not see their way clear to accept the terms of some employer, it is their right to seek employment elsewhere; but it is not their right to intimidate the employer, by a show of force or otherwise. If those in search of laborers to work for them do not see their way clear to grant the terms of their would-be employes, it is their privilege to look elsewhere for laborers; but it is not their privilege to use monopolistic efforts to compel laborers to come to their terms. For either side to resort to monopolistic or coercive measures to compel the other side to yield means a fight to crush out human freedom.

The principle of liberty of conscience and freedom of action, so long as we do not trample upon the liberties of others, is embodied in the Bill of Rights found in the Constitution of the United States. Had this principle been honored by both miners and mine owners, the disastrous strike which means suffering and privation in millions of homes would never have taken place.

The spirit of monopoly, whether fostered by organized capital or by organized labor, is not only destructive to human rights but is also the cause of much trouble and distress wherever it is found. America stands in need of two revivals: (1) a revival of genuine orthodox Christian religion; (2) a revival of a proper regard for the rights of others—which means living for the good of others.

—*Daniel Kauffman*

1940

Let Us Suppose

1. That Hitler will succeed in reducing London to a mass of ruins and that England will be beaten into submission, her vast empire completely obliterated; that Italy will accomplish in the South what Germany is doing in the North, and that the old Roman empire will again come back into an actual reality. Or,

2. That England will in the end beat off the German invaders, come out victorious in the

end, and that Germany and Italy will be reduced to second rate powers.

In either case, how would the results compare with another supposition that we shall list; namely,

3. That all the world, tired and disappointed because of this dreadful carnage, would turn aside from these "wars and rumours of wars," become true followers of Jesus Christ the Prince of Peace, beat their swords into plowshares and their spears into pruning hooks, and millions be saved for a blissful eternity.

This comparison naturally raises the question: Why should men give themselves over so completely and enthusiastically to either of the two first suppositions, and take only a passing interest in the last, which if achieved would yield results infinitely better and more desirable than those which any gigantic struggle in the carnage of destruction can possibly bring about? Why not devote ourselves wholeheartedly to the work of salvation rather than that of destruction? Let us therefore

"Follow peace with all men, and holiness, without which no man shall see the Lord."

—Daniel Kauffman

The 1940 World's Fair

by George R. Smoker

At the World's Fair humanity is shown arrayed in his best clothes and wearing a kindly, smiling mask. In war the mask is torn away and man is seen as he actually is apart from God—and the sight is truly terrifying. The fair glorifies man and his vaunted progress; war reveals his degeneracy.

It is a characteristic of Satan's working that he dresses up his wares attractively and offers a good excuse to the reason to indulge in what one wishes. He says that the commercial movie is educational; and once in a while one may be, even though movies are admittedly graded to the level of the moron and most people would hardly like to admit that their education has not advanced beyond that stage. Movies are educational, it is true—educating

boys and girls in lust and vice and crime. Satan says that the dance is healthful and that it develops grace, but he leaves unsaid the fact that the dance is the road by which girls are seduced by the tens of thousands yearly. Satan says that card-playing sharpens the wits, but he fails to add that if it sharpens the wits it does so only for card-playing and nothing else, and besides that it consumes a colossal amount of valuable time and makes professional gamblers of many. Satan says that smoking gives one a lift, but there is no explanation that the seeming lift of the cigarette is only that out of a depression which previously smoked cigarettes have caused. So with intoxicating drink that is held up as making life a rosy dream; the advertisements say nothing of the fact that at last the wine bites as a poisonous snake.

When it is said that the World's Fair is educational we must examine to see whether perhaps something has been left unsaid. No one will dispute that there are many educational exhibits at this Fair. What these are, need not be set down here; for they have received plentiful and high-powered publicity. There is a great deal that is good and worth while to be seen. However, the Fair by no means holds a monopoly on educational exhibits. While living in New York I talked to a number of friends who attended the exhibits, and I was informed that similar things may be seen in New York City in the permanent displays at the museums, art galleries, botanical gardens, and so on, which things are not connected with the objectionable features that the Fair is. One young man told me that the whole thing impressed him as being mostly advertising "and spread pretty thin at that."

It must be borne in mind that the educational feature of the World's Fair is really the sideshow. The amusement zone is played up as being the center of attraction by the New York papers. One newspaper asserted that no fair can possibly be a success without the showgirls. As you may have noticed, the 1940 World's Fair is deliberately playing up the amusement end of things. A number of educational exhibits have withdrawn this year, and numerous amusement concessions have been taken on.

This brings us to consider whether we as Mennonites can conscientiously attend the World's Fair. The three considerations that follow would seem to argue against it.

The Matter of Amusements

The Mennonite Church opposes all unnecessary Sunday business. The World's Fair opened on Sunday last year at the time of the morning church service and has continued to operate throughout on Sundays. Those working in the New York churches know the effect this had upon church attendance on the part of some. Such competition with the Church is certainly not good. The Mennonite Church has consistently maintained a witness against promiscuous bathing in public resorts, against dancing, against the theater, against strong drink, and such like, all of which are highly featured at this Fair. Our Church has found it necessary to raise its voice against various local fairs because of certain objectionable features; how then can she stamp approval on this supreme of all fairs, where the objectionable features are infinitely multiplied?...

The Matter of Stewardship

It costs time and money to go to the Fair. It was said last year that one could visit all the exhibits at a cost of $15.00, but no one attends all of them and there are many free exhibits. The fees for entering and viewing the Fair are the least part of the cost. In these days when tremendous sums are needed for missions and for relief work—five million refugees are on the roads of France and many more millions in China, where a cent or two will amply care for one refugee for a day—in days such as these stewardship of the wealth God has entrusted to us is a serious matter indeed. Who can spend money freely for selfish pleasure in these days?

I lived in New York, however, and could have gone to the Fair without traveling expense—except for a ten-cent subway fare—and without loss of working time. I was on several occasions offered tickets by which I could have gone without expense. The stewardship matter thus eliminated there still remained one consideration that deterred me.

The Weaker Brother

We say that as established Christians we know what to see and what to keep away from, and we must certainly learn to do that in a world of mingled good and evil. But is it not most selfish to say that I will go to the Fair because it won't hurt me to do so, when the course I follow might harm a weaker brother? Most of the allurements of this world in their most attractive form are to be found at the Fair. Dare we subject our brother, who may not have the taste for purely educational things that we have nor the stamina for resistance that we possess, to the influence of Satan's most powerful traps, simply because our attendance has set a precedent for going?

It was a profoundly important principle enunciated by Paul when he affirmed, "If meat make my brother to offend, I will eat no flesh while the world standeth, lest I make my brother to offend" (I Cor. 8:13)....

Scottdale, Pa.

1941

Christian Snake Stories

by H. N. Troyer

Several years ago a prominent editor of a western religious magazine printed a lengthy article about a former infidel by the name of Chester Bedel, who is buried at North Benton, Ohio. He illustrated his article with a number of pictures showing the burial plot with a life-size monument of Mr. Bedel, as well as pictures of snakes found on the grave with snow on the ground. This made such a sensation that numerous editions of tracts were gotten out with much the same story.

In one of these editions the editor is made to state that he himself was in very close touch with the situation and that the infidel stated that if there was a God that his grave should be full of snakes. He then says that at the funeral they had quite a time cleaning out the snakes before being able to lower the coffin, and that ever since there were often from fifteen to twenty-five snakes seen on the grave at once and even on nearly any winter day however cold.

The writer of this article lived within thirty miles of this place for a number of years. His first visit was made on an ideal hot sultry day. Upon stopping in the center of North Benton for instructions as to how to reach the graveyard the directions came as if memorized without the giver even looking up. One could not help thinking that a good many others must have likewise asked directions. About two miles out the monument was easily recognized from the pictures. But not a snake was to be seen. After spending some time there hoping the snakes would appear, the trip back to town was begun. However, after going about one half mile, an old white-haired man was spied and the auto at once headed in. After a little conversation the subject of snakes was brought up. The explosion of the old man was about as expected from one who had always lived there, had known Mr. Bedel while still living, and had been to his funeral at which nothing unusual had occurred. He lived within sight of this graveyard all his life and had traveled past this place over and over as well as inside but never saw any snakes. He then went on to say that this snake story was the biggest hoax ever pulled off on the American people. The summer before the roads were lined continually with cars from all over the United States—All looking for snakes.

A few weeks after this the writer was again in this community and drove in. The story about these snakes was written in such a convincing way that one could hardly mistrust. This time however he planned on surprising the snakes since he thought they might have become educated to watching the road. Accordingly the car was driven past the graveyard and, by sneaking around, he was able to come from another angle. But another disappointment. No snakes! Later the writer's family visited the spot and again no snakes.

Later, in the Plainview Church, this was used as an illustration of how we repeat things that can easily be checked on, and, if not so, bring Christianity into ill repute. A show of hands was called as to how many had been there and a large number of those present had visited the place. Then a show of hands was called for as to how many had seen snakes and not a hand went up.

Even should a snake be found there it would prove nothing, for the writer found one recently in his own yard. Last summer a prominent writer for the "Cleveland Press" investigated this story and his discoveries agree with the above. He, however, found that some evangelists wanted a snake so badly that they tramped the meadows till one was found, killed, and then carried to the grave. That evening they would exhibit the snake and call attention to how they had "picked it up on his grave."

Millersburg, Ohio.

Prophecy

Wartime brings an increased demand for prophetic teaching. This demand arises in part because the "manifold trials" that come upon the Lord's people in such times serve to focus attention upon the Blessed Hope of Christ's return. There is also a desire to know how world events are fitting into God's plan for the ages. Spurious interpretations and fantastic speculations are much in evidence today, as radical teachers endeavor to give the public what they want.

The Mennonite Church recognizes as "orthodox" two schools of prophetic thought—amillennialism and premillennialism, the membership being perhaps equally divided in their adherence to these schools. The columns of the Herald are accordingly open to adherents of both viewpoints who will present their views sanely, soundly, and Scripturally. In the discussion of a theme concerning which there is sharp difference of opinion it is most important that the discussions be written in a spirit of deep humility and with a kindly forbearance and sincere love for those with whom we differ, giving answer "to every man that asketh a reason . . . with meekness and fear."

Both premillennialists and amillennialists

believe that what the Bible says is unqualifiedly true. They differ in the principles of interpretation which they employ.

Both sides hold that the world is getting worse and worse, leading up to a final great catastrophe in which the righteous will be rewarded and the wicked, punished. One group holds to a general resurrection and general judgment, the other separates the resurrections of the righteous and wicked by a thousand years and teaches that there will be a number of judgments.

Both sides hold that we shall reign with Christ forever and ever in the new heaven and new earth. One group holds that for a short interval of one thousand years this reign will take place on the earth approximately as we find it now, with restoration to Edenic conditions.

Both prophetic viewpoints are open to criticism. Premillennialists have found amillennialism too negative in its approach, disclaiming many prophetic interpretations without supplying positive prophetic teaching. They have said the view is too intellectual in its approach and that it tends to cast doubt on the imminency of Christ's return. It is feared that many Scriptures are "spiritualized away."

Amillennialists have found in the premillennial position a too-elaborate depicting of events surrounding the Second Coming. They fear that this viewpoint loses sight of the spiritual nature of Christ's Kingdom, and feel that the teaching that people will somehow be saved after Christ's appearance is dangerous.

The truth is that there are a great many problems connected with either viewpoint, so that humility is a comely virtue on the part of all prophetic interpreters.

Tremendous world events completely baffle our thinking. We do know, however, that civilization is crashing and that things are going badly with the Jews and with the professed Christian church. "What meaneth this?" men are asking again today. Our Bible teachers ought to tell us what they know and be frank to state what they do not know. We want to know what the Bible has to say about these days in which we are living.

—S. (*Likely George R. Smoker, Office Editor*).

1942

Where there is a will there is a way. If you can't get gas use a bicycle or a horse. Give the Lord a chance and cooperate with Him.

What Will You Do About No Tires and Gas Rationing?

by C. F. Yake,

"It just is impossible to have Summer Bible School this year. We always had Summer Bible School in the evening and our teachers came from a distance. With gasoline rationing and the tire shortage it is impossible to have the teachers come this distance to teach Summer Bible School for nothing. Besides, we haul quite a number of our children to Bible school and that means tires and gasoline for trucks or automobiles. It does not seem practical this year. I guess we will have to give up the idea of a Summer Bible School," was the conclusion of a city mission superintendent. A similar story was heard by a superintendent of a rural school drawing its pupils from a large rural area.

And this problem is no easy one. It is a cause of serious concern. It will be impossible to secure new tires or recapped ones for a long time. In most instances gasoline rationing will make it possible for the drivers to get only a limited amount of gasoline in certain areas. This cuts down the driving. These two things together seem an insurmountable mountain. What is to be done about it? Shall we give up and have no Summer Bible Schools because of these two factors which cannot be eliminated?

If obstacles cannot be removed, then

C. F. Yake: Surely summer Bible school teachers will not give up because of the tire shortage and gasoline rationing. Why not use a bicycle?

frequently it is possible to get around them or over them. Is there not a possible way to get around the gasoline rationing and the tire shortage? Must teachers be secured from such a far distance? Or if they do come must they come in individual cars? Could they not combine and a half dozen or more come in one car or by bus? Would it not be possible to secure teachers nearer at hand? A number of questions like this properly considered may make it possible to get around the obstacles and open the way for Summer Bible School.

Again, why is it necessary to have such a large school at one place and haul the children so far? Instead of one large school why cannot there be two or three or four small schools? Why cannot teachers in territories where such schools would be held direct and teach school? In many ways such schools could give better service to our boys and girls than a large school possibly would do. Anyway it is something to think about.

It is not always necessary to have a church house in which to conduct a Summer Bible School. A tent may be used, a trailer may be used, and an open air school conducted. Several rooms in homes can be used, and two or three teachers can operate a Summer Bible School. There are really a dozen-and-one different ways in which we can get around the tire shortage and the gasoline rationing.

Where there is a will there is a way. And the Lord has challenged us to bring the problem to Him. In prayer and by the use of our natural endowments, ways and means can be worked out whereby Summer Bible Schools can be held, and the boys and girls can be given the Bible instruction which they so much need in these dark days.

Surely you will not fail us because of the tire shortage and gasoline rationing. Even if teachers may have to come from a distance, why not use the bicycle? Perhaps some might come on horseback. And what about the horse and the buggy? It is still one of the best ways for social travel! Give the Lord a chance and co-operate with Him, and He will make it possible for you to have your Summer Bible School in your district. Here is wishing you the Lord's richest blessing and good success.

What Does the World Think of the Mennonites?

by Beulah M. Weber

The world is in turmoil these days, and the Christians have a duty of living closer to the Lord and spending more time in prayer. If we spent one hour a day or even one hour a week in meditation and prayer with the Lord in secret, we would be better lights. We do not need to be missionaries in foreign lands; we can use our means of service by living a life, "holy, acceptable unto God." If we spend time in reading and studying God's Word and in prayer we will not do things that the world will look on and say, "I thought they were conscientious people."

We are a peace-loving people. We then must live so that they would have no reason to accuse us of not living up to our standards. There are some people who do not like to go among worldly people because they are afraid they will be made fun of. The world respects the true Christian and appreciates his clean and holy life.

Once a policeman (in reference to a Mennonite) said, "If everyone lived like that we would need no jails or policemen." As not every one lives like that, let us do our part toward making the world better by living our own life right instead of finding something wrong with the other person.

We need to be sober, but that is no reason to go around wearing a long face. Let us be cheerful and show to the world that we enjoy living for Jesus who died that we might be saved. I once heard a woman say about two Mennonite girls, "I think they would have a dry life of it. They can't go to the movies or dances. What do they have to do?" The other, a gentleman, replied, "Do you hear those girls laughing?" "Yes," she replied. "Well," he said, "those are the two Mennonite girls you were speaking of. They have their fun within them. They go to singing and can entertain themselves, where you have to go to the movies and dances for entertainment." Let us stay away from those places of entertainment and seek the fellowship of God's people.

Take time to be holy, speak oft with thy Lord;
Abide in Him always, and feed on His Word.
Make friends of God's children; help those who are weak;
Forgetting in nothing His blessing to seek.

Take time to be holy, the world rushes on;
Spend much time in secret with Jesus alone—
By looking to Jesus, like Him thou shalt be;
Thy friends in thy conduct His likeness shall see.

Hagerstown, Md.

1943

Colleges, like the churches they serve, are an average cross section of the churches from which the students come.

Reflections After the 1943 Evangelistic Meetings at Goshen College

by C. F. Derstine

College staffs and students are very much like the rest of us; they sometimes appreciate a word of encouragement, particularly since faculties, like most ministers of the Gospel, often get more than their share of criticism. Scriptural ground for speaking words of encouragement is found in that admirable passage in Phil. 4:8: "Finally, brethren, whatsoever things are true, whatsoever things are honest, whatsoever things are just, whatsoever things are pure, whatsoever things are lovely, whatsoever things are of good report; if there be any virtue, and if there be any praise, *think on these things*." This we want to do. Some kind reader may ask, "Why not tell us some things in which the college should be different, or improved?"

This we did—but to them. How did they take it? Here is an official reaction. I quote from a letter written for and by the student body: "We all feel that the sermons and the short talks which God gave us through you have enriched our lives and will help us live more consecrated lives in future days." Then the writer adds, "I personally, would like to thank you for the very practical thoughts you gave us for our Christian lives. So often messages which theoretically are beautiful, don't stress practical, common, everyday living." Then some personal touches, ending with this appeal, "Remember us as students at Goshen College that we may live richly for Christ." No evangelist could wish for a more consistent reaction.

The manifest presence and power of the Lord was realized from the first meeting to the last. A number were moved to decide for Christ and more than a score reconsecrated and dedicated themselves to God. The thirty-three prayer meetings conducted throughout the campus every evening by the faculty and student body, made their own effective contribution.

The entire faculty gave their full cooperation and support. They would gladly give the Mennonite Church a perfect college if this were possible. Colleges, like the churches which they serve, are an average cross section of the churches from which the students come. They represent the strength and weakness of these scattered congregations. A college president once remarked, "Don't expect us to turn out the best mahogany furniture when you send us pine boards." Personally, I have listened to critics of our church schools, the members of whose own congregations did not live consistently or spiritually. We as pastors, as congregations, are responsible to send to these schools students which make for strong Christian colleges.

In thirty years of evangelistic work, the writer has never received in advance so many letters which craved "a real work of grace in the hearts of all," as he received from the faculty and students of the college. This deep desire the Lord satisfied. This attitude is much better than the self-satisfied condition so often contacted, which is aptly expressed in the Word, "I am rich, increased in goods, and have need of nothing."

A great amount of Christian work is being carried on by the faculty and student body in the college and around the college area. The North Goshen congregation has grown to a separate congregation from the college church with its own pastor and deacon, and lately the pastor, Bro. Paul Mininger, was ordained bishop in charge. One Sunday morning I was taken to East Goshen, a mission work conducted by College students, where the house was filled with workers, parents, and children. After the sermon, with deep conviction manifest all through the audience, a young lady accepted the Lord Jesus Christ. Others have done so before this. Fruitage is evident in many lives and homes. Another mission Sunday school is conducted at Locust Grove near Elkhart, where twelve recent converts are under instruction. Jail services are conducted each Sunday afternoon. With trained teachers and good special singing, many doors of opportunity swing open. Some have accepted Christ in the jail services conducted by the student body.

Thirty-three brethren and sisters have volunteered for full-time service. How I wish that some of the congregations whose pastors are advanced in years, good men who need youthful assistance, could be brought into contact with our pastorless congregations. This is an opportunity for the general church boards to take some joint action to utilize these resources. The writer feels that the Church owes a great deal of appreciation to our school faculties who labor for small salaries when they might be earning much more in other institutions of learning. Their loyalty to the Church calls for definite appreciation.

Occasionally, some tell us that the colleges are not greatly helping the Church. They question the loyalty of faculties and student body. The writer conducted his last series of meetings at Goshen College thirteen years ago, and his candid reaction is this. **There is more loyalty to the faith and Church manifest in the school today than at that time.** This, if space would allow, could be shown in at least five or six directions. . . . Christian colleges do not solve all our problems—but by and large—we are better off with our Christian colleges than with the worldly, liberal, modernistic—and be times—atheistic educational institutions about us.

Kitchener, Ont.

꩜

Mennonite Men in the Army?

by H. S. Bender

There is ground for real satisfaction in the loyal way in which the young men of the Mennonite Church on the whole have met the test of conscription. In large numbers they have taken their stand for sincere and complete nonresistance and have by their choice of Civilian Public Service (IV-E) instead of either combatant or noncombatant military service, witnessed, to all men, of their faith and their conviction that war is sin, and that Christians can have no part in it. Likewise in a splendid way the Mennonite Church has stood by her conscientious young men and provided for them by the establishment and maintenance of Civilian Public Service camps. This is the encouraging side of our war record.

But there is another side that is not at all encouraging; namely, the record of numerous Mennonite men who have entered the army and are now taking part in the war. Disturbing reports of the number of such men led the Peace Problems Committee to take a census of all our congregations to secure reliable information. The results of the census have recently been compiled and are exceedingly disquieting. We now know that approximately thirty per cent of all drafted men accept army service, and that one half of this number enter regular combatant units. On Nov. 1, 1942, the date of the census, in round numbers eight hundred (800) members of the Church were in C.P.S. camps, while three hundred twenty (320) were in the regular army as soldiers. A detailed report of the census will be released later. This covers only the United States congregations, but the Canadian record is about the same.

A thirty per cent failure is a bad record. If we have been complacent, this report should put an end to our complacency. Nor is any one part of the Church much better than any other. From East to West, the record is much the same. Quite a number of congregations show up in the census with all their draftees in the army and none in C.P.S. One congregation has seventeen men in the army.

Why this shocking record? It is true, of course, that many of those who went to the army were not strong and active members, and some no doubt were genuine backsliders. Few were warm Christians, workers in their home congregations. But this is no explanation. The real question is, Why are so many of our young men in the prime of life so weak in their Christian life and convictions? The test of war is flashing the spotlight on our weakness at home. This record is a direct challenge to our bishops and pastors, to our congregations, to our parents. Only seventy per cent loyal! Is this a passing grade for the Mennonite Church in God's great record book?

Goshen, Indiana.

H. S. Bender: Only seventy percent loyal! Is this a passing grade for the Mennonite Church in God's great record book?

"Fare Ye Well"

These were the concluding words sent by the conference in Jerusalem (Acts 15) in a letter to the church in Antioch. They are also to be the concluding words in this message, by your unworthy servant, to the readers of the Gospel Herald. As most of you probably know, at the close of this year the editorship of the Gospel Herald is to be assumed by Bro. Paul Erb, Goshen, Ind., well known to the body of our readers.

In October 1899, I was informed by a letter from Bro. J. S. Hartzler, then (as now) one of our most widely known church leaders, that at a meeting held by interested brethren (from a number of states) in Wayne Co., Ohio, it was unanimously decided by those present that the time had come when a new church paper was urgently needed, and that my name was selected as one of the editors. I was interested, but it was more than five years before the proposed new paper finally appeared. In the meantime, a number of similar efforts had been made, the one nearest successful being the periodical published for several years under the name of "Gospel Truths," with Bro. O. H. Zook of Belleville, Pa., as editor.

In January 1905, while Bro. J. S. Shoemaker and I were laborers together in a Bible conference near Palmyra, Mo., he informed me that he had been requested by Bro. Aaron Loucks of Scottdale, Pa., to find an editor for the church paper for which many of our people had been planning and praying for a number of years. After several days of prayerful and serious consideration, we decided to open up a correspondence with Bro. Loucks, which resulted in the publication of the Gospel Witness on April 5, 1905. We found enough general interest in the church at large, so within that three years there was a church-wide organization in existence, known as the Mennonite Publication Board and composed of representatives of the Mennonite General Conference and Mennonite district conferences. This board then took charge of practically all of our church publications through a merger of church periodicals then in existence. Through this merger the Herald of Truth, published at Elkhart, Ind., and the Gospel Witness, published at Scottdale, Pa., were combined under the name of Gospel Herald. The home of our publication work became the Mennonite Publishing House, located at Scottdale, Pa.

After an editorial experience of nearly thirty-nine years, the editor is now ready to lay down his pen and leave the work to younger hands. We desire to thank our people for their hearty support during these years, and we trust that the same hearty co-operation and support may continue during the years to come. So long as we continue to praise the Lord and give Him the glory for all that He has done for us during these years we have the sure promise, "Lo, I am with you always, even unto the end of the world."

In laying down our editorial pen, we do not mean to retire from active service. Our prayers shall continue to ascend in behalf of the work to which we have given the greater part of our life. May the Lord richly bless the labors of all who are devoting themselves to the furtherance of this great cause. As long as God gives us breath, our affections, minds, hands, feet, tongues, and pens should continue to be wholly upon the altar of the Lord. With this as our aim and ideal in life, may we press on in the service of our Lord as He gives us grace and do our best to the end that the standards of the Gospel may at all times be maintained as the standards of our church and of our homes. As long as God gives to our readers the grace and the power to continue faithful in His service, we are glad to say, in the language of inspiration, "Fare Ye Well."

—*Daniel Kauffman*

1944-1962

THE PROFESSOR

He left behind the comparative security of a college professorship to come to Scottdale. At first he was hesitant, but on reflection, he is glad he did.

Paul Erb

1944-1962

The Professor

To Paul Erb, the editorship of the *Gospel Herald* came as an unwelcome interruption in mid-career. He had already changed direction several times before. Now at near the age of 50 he was ready to settle down and teach English at Goshen College for the rest of his working days.

Erb, as he used to call himself on the inter-office phone, had grown up in central Kansas in the heady days of the borning century. His father was Tilman Erb, a bishop and a leader in the founding of Hesston College. Paul attended the college for two years (where he eventually married Alta Eby, one of the teachers) and got a bachelor's degree from Bethel, the General Conference Mennonite College at nearby Newton.

The Erbs were set to go to India as missionaries, but World War I came and the British declined to issue a visa to people with a German sounding name like Erb. So they taught at Hesston College and he eventually became dean. Then H. S. Bender called him to Goshen College at the beginning of the forties. Before he was quite settled, Mennonite Publication Board summoned him to Scottdale to edit the *Gospel Herald*. The minutes of the Board reveal that there were negotiations.

The first vote on the board was 13 to 12 in favor of Paul Erb. (The other candidate was a Publishing House employee and a Kauffman understudy.) This vote was considered too close for an immediate decision and a committee was appointed to work further on the question. The committee recommended Paul Erb. A. J. Metzler was a member of this committee and I asked him why they decided in favor of Erb. "I had worked with Erb in the mid-thirties and I saw how well he worked. [The other candidate] was a good man, but he was a carbon copy of Daniel Kauffman. Erb was from the West with a broader perspective."

But still he had to be convinced to take the assignment. "I approached him at Goshen but he kept putting me off. So I got the Board executive committee together and talked to him like a 'Dutch uncle.' I gave him such a rough time that years later I apologized to him."

Erb too remembered the experience in an interview he gave in the fall of 1980. It had been less than four years since he had left Hesston College. "Having sold my home in Hesston and bought a home in Goshen I had nothing else in mind than this is where I spend the rest of my days. The very day I bought the house in Goshen, Otis Johns from the Publication Board came to see me asking me to become editor of the *Gospel Herald*.

"At first I said no. I couldn't let myself do that especially as I had achieved success as an English teacher. I had gone through all those summers of graduate work and, as I said at that time, 'All that to go to Scottdale and edit the *Gospel Herald?*'"

H. S. Bender's support of the move finally convinced him. As dean of Goshen College, Bender had brought him to Goshen and if Bender would release him to go to Scottdale, so be it. "I never heard him say this," Erb reflected, "but as I look back on it, he saw that with him at Goshen and me at Scottdale, we had the Mennonite Church going in the right direction."

In *Gospel Herald* for January 6, 1944, the first which was his responsibility, Paul Erb wrote a testimony on behalf of Daniel Kauffman, his predecessor. "Your incoming editor will not fill Bro. Kauffman's place. It is not necessary that he do so.... We shall endeavor as the Lord gives us grace and as the church continues her prayers, her contributions and her counsel, to continue the *Gospel Herald* as an efficient organ of the church, fully expressive of her life, her thought, her activities. We trust that the atmosphere of the *Gospel Herald* editorial office will never get beyond the influence of our faithful predecessor."

There are 38 boxes of Paul Erb's correspondence in the Mennonite Archives at Goshen, Indiana. There was not time to survey them all but some spot checks were made with the help of two research assistants, Dennis Hertzler and John Sharp. At least the samples provide some sense of Erb's approach to persons who raised questions with an editor, some questions petty and others profound.

We examined the "A" folder because it was first, the "B" folder to make sure we got the benefit of correspondence with H. S. Bender, and the "K" and "M" folders to get other samples and to look for correspondence with Orie Miller, another prominent Mennonite churchman of Erb's era. In "A" we found William Anders from Franconia Conference who said that he enjoyed the *Herald* but that a bishop in the conference was openly critical. We found extensive correspondence with J. John Allison, a prisoner who wrote about physical and spiritual healing, the Revised Standard Version of the Bible, and intermarriage among the races.

There is a note to Don Augsburger urging him to cut out big words (presumably in articles for publication) and to Myron Augsburger upon the appearance of a publication called *Voice of Truth* which was evidently related to Myron's work in revival campaigns. Erb expressed concern about the multiplying of publications, but Myron sought to assure him that it "rises out of an interest to gain prayer support, not to compete."

In 1952, a letter from Erb to Dean Acheson, U.S. Secretary of State, seconded the nomination of Charles Malik for the office of Secretary General of the United Nations. In 1961, he corresponded with John Amstutz related to nonconformity as practiced by Mennonites. Amstutz felt the current interpretation stressed too much the outward appearance and not enough the inner spirit. Erb replied that nudists might say that the inner spirit is what counts and he thinks a line must be drawn there.

In his first year as editor, Erb appears to have stood on the sidelines while J. L. Stauffer, Sanford Shetler, and H. S. Bender exchanged vigorous letters over the authority of Mennonite General Conference, with carbon copies to Erb. Bender had written an article describing the role of the conference as he understood it and Stauffer and Shetler wrote to insist that it must be permitted to take stronger specific actions.

Between 1947 and 1959 there is correspondence with S. C. Brubacher of Kitchener, Ontario. The first letter from Erb seeks to clarify his position on millenialism. Some other letters from Brubacher were critical and some just friendly conversation. After receiving a lengthy letter from Brubacher, Erb wrote on May 16, 1951, "I must congratulate your typewriter on being able to turn out a lot of words. Of course you have something to say, too."

He wrote to Robert J. Baker and Edna Beiler to encourage them in their writing for the *Herald* and to Carl S. Keener to acknowledge a letter of encouragement. "I do not worry too much about the attackers," he wrote on October 24, 1951 . . . . I have learned to do the best I can and then leave the results with God."

To M. T. Brackbill, a teacher at Eastern Mennonite College and one whose contributions Erb was glad to receive, he wrote in January 1945, "Why don't you resign your position and send me an article every week. Or maybe keep your position and send me one every week anyway?" In October 1949, he responded to an article received, "God bless you, you up-to-date fogy. Somehow God has given you the knack to say the thing that needs to be said and say it in a way that people will read it, and for the most part agree with it."

To Marvin J. Miller he wrote on July 30, 1956, concerning music in the church. "My chief argument against instrumental music is that it will do something to our singing that we don't want done. It will reduce the emphasis from full congregational participation to some kind of a professional performance."

On October 10, 1949, Erb wrote to Mrs. Elmer K. Beiler who was distressed because he had not printed the obituary of her "little boy" in its original form. She had written twice requesting it to be printed properly and now complained about his "insensitivity." Erb responded warmly and with sympathy, identifying with her loss, but standing by his editorial policy.

The Daniel Kauffman mantle of Mennonite leadership was not passed on in one piece. Erb, for example, was not called upon to update *Doctrines of the Bible*. Indeed, in December 1943 when Daniel Kauffman had only a month to live, H. S. Bender delivered an address called "The Anabaptist Vision" which was to become the theological point of reference for a new generation.

But Erb had plenty to do even while sharing leadership with others. For one, although he was conscious of the power of the Kauffman tradition and the need to respect it, he was aware also that some things had slipped in the waning years of Kauffman's life. "We were right up there in the days of the second world war with Civilian Public Service and so on and I had to speak for myself. Daniel Kauffman never spoke on these issues. People at Scottdale had tried to get him to resign. He didn't hold on to the editor's job from any ambition, but I think plenty of people told him things would go to pieces if he would resign." One thing that Erb sought to do was to make the editorial page a place of significant comment. There were those who "were thinking that the editorial page of the *Gospel Herald* doesn't represent front line thinking anymore. I had to make a reputation on that for myself."

Erb was conscious that he represented a different millenial point of view from Kauffman, who had written to H. S. Bender in 1928, "Personally I hold to the theory now commonly known as 'amillenialism,' but will be very glad to have a part in a literal thousand year reign in case that will prove to be our Saviour's program."

Erb had been trained to anticipate as literal the thousand-year reign of Christ described in Revelation 20. This was a divisive issue in the church and Erb attempted to mediate through his book, *The Alpha and the Omega*, published by Herald Press in 1955. He stated in the preface the hope to "lift the discussion of unfulfilled prophecy out of the profitless argument between different schools of thought into which it has fallen." Near the end of the book he wrote, "Christian hope shows most brightly against the background of darkness in which we live today. . . . Not even concentration camps and communist prisons and shadows of atomic clouds can take away the confidence of one who can muse upon the hope of an *eschaton* that our Omega is bringing."

In 1968 A Spanish edition was published and although the English edition is out of print, the Spanish is still available. Much of his earlier thinking is reflected in his more recent book, *Bible Prophecy: Questions and Answers* (Herald Press, 1978.)

In 1958 Erb became executive secretary of Mennonite General Conference. This was a new office; he was the first staff person for the conference and served until 1961. There was evidently no adjustment in his editorial load as a result of the new responsibility. In his report to the executive editor for 1957 he wrote, "My work load is very heavy, and there should be cooperative planning between the General Conference Executive Committee and the Publishing House to relieve me in part or entirely during the next two years."

A year later at the age of 65 he wrote in his report for 1958, "I am in full accord with the proposals for further assistance which will permit me to retire over a period of several years." In 1960 he became book editor also at Mennonite Publishing House and Paul M. Schrock was appointed as assistant editor of the *Gospel Herald*. In 1961 Erb wrote, "I am happy that the Publishing Agent has been able to appoint my successor

[John M. Drescher], and I plan to make an easy transfer of the magazine to his editorship at the arranged time in 1962."

Although he did not complete a doctrinal book on the level of *Doctrines of the Bible*, Erb did write a series of articles based on the 1963 Mennonite Confession of Faith. These were published in *Youth's Christian Companion* in 1967 and by Herald Press as a book called *We Believe* in 1969. The book is still available. In January 1983 at the age of 88, Erb met with the youth class at Scottdale Mennonite Church for a discussion of these beliefs. David Hostetler was present and reported that "his contribution was to call them to awareness of the need to have 'beliefs' and that they make a difference."

Erb raised editorial writing in the *Herald* to a new height. In tacit recognition of this, Herald Press published a selection of his editorials in 1962 with the title *Don't Park Here*. In the table of contents they are classified under five headings: Part I, Dynamic Living; Part II, In Christ; Part III, Conscience Sharpeners; Part IV, The Real God; and Part V, Christian Service. The headings are probably not his, but the titles are. Examples include: Losing in the Last Lap; Revival by Imitation; Mottoes and Mud; Majoring in Minors; Gossiping the Gospel.

His final editorial on June 26, 1962, was entitled "The Mennonite Church at Mid-Century." He noted that the period of his editorship had been a time of "accelerating changes." Some, he noted, see this as good, others as apostasy, and possibly still others in between are not sure. He acknowledged the potential difficulties and observed, "To be a Mennonite in these days is still a great privilege. But it is also a fearful responsibility. How can we be the people God wants us to be?"

In the following issue his successor John M. Drescher wrote of Erb, "Outstanding in his ministry as editor has been the optimistic and positive spirit which he manifested in his writings." In *Paul and Alta* by Phyllis Good (Herald Press, 1978) Carl Kreider characterized him as a statesman and said, "Paul had the ability to bring divergent groups together" (p. 108).

Did Paul Erb have an easier time as editor than those before and after? One of the researchers who had spent time with Kauffman's file and then moved to Erb's, thought that "Things flow smoothly in the fifties, perhaps a reflection of the settling down after the war, perhaps because of economy being in good shape, perhaps because Erb is an efficient operator."

It was just an impression and cannot be documented until the dynamics of the period are subjected to further study. At this point we can only note that the church called him and after some hesitation, he came. Reflecting on the experience in the fall of 1980 Erb said, "This added a new dimension to my life that had been absent: the acceptance I found in the church and the many ways I learned to serve in the church. It put me on boards and committees, and so on. It meant that I would be introduced not as head of the English department of Goshen College, but as editor of *Gospel Herald.* Daniel Kauffman had made that a big position in the church and to step into that man's shoes was something that was given to me. I didn't achieve it of myself. I created a new dimension for my life by coming to Scottdale. I don't regret it a bit."   —*Daniel Hertzler*

1944

The new editor begins to develop his platform on issues such as personal, parental, and social responsibility.

Nonconformity

"Be not conformed to this world" (Romans 12:2).

The doctrine of nonconformity to the world is clearly taught in the Scriptures, and it should be obvious that the life of a Christian must be conducted on principles different from those which govern the non-Christian man of the world. The church must of necessity from her very nature as a called-out body teach and practice nonconformity.

In the circles of our own church it is probably true that the term "nonconformity" suggests the subject of clothes and personal appearance. But nonconformity is a broad term with applications to every phase of Christian living. There are extreme positions which one might take on the application of this term to the clothes question. One is that nonconformity has nothing to do with clothes. The specific teaching of Scripture as to how we should and should not dress makes it impossible for us to agree with this position. The other extreme position would be that nonconformity has to do chiefly or even entirely with the subject of clothes. The reaction that most of us have to the sight of a man in a plain coat, or a woman in a bonnet, smoking a cigarette makes it clear that nonconformity must include much more than our dress.

Those to whom we would teach the doctrine of nonconformity, both inside and outside the church, will probably be far more easily convinced of the truth of this teaching if we give nonconformity its complete and scriptural sense. To be nonconformed to the world is to be Christian in every phase of living. It does have to do with our clothes; but it also has to do with our homes, our use or misuse of the various inventions of our age, our talk, our reading, our interests. No phase of the subject can be excluded. A woman who is immodestly dressed is conforming to the world, no matter how much interest she may have in saving souls. A man who lives for money and worldly prosperity is conformed to the world, no matter how plain his dress may be. A person who indulges in gossip and in uncharitable judging is worldly even though he does not drink or use tobacco.

Probably we lack the right term for our teaching on Christian dress. To describe it by "nonconformity" seems to limit the connotation of that term to dress. This is unfortunate. It is important that our discussions of the nonconformed life cover the whole field and not only a part. The limited use of this term gives an unwarranted appearance of orthodoxy to a man who emphasizes only one phase of the doctrine. Probably when we mean to apply nonconformity to the subject of attire, we should use the full term, "nonconformity in dress." Our testimony to the world will be most effective when we have a balanced emphasis, both in our teaching and in our practice.

—*Paul Erb*

Parental Delinquency

Juvenile delinquency percentages continue to rise. Governmental as well as religious authorities are greatly alarmed. Certainly our national well-being has no greater threat than the moral breakdown which is evident among the young people of our country.

But conditions have causes. Juvenile delinquency is merely a symptom of some kind of adult delinquency. The nation, the church, and the school must carry their share of the blame. But undoubtedly the most serious breakdown is among the parents of our young people. F.B.I. Chief J. Edgar Hoover wrote recently: "Our homes have seen a form of treason closely akin to giving aid and comfort to our enemies. I refer to the betrayal by parents of their trust through their failure to provide the loving guidance and devotion which are the endowment and birthright of every child. Many instances have come to my attention where mothers and fathers have actually stated they do not wish to be bothered with their children, and thousands of case histories prove that these sentiments and actions are growing more widespread." This is a proper recognition of the great importance of the home and of home training.

As a Mennonite people we may think this problem is not ours. But it is probably true that in so far as there is a breakdown of the religious and the moral ideals of our Mennonite past, the homes of our church are chiefly to blame. If our young people are delinquent, there probably lies behind that delinquency some sort of parental failure. There are few things that are more pressing in Mennonite life than the necessity of getting back to the business of bringing up children in the nurture and admonition of the Lord. For our failure to do this faithfully and diligently we may have to pay dearly in the years to come.

—*Paul Erb*

1945

The Christian-Scholar

The sudden and early passing of our brother, Edward Yoder, has created among all who knew well his work and the significance of what he was doing a sense of genuine loss. The Mennonite Church has no surplusage of leadership anywhere, but comparatively speaking we seem to be rather well supplied with good preachers, with strong administrators, with efficient teachers, with able writers. When vacancies occur in our ranks in these various areas of activity it seems not too dif-

Edward Yoder, 1893-1945. On the occasion of his passing, Paul Erb commented on the need for and the value of Christian scholars.

ficult to lay hold upon young men who can fill the vacancies with ability and credit. Only recently has our church enjoyed the services of what one might call scholars. The supply of Christian scholars is sorely limited. Bro. Yoder was one of these few. It is for that reason that his early passing creates such a sense of loss.

A scholar is one who does more or less original research and study. He does not merely absorb the learning of others and after some rearrangement pass it on. He rather creates learning. He discovers facts that were not known before or which at least had been allowed to drop into forgetfulness. He is one who has a passion for the truth. Facts are for the scholar not only very stubborn things, they are very precious things. The scholar recognizes the necessity for interpretation and evaluation. He is not a mere collector of curious odds and ends of knowledge, but he is keenly aware that mere opinion and dogmatic assertion have little value. The scholar is interested in facts and he follows in his thinking where these facts lead him. He does not reject what he learns because it may happen to displease him. If he discovers that what he has been saying before is wrong, he throws away not the facts which have set him right but the error which he had before been teaching. His writings and speeches are complete in their reference to his sources so that others who follow him may be able to judge the correctness of his conclusions.

It may be that the Mennonite Church does not need many scholars, but we do need some and probably we need an increasing number. We need men who while retaining their faith in the Bible as the Word of God can with scientific accuracy guide us in questions of textual and expository understanding. We need men who can carry on the fine start that has been made in research in Mennonite history. We need men who can devote themselves to the fact-recording and the fact-finding which is necessary if we would intelligently understand what is going on in our church and in the world about us. And we would all be better off if we were more capable of an objective search for truth apart from our prejudices and preconceived notions. May God raise up Christian scholars among us who with the utmost reverence and loyalty to God and His Word will be able to contribute to the church facts and fact-finding techniques.

—*Paul Erb*

An Unusual Incident

by George J. Lapp

A missionary had come to India to serve the educational interests of a mission, also to serve as a chaplain to army troops and as a pastor of an English church. But he seemed cold and indifferent to the spiritual interests of those among whom he worked. He seemed to regard his service as a profession rather than a calling. Indian teachers and church leaders who became associated with him failed to see in him what they expected of a missionary who was called to India to take his part in the great missionary program of proclaiming the Gospel of Jesus Christ with a heart filled with His love. After a few years they became concerned about this missionary's spiritual condition and were very anxious that he come into the same

spiritual experience which they had and which they believed that other missionaries they had come to know also had.

These Indian workers talked over this disappointing condition of the new missionary, for they saw in him the making of a very useful servant of the Lord if only his heart were filled with the love of Christ. They finally decided to meet as a little group in a sequestered spot on the mountaintop where once a week at a certain time they would unitedly pray for their missionary. For more than a year they met regularly and pleaded with God in his behalf.

Then a mysterious break came in his experience. Something bore down upon him which he could neither describe nor analyze. He began to be concerned about his own spiritual life and to look about him for help. He found it in missionaries of his own and other denominations, especially those who had been gathering in the small group prayer meetings where they had been holding him up before the throne. The Lord answered prayer in a definite change in his life and attitude, but no one outside of this little prayer circle knew just why. The love of God began to shine out' through his life and interests. He began actively to bring the light of life to the unenlightened and earnestly to seek to save souls. He confessed to his Indian brethren and others his sins of commission and omission and also his lukewarmness. His own church was formal, but he realized its, and also his own, failure to witness effectively to the grace of God.

One year—many years ago—when we were privileged to attend a convention in this Himalayan city we noted his intense spiritual interest and enjoyed his warmth of soul and wondered. One day in a meeting of praise and prayer he asked for the privilege of giving a special testimony. He told of his lukewarmness in the past and of the change that came into his life and attitudes, and then with great emotion he told us the reason why. He said, "This change came about in me through the operation of the Spirit of God in answer to prayer by my Indian brethren who, unknown to me, met each week on a certain hilltop to pray for me." We all shed tears of rejoicing and sympathy with him and within ourselves vowed more deeply to consecrate ourselves to the spiritual interests for which we were called in India....

This missionary is still active in the work of the Lord and manifests the same spiritual interest he did after the change came into his life.

Dhamtari, C.P., India

1946

Looking Toward Death

"So teach us to number our days, that we may apply our hearts unto wisdom" (Psalm 90:12).

The other day we received a deed for a lot in the Scottdale cemetery. It is a beautiful place on a green knoll among the rolling lands of western Pennsylvania. It looks away to Chestnut Ridge, the first range of the Appalachian Mountains. It is such a spot as one might choose for a last resting place of that part of him which is earthy.

There are those who do not like to contemplate death. To come to the end of a pleasant earthly road, to lay down the work one loved, to bid a farewell to loved ones and friends, to submit to whatever unpleasantness there may be in disease or physical deterioration, to go from the light of this known world to the dimness of that which is unknown—all this may give pause to any of us. To the ungodly man, contemplation of death may bring terror or rebellion, or perhaps a numbing bravado. If death is the end of all, if these few years are all that we have for the enjoyment of existence, if the future is totally dark, then one may well feel a repulsion concerning death.

But God has given us an outlook which is full of hope and joy. The Christian may face death without fear, distaste, or even regret. He may arrange for his resting place; he may plan his funeral service; he may write his will and give final instructions to those who will be left

behind with the freeheartedness of one who is about to graduate to something better. For the Christian knows that though the body returns to earth, the spirit returns to God who gave it. He has the promise of God in His Word and the assurance of his Lord and Saviour of a house of God eternal in the heavens. He may actually anticipate with longing the transfer from the imperfections of this life to the perfections which are beyond. Christ is His manifold salvation, and in the hope of eternal life which He has brought, has taken the sting from death. It is an enemy, but it is an enemy which has been conquered. "Death, thou shalt die," was the triumphant exclamation of John Donne. That cemetery lot shall someday be invaded and the body which has been laid to rest shall be resurrected in glorious vitality and immortality. Yes, the coming of Christ with its translation of the living saints may prevent its ever being used. The grave for the Christian is only an incidental in his forward look. It is not the last resting place for those who have found their eternal rest in God. We are headed, not for our green knoll in the Pennsylvania hills, but for a mansion which is being prepared for us. Praise God for a faith that cannot be buffeted by the prospect of death.

—Paul Erb

Paul Erb in 1983 at cemetery lot he purchased in 1946, on a green knoll which looks away to Chestnut Ridge, the first range of the Appalachian Mountains.

Concerning Chenaniah

by Milford R. Hertzler

It is always a great satisfaction if, upon the consideration of any worthwhile subject, we can go to the Bible for inspiration. The subject of music and musicians, singers and singing, is no exception.

In I Chronicles 15 we read of the elaborate preparations made by David to bring the ark of the covenant of the Lord out of the house of Obed-edom into the tent erected for it in the city of David. He called all Israel together to Jerusalem; the priests and Levites were numbered; then he called for Zadok and Abiathar, the priests, and for the chief of the Levites. He said to them, "Ye are the chief of the fathers of the Levites: sanctify yourselves, both ye and your brethren, that ye may bring up the ark of the Lord God of Israel unto the place that I have prepared for it" (v. 12).

Now David himself was a musician and singer and many times had written a song as an expression of his innermost feelings. Accordingly, for this important occasion, David composed a song. He also instructed "the chief of the Levites to appoint their brethren to be the singers with instruments of musick . . . lifting up the voice with joy" (v. 16).

Then follows a list of appointments of singers and musicians, and of doorkeepers and shouters. But standing out, uniquely, in the midst of these many offices is the name of Chenaniah. "And Chenaniah, chief of the Levites, was for song: he instructed about the song, because he was skillful" (v. 22).

I have often wondered about Chenaniah and have wished that the sacred record would tell us more about this ancient songmaster. However, let us examine the Word again and consider the several interesting things that are revealed concerning him.

In the first place, Chenaniah was a sanctified man. He was a Levite by birth; his calling was to minister in the sacred things of God. This heritage, however, was not enough; he needed to be cleansed. His body he had washed, and his clothing were without spot or wrinkle. While this suggests to us neatness and cleanliness on the part of a chorister, the real significance is a spiritual cleansing. "Let us draw near with a true heart in full assurance of faith, having our hearts sprinkled from an evil conscience, and our bodies washed with pure water" (Heb. 10:22). Also, notice in Colossians 3 the significant words "mortify" (v. 5); "put off" (v. 8); "put on" (vv. 12, 14); "let" (vv. 15, 16); and "be" (v. 15), all associated with the thought of acceptable worship in song. Choristers, yours is a place of leadership in the worship of song; let your leadership be with power and influence because your work is done with "clean hands and a pure heart."

In the second place, Chenaniah instructed about the song because he was skillful; doubtless, he had great natural ability. Just so, today, there are those who have great musical talent and those who have less. Natural ability or skill will deteriorate unless there is a continual exercise of it in study and practice. Because a lesser degree of skill can be greatly improved by a determined application of time and effort, every chorister should avail himself of every reasonable opportunity to increase his musical skill. Chenaniah was "master of the song." He, no doubt, knew the music from beginning to end and could sing it. He was familiar with the text and, like the Apostle Paul, sang in the spirit of the composer

Also, to Chenaniah was given the responsibility of instructing the large group of singers. No doubt they practiced for this great occasion. He, their master of song, could lead them by tone of voice, and by direction of the hand. He could tell them when to sing in subdued or solemn tones and when to break forth in loud and joyous strains. He would indicate when this group should sing or when that; when the tenors and when the basses; or when they all should join together in harmony. . . .

Notice, lastly, Chenaniah was clothed with a robe of fine linen. Verse 27. It was a plain, simple robe with no ornamentation. It spoke of humility, of man—unworthy, sinful man— drawing near to the presence of a high and holy God. The high priest, when he entered the holiest place on the day of atonement, laid aside his robes of splendor and clad, in a simple linen robe entered into the presence of

God. Even so, the spirit of simplicity and humility should possess the heart of every chorister and should manifest itself in his outward appearance and conduct. Why should there be any tendency toward pride or conceit in our song leaders? There is, indeed, too much to be accomplished to allow such hindrances.

The Apostle Paul says that "David after he had served his own generation by the will of God, fell on sleep" (Acts 13:36). I like to think so, also, of Chenaniah, David's master of song—he served his own generation by the will of God. And in this generation, when there is so much room for improvement in the music part of our church worship, we need men who will serve, men who are "masters of song," after the order of Chenaniah.

Joanna, Pa.

1947

House Wrecking

Below our window they are wrecking a house. Room must be made for the addition to the Publishing House, and this residence must go. We all rejoice in the prospect of more room in our crowded plant, and so we are glad to see these preparatory operations begun. The wrecking is a promise of building; something must be taken away so that the greater may rise in its place.

And yet, house wrecking is a sorry business. Where once the warm light shone out after nightfall, there is now only cold darkness. Where once there was a cheery sound of happy living and the welcome invitation to strangers, one hears now only the thuds and the screeching of a house being torn apart. Somehow one cannot forget the "heap o' living' " that made that house a home. Something that lies close to our hearts has gone out of our immediate community.

The workmen are proceeding carefully so as to save the material, but yet one can see that it is easier to tear down a house than to build one. Construction in reverse doesn't take the skill that the original planning and execution did. It would hardly be to anyone's credit to be known only as a successful wrecker. Delight in destruction is hardly a good attribute.

It is much easier to wreck a character than to build one. It is much easier to spoil a reputation than to create it. A few indiscretions, a few lapses can undo the careful and painstaking work of years. And it is much easier to wreck a church and community than to build one. The toil and tears of many generations, come to fruitage in a peaceful community and a functioning church, may be brought to ruin in a short time by selfish and sinful words and deeds. Sometimes some wrecking may need to be done in order that the greater structure may appear. But who would want to be written into history as one whose influence had been chiefly negative, tearing down what other men had built? The wrecking bar is a tempting instrument, for one can do much with it in a short time. But the architect's pencil and the builder's level will bring one more blessing from the generations to come. God, make me a builder and not a destroyer. Help me to be obsessed, not with that which now is and may be done away with, but with that which is not yet but which may be.

—Paul Erb

Using Criticism

In a recent issue of *Time* magazine there is a story concerning foreign minister Wang of China. Wang was under fire for his foreign policies. Stung by the criticism, Wang resigned. One member of the party commented, "When anyone criticizes a minister, he wants to resign. A minister must accept criticism and strive to correct his faults. Wrong attitude!" Generalissimo Kai-shek said, "Everybody wants to resign. To whom can I resign? You go back to your post." According to the story, Wang did.

Probably everyone at some time or other becomes the object of criticism. The more contact you have with people, the more you are in the public eye, the more criticism you will get. The more work you do, the more criticism you will get. Criticism is not to be wondered at; it is to be expected by any public servant in nation, community, and church.

The important question is, what shall one do about criticism? It is natural to resent the criticism and to "resign" in one form or another. This is the smallest and most futile attitude to take toward criticism. Sometimes one must bow to common protest, but to flee from a difficulty is usually small and profitless.

The better plan is to meet criticism fairly. One must look it in the face and see why it was given. Even the most violent critic sometimes presents a grain of truth; perhaps there is much truth in his point of view. Most of us can profit by criticism that we receive. It is egotistic to assume that one makes no mistakes. The only people who make no mistakes are those who are dead. The man who wants to learn should thank his critics. They may not be right in every particular; they may be most unkind in the way in which they present their criticisms. One's opportunity is to sift from the criticism that which may be true, at least that which may be helpful, and then to profit by it. When criticism by others becomes a means to helpful self-criticism, then some profitable fruit is reaped.

The pruned tree does not resign. The suggestion that there is too much wood is a truthful one. The wise tree yields to the pruning and produces still more fruit after the painful process is over. Ministers, administrators, teachers, editors, parents, even friends will probably get their share of criticism. Let this criticism become a means of grace, and we will be thankful for it.

—*Paul Erb*

1948

Fogy

by Maurice T. Brackbill

I just now looked up in the dictionary the meaning of a word I have occasionally heard used in years gone by. I do not remember that I ever inquired into its meaning before. I thought I nearly knew it, and put it down from the usage that fogy was something, whatever it was, I did not particularly wish to be, and certainly did not wish to be called. Webster defines a fogy as one who is dull, behind the times, and overconservative. Another word next to it is fogram with the added qualification of being old-fashioned. Well, that isn't too bad. There are many things I'd rather NOT be. Indeed I have come to think that a little fogyism is a good thing to have around, and that all of us should have at least a little of it personally. I do not favor the "over" part of it, however; I do not like extremes in anything, and I hope one can be old-fashioned and conservative without being particularly "dull" about it. To make it sound worse, the word "old" is prefixed to fogy, but one doesn't need to be old to be a fogy.

I do not like at all the sound of the word. It probably originated in derision of the thing it stands for, and the sound was suggestive. It reminds one of bogy and no one wants to be that either. We need a new word to mean what fogy implies, but which sounds complimentary. Can't someone coin a word! I think it should not have a long o sound, and initial f's are definitely out.

It has been my observation that fogies are always spoken of in a spirit of contempt or ridicule. But in the catalog of fogies there are many very worthy folks. There are dozens of them among the Bible heroes: Noah, Abram, Lot, Samuel, etc., and everybody greatly admires them today. The old fogies are not all dead, but it seems that the admired ones are. It is queer that we should be so farsighted. To our seeing eyes living fogies are out of focus, and it takes a historian to set up a glass, a telescope, to enable us to see them clearly afar off in the past. But it was always that way.

The fogies usually make good brakes to progress. It is a bit strange that most of us, perhaps, should see the need of brakes on everything that moves but progress. Progress is just as dangerous without brakes as a locomotive. Man can not stand too much speed in anything; indeed, man can increase speed safely only to the extent the adequacy of brakes can keep up with it. An example of this is the progress made in nuclear fission. A few years ago I heard an astronomer in a large university say that a number of his colleagues became much alarmed when they learned how near physicists were achieving the atomic bomb, and they prayed, these hardheaded men of science PRAYED, that it would not be achieved. Now they, I suppose, could have been dubbed old fogies. But what have we today because of chain-reaction—the most worried world of all time. It isn't sitting on a volcano—it is sitting on an atomic bomb! A world-famous astronomer is reputed to have said: "Soon the Lord will look out from the Nebula of Andromeda and see a nova in our direction and will exclaim: 'Ha, another of my worlds has learned the cosmic jest!' " I do not claim to know, but it does look to me that progress in subatomic research has gone on too fast. The world isn't ready for it. It might be safely used in the millenium. We can go too fast in anything, and we just must have some fogies around to keep us from going to destruction.

Satirists are mostly old fogies, but we say they do society good by holding up to ridicule strides in wrong directions, and too rapid changes. A few satirists, like Voltaire, have laughed at the fogies, but they themselves were fogies in reverse to evil ends. And I think one can be fogyish for no good reason: just because of an inability to change or to see any virtue in changes, or just because of jealousy or something else inexcusable. One can be a fogy by worshiping traditions like the antique faddist who will have nothing in his house but ancient furnishings and contraptions.

You might have guessed this paper is in defense of the fogy, and that is right, but, as already intimated, with some slight modification. I think a fogy should be guided by wisdom and charity and open-mindedness, and he should be capable of at least some fine adjustments. But then maybe some would say he would no longer be a fogy. Well, anyway, here is an open declaration of my admiration of the old fogies who know the Bible and a few other things, who are willing to lend their hand to the brake lever when the traffic light to any progress goes red, who can take it when their warnings go unheeded or when the ridicule stings their faces. I do not mind being a fogy myself. My chief objection is to the sound of the word. And I would hesitate to brand any one a fogy, not only because it doesn't sound "nice," but because of the dispute the word has always borne, and also because it is a colloquialism. But I'd rather be a fogy and be called the same than be too far afield in the other direction and be called something that sounded commendable.

Harrisonburg, Va.

M. T. Brackbill: We can go too fast in anything and we just must have some fogies around to keep us from destruction.

1949

There is something almost profane in our continual hurry. We need to learn what we can do on a decent schedule and leave the rest to God.

What's Your Hurry?

Somewhere we have read of a man who watched in amazement the hurrying, rushing, milling throng on a New York subway platform. They ran, they pushed, they darted toward every opening in the crowd; they raced toward a moving train as if there never would be another. Where can they be going? he wondered. What terrible urgency makes them risk life and limb, breaking every law of courtesy and kindness in order to get to wherever they are going a few seconds sooner? Finally he thought he would answer his question. He picked out a particularly hasty man who came out of the subway car on the run. He followed him closely as he elbowed his way, taking advantage of open places on the stairway to take the steps three at a time. That package of paper under his arm, thought the pursuer, must be some important document that some board of directors is waiting for. The hurrying man dodged honking cars and trucks as he crossed the busy street. Sometimes running, sometimes walking rapidly, he fought against the current of traffic on the sidewalk. Soon he took a path into Central Park. But seeing an empty bench he slumped into it, and quickly opening his papers he began poring over the contents. When his pursuer casually walked behind him he noticed that the subject of study was the comic page of the newspaper. For twenty minutes the man sat there following the foolish fortunes of the comic personages. And that was what all the hurry was about.

But there are a lot of us like him. We hurry out of childhood into youth, into early maturity, middle age, and old age, fairly leaping from our cradles into our graves. We can hardly wait to start to school, and then to get through with school and into a job. We crowd for promotion and quick success. We become stoop-shouldered going after early fortune, and dyspeptic from bolted meals....

"He that believeth shall not make haste," says the prophet. One of the greatest contributions we can make to our spirituality, both as individuals and as a church, is to recover our composure. There is something almost profane in our continual hurry. We need to learn how to meditate. We need to do what we can on a decent schedule, and then leave the rest with God. We have but a few years, it is true, but God has milleniums. His work goes on continually, but with a stately decorum. Let's fall into step with Him. What's your hurry?
—Paul Erb

The Shepherd Psalm

by Edna Beiler

I think that through long star-enchanted
    nights
With gentle crunch of woolly flocks near by
Young David felt these truths pierce to his
    soul;
That over and around his own concern
For each least lamb of his, he knew God's care;
And as they walked the lonely trails together
Seeking fresh pastures and still little pools
God must have guided David's secret thought.
So when the Holy Spirit whispered, "Write!"
He Took the simple fabric of his past
And wrote such words as through the shifting
    years
Have never lost their God-inspired glow.

Phoenix, Ariz.

Toggenburg Goats and New Hampshire Chickens

The report on the goat project at La Plata and an article on raising chickens in Puerto Rico appearing in this issue of the Missions section are especially significant to us because of our emphasis on the dedication of one's whole life to the Christian purpose. Since the physical life cannot be separated from the spiritual, any effort which promotes the physical and which in turn promotes the spiritual can therefore be designated as spiritual. Toggenburg goats and New Hampshire chickens in the hands of Christians do play a part in the extension of the kingdom of God.

There are those who claim that the teaching of farming in a mission program is the social Gospel, is a waste of time, and is the devil's handiwork in delaying effective preaching and evangelization. The Christian is to do direct missionary work. Yet, we have learned that an unhealthy body cannot worship God properly. The semi-starvation unit of Civilian Public Service men at the University of Minnesota several years ago proved that with physical deterioration goes a significantly parallel downward trend of morals and ethics. Stalwart Christians, enduring the pangs of hunger, stole food even though their consciences told them not to.

How then can Puerto Ricans, or any other group of people, live the Christian life regularly if their bodies are malnourished? We, in well-fed America, know that it is difficult to think of the attitudes of God when we have a splitting headache, when we are expurgating that nauseating food, or are too weak to even talk. A vigorous body, with an accompanying sound mind, help us worship God more than we often consider or admit. . . .

Our church, with her valuable rural and farming heritage, can play an important role in developing unproductive land, in working by the sweat of the brow, and in teaching that good soil produces good food and that good food produces good bodies and that good bodies produce good mental preparation for good spiritual growth. With all of the capable farmers in our constituency we should think of sending out agricultural missionaries by the dozens. Most of them could perhaps soon be self-supporting. Some could be sent to aid our missionaries establish a Christian community. The Chaco of Argentina, the wilds of Africa, and the jungles of India have soil that should be used to the glory of God. Toggenburg goats and New Hampshire chickens are meant for Christians in other lands too.

—F.B. (*Ford Berg, Missions Editor*).

1950

The House by the Side of the Road

by Paul and Alta Erb

"Let's cut out paper dolls."

"But we can't. Mother threw away the old catalog so we wouldn't mess up the house."

"Then we'll go over to our house. Mother kept ours just so we could use it to cut out. She isn't using the sewing room today, and she won't care how much of a mess we make."

The car with two young couples in it drew up in front of the roadside refreshment stand.

"Let's not go in here," said one of the girls.

"Where can we go?" asked her escort.

"Why, to our house," she eagerly replied. "Mother said there would be plenty of ice cream in the refrigerator if I brought any of my friends in. And I want to hear the Messiah recording that we just bought."

"I'm just too ill to drive on home tonight. Can't we stop some place?"

"But there's not a decent tourist home, camp, or hotel for many miles," her husband replied. "There are many Mennonite homes all along here, but it's almost eleven, and I hate to impose on people."

"But we must. I can't go farther."

"Well, about a mile farther on is _____'s. I'm not afraid to stop there. We're sure to be welcome at their house, even if they have already gone to bed."

"Oh, yes, I know they'll take us in."

"Lady, could I please have a sandwich? I haven't eaten all day."

"Yes, step in out of the wind. There's a basin if you would like to wash. Then sit at the table over there. I'll make you some hot coffee. And we have some good cold beef to slice."

"Thank you for your kindness. I'm ashamed to bother you. But I lost my job, and I knew I could—"

"Oh, you are very welcome. I could not say 'no' to a hungry man. One never knows how soon she might need some help herself. I share because I am a Christian."

"Thank you, lady. That's the kindest word I've heard for many a day."

"How do you do? My name is Plank. We are glad you stopped at our church, Mrs. Snyder. Won't you go along for dinner? We were hoping some strangers might show up to help us eat the roast in the oven. We always prepare to entertain the chance visitors. That's one of the nice things about having our church near the highway. You follow our car, that Ford over there."

"Can't you come over for supper Thursday evening?"

"Oh, it isn't our turn."

"That's no excuse at all. We don't keep books on our friends. We want to talk to you—nothing special—we just like to be with you. And I'll make a meatloaf on that new recipe. You'll like it. We'll look for you."

"Mother, who'll we have for Christmas dinner this year? The relatives can take care of themselves this time. Let's invite that D.P. family that just moved in down the road. I'd love to give them the happiest Christmas they have had for many a year, O.K.?"

"Yes, the smaller house would be handier and less work. But there's just one bedroom, and the living room and the dining room are so small we never could have all the children home with their families. That's no house for a real grandmother. I don't want a cubbyhole to grow old and die in. I want a house that's big enough to invite folks to."

"All right, Fanny. I thought that's what you'd say. We'll stay right here."

"Let me live in a house by
      the road,
And be a friend to many."
    Scottdale, Pa.

Paul and Alta Erb: Let's invite that DP family for Christmas.

The Korean War

Are we hearing now the opening guns of the Third World War? Or is this merely a skirmish on the line which separates the Communist and Western worlds? Will the tide of victory in Korea merely locate or relocate that line? Or will it be the beginning of an armed conflict that will once more engulf the world in bloody death?

At the moment of this writing it seems to be going badly for the American forces, and it appears possible that anti-Communist lines in Asia will need to be reformed in Japan, Formosa, and the Philippines. But it may be possible, as the military might of the United States and its supporting friends comes to fuller strength, to drive the Communists back to the original thirty-eighth parallel. In that case, there will no doubt be a loud popular cry to go on and finish the job, driving the Communists entirely out of Korea. It is hard to see how either side can save face by agreeing to leave things just as they were before hostilities began.

Bombarded as we are by the incomplete and nationally biased interpretations of press and radio, it is important that, as Christians and as members of a nonresistant church, we have clear understanding of the situations in the world and of our relation to them. There is great danger that we will find ourselves agreeing with the popular cry that since the Communists have begun hostilities, and since what they are doing in Korea is only a sample of what they will do, if they dare, along the whole Communist front, there is nothing else for the United States and the other non-Communist countries to do than to use all the military power that is needed to stop such aggression. . . .

These are days when we need to base the ethics of our living, not on headlines, newspaper editorials, or radio interpretations, but on the unchanging Word of God. We need to read again and again what Jesus and Paul and Peter and John have to say to us.

We need to open our hearts wider than ever to the Spirit of love that breathes through the sacred pages, and we need to pray for grace to suffer wrong, if need be, rather than to do wrong. True Biblical religion never takes a vacation during times of crisis and national emergency.

In the second place, we need to keep ourselves from thinking and saying that what our nation is doing is the right thing, only that as Christians we cannot participate. It is true that it is not our primary responsibility as Christians to tell the government how to conduct itself, but it is our responsibility to hold high the light of truth and to proclaim as widely as we may what God's will for mankind is. We need not only to be assured, but also to proclaim, that those who take the sword shall perish by the sword, that the road of military conquest can lead only to destruction, even for the victor. . . .

We are in the smoke of battle, and it is difficult to see clearly. We may be sure that now, as always in the time of conflict, truth is distorted and passions rule. As Christians we need to strive earnestly to keep our thinking clear and our hearts warm, not only toward people of our own color and nation, but also toward the peoples of other colors and nations. Our hearts should bleed not only for the American soldiers who are losing their lives in this struggle, but also for the hundreds of Koreans who are lying dead on the battlefields, and for the thousands of other Koreans who are losing their homes and their means of living. Our hearts should bleed for the millions of Chinese who are starving, and for the millions in other parts of Asia who live continually on the very edge of subsistence.

But particularly we should be concerned that all this trouble and suffering comes upon men because they do not know the way of God nor the salvation and way of life which Christ taught. These are days when we need to expend our means and our personnel not to destroy but to save, not to fight Communism but to teach and demonstrate the way of life and love against which Communism can have no argument.

May God keep us true to our call and our essential Christian commission.

—*Paul Erb*

1951

On Marriage Customs

by John A. Hostetler

Our marriage customs have their origin in the oblivion of the great past. They are a strange combination of the survival of ceremonies and "relics" of many tribes and peoples. There is nothing distinctly "Christian" about the marriage vow, the ceremony, the arrangement of flowers, or the honeymoon as practiced by Mennonites of today. Not even a hint can be found of a formal religious ceremony connected with marriage in either the Old or New Testament.

Jesus seems to have accepted marriage as it existed in the conventionalized civilization of the Jews, with but one exception (divorce). There is nothing in the record which suggests that He added or took from marriage any custom, or that He gave any new meaning to it. Neither did the apostles.

There is a tradition, however, which follows the ceremony among Mennonites today that has some resemblance to the practices of "uncivilized" peoples. I do not mean the high cost of all the paraphernalia that goes with a wedding, the festivity that follows the ceremony, the luxurious display of fancy dress, or the picture-taking craze, although our religion and concept of morality would have much to say on these points.

I refer to the enthusiastic spirit of some, perhaps most often young adults, who are so zealous in demonstrating their "good wishes" to the newlyweds. This form of expression frequently does not stop with rice throwing, pranks of various sorts, and glaring streamers attached to the auto of the bridal party.

Particularly in a mob, even well-meaning friends do things that ordinarily in their good senses they would not think of doing. In a car dabbed over with words or phrases, or with perhaps part of the vehicle dismantled, and a dozen varieties of tin cans fastened to the rear, the bridal party may drive ten or twenty miles trying to escape for their honeymoon, while three to six cars follow with blasting horns. Granted that there is nothing wrong with such things as tin cans and rice, one hilarious prank leads to another until no one seems to know when to stop.

This is an initiation of the kind which may by some use of the imagination be likened to the ceremonial rites of the Andaman Islanders, or the puberty rites of the Canoe Indians of Tierra del Fuego. More often than not, the practice brings frustration instead of joy to an already overtaxed and strenuous day—a day on which the couple takes the greatest venture in faith ever possible during a lifetime.

Custom may add meaning to the dignity of marriage, or it may subtract from its spiritual significance, resulting in the degradation of a divine ideal. This is one area in which Mennonites have borrowed from the heathen and "Christian" culture about them, and does it not suggest the need for an appropriate substitutionary form, in harmony with the rest of our Christian way of life?

State College, Pa.

John A. Hostetler: Custom may add meaning to the dignity of marriage, or it may subtract from its spiritual significance.

Not by Might

"Not by might, nor by power, but by my spirit, saith the Lord of hosts" (Zech. 4:6b).

In the days of the restoration Haggai and Zechariah gave prophetic encouragement to Zerubbabel the prince and to Joshua the high priest. The temple of the restoration had not been built on the scale of the former temple. The human resources available were greatly reduced from the days of the wealthy Solomon. The enemies of the Jewish people were only describing what they saw when they talked about "these feeble Jews." The old men who had seen Solomon's temple wept at the reduction of grandeur. To such a time Zechariah declared, "Who hath despised the day of small things?"

In his letter to the Corinthians Paul reminds us that the Lord loves to use weakness through which to reveal His might. The great letter to the Romans was carried by Phebe, a feeble woman. A Jewish captive boy preserved Egypt and the surrounding countries in the time of famine. A shepherd lad slew a great giant with a sling shot. Redemption was brought to the world through the Baby Jesus. The great Messiah was a peasant of Galilee. An obscure monk at Wittenberg sounded the note of the Reformation. A persecuted little group of Anabaptists brought into being for the modern world separation of church and state. The Publishing House in which we write this editorial has grown in a few years from an attic press in a house down the street. God does not choose to work by the might of numbers. One with God is a majority. An institution is the lengthened shadow of a man. The evangelistic movement in the Mennonite Church grew from the conviction and the effort of J. C. Coffman. Our far-flung mission program has grown from the work of a few faithful ones in Chicago. A Sunday afternoon conversation resulted in Hesston College. The most significant things are done by minorities. God loves to work through a few far-seeing ones who are willing to attach themselves to a worth-while but unpopular cause.

Nor does God choose always to work by the might of wealth. One of our greatest fallacies is that money is all-powerful. One of the best ways to kill a cause is to swamp it with money. Bitter necessity is the mother of invention. Resourcefulness of personality is often increased by the sheer struggle for existence. The budget is not the final word on the possibility of a line of action. Equipment, which usually depends on wealth, is not the chief means to accomplishment. The man makes the tools, not the tools the man. A calendar picture shows a boy with a string of fish which he caught with a crooked pole and a small hook on a cord. A fisherman from the city with an elaborate reel and a whole box of fish lures, but with an empty creel, looks on in astonishment. Everyone has heard a college defined as a log with Mark Hopkins sitting on one end of it.

Nor does the Lord always choose to work by the might of talent. The high I.Q.'s walk out with their diplomas and are frequently never heard of again. The best pastors are not always eloquent preachers. Soul-winners need not be skillful debaters. Water does not need to flow through golden pipes, or even through copper ones. The tin cup by the well was the most-loved utensil down on the old farm. It was clean and it was always there. It isn't talent we lack; more likely it is consecration and a passion to do the Lord's will.

The might of the Lord manifests itself in its own way. Divine power is not to be laid hold on and put to work according to our desires and notions, like electricity or steam. The Old Testament narrative says, "And the Spirit of the Lord came upon him." Then the wonders began. God enters into human flesh, into human mind and heart, that through this human agency He might manifest His power and do His work....

Through the Spirit God empowers for witness and testimony. Peter the fearful becomes filled with boldness. Thomas the doubter establishes a church in India. Runaway Mark writes a Gospel. D. L. Moody of the stumbling tongue preaches to multitudes. Weak words and faulty homiletics are seized by the Spirit and become means of salvation and edification. The Holy Spirit is seeking minds which

He can inspire with truth, hearts which He can warm with divine love, and tongues through which He can speak to those whose hearts He has opened. He creates the occasion and then brings the word for the occasion. Let us be assured that only as the Spirit of God works will the work of man be effective.

—*Paul Erb*

1952

There are many questions involved which make an arbitrary answer impossible. This is an area where we may counsel, but not judge.

Interracial Marriage

"Marry from among your kind of folks." This is a traditional counsel that has a great deal of wisdom in it. It was not mere prejudice against the people of his adopted land which made Abraham send his servant to Haran to find there among their kindred a wife for Isaac. Nor was it mere personal preference that made the daughters of Heth, Esau's wives, a grief of mind to Isaac and Rebekah, so that they urged Jacob to find a wife in the ancestral stock.

The adjustment which is a part of every marriage is certainly made easier when the husband and wife bring from their background a great many things which they hold in common. The more disimilar the background, the more different the marital problems may be. This is one of the reasons that interracial marriages are considered by most people to be unwise.

Problems of race relations are pressing for solution in today's world. In America, in Africa, and in Asia there are tensions that must be eased if disastrous conflicts are not to result.

Many people who try to think through the implications of Christian love and brotherhood feel that the patterns of segregation which have developed through the years in many areas are wrong and ought to be abolished. But very often when such ideas are set forth, someone comes up with the question, "Are you advocating marriage between the races?"

It is often an unfair question, thrown up as an argument for social segregation. People who argue for racial equality are thinking, for the most part, of equal political, economic, and social privileges. They may still feel that people will be happier if they marry within their own race. The less privileged races will usually say that they are not asking for intermarriage, but only for an equal chance of employment, and the privilege of living, eating, sitting, traveling, and worshiping where they will.

But what shall we say if young people of different races who do go to school together, who worship together as members of the same church, who live in the same block and work at the same employment, should fall in love and desire to marry? Has Christianity a clear directive in such a case?

There are many questions involved which make an arbitrary answer impossible. In the first place, what is a race? When is a marriage only international, and therefore presumably unobjectionable, and when does it become interracial? There are national physical traits, as well as racial physical traits. When is a person of pure racial blood? The Jews, who for religious reasons were forbidden to marry non-Jewish people, actually absorbed much Gentile blood, so that David, the outstanding king of the Jews, was a descendant of Rahab the Canaanite and of Ruth the Moabite. God became incarnate in a descendant of this line. None of us can be very sure of just what blood strains we are compounded.

What Scriptural arguments can we give against interracial marriage? We are told to marry only in the Lord, a commandment still in full force, and we are wise to specify further that one should marry in his own church; but there is no commandment that a Greek should marry a Greek, or a Roman a Roman. All we find is a minimizing of racial distinctions in the clear light of the fact that God has made of one blood all men, and that we all become one in Christ. We may call interracial marriage unwise, but we can hardly call it unscriptural.

One of the pioneer missionaries to China, in his sincere desire to become one with his people, married a Chinese woman and adopted Chinese manners. Few would agree with his idea or practice as a technique of mission strategy, but we have never read that anyone thought he committed a moral fault. If we should enter the mission field in Brazil, where interracial marriage is not only accepted, but encouraged, we should probably not try to make a moral issue of the matter.

Which brings us to the position that the arguments against intermarriage are social arguments. They are still, it seems to us, very strong. We have to live in our society as it is. If that society has prejudices and makes distinctions, and we choose to flout those distinctions, we must be prepared to accept the consequences. For ourselves that may not be too difficult. People secure in each other's love can disregard the slights of friends and neighbors. But people who marry must think of their children. In a segregated society the children of mixed marriages are classed with the less privileged race. Their parents must be prepared to explain and to comfort the hurts that are pretty sure to come.

One may follow the Apostle Paul in saying to interracial lovers that, if they will, they may marry, but, since "they will have trouble in the flesh" (I Cor. 7:28), it would seem the wiser thing to marry among one's own kind of folks. This is an area where we may counsel, but where we should not judge.

—*Paul Erb*

1953

Perhaps some sculptor ought to mold for us a new "Thinker" not meditating in solitude, but listening respectfully and thoughtfully to one who is addressing him.

Listening to Others

He planned his schedule so that he would be present when his own speech was on the program. That was important. It was a topic he liked, and he had made careful preparation. His message would, he felt sure, be a real challenge to the audience. He expected it to change attitudes and to bring about needed reforms. He visualized that everybody would be there to hear it. His speech, in fact, was the real center of the program.

He worked so long on his preparation that he did not arrive in time to hear the speeches before his, except the one that immediately preceded. Even then he was putting some last touches on his notes. And he didn't stay to hear the speeches of his brethren that evening and the next day. In fact, to make the six o'clock train he had to leave before the benediction was said. One could hardly expect a man with such a busy schedule to hang around a conference for two or three days. It made him nervous too, to just sit and listen.

There were people who had wanted to speak to this experienced church leader, but he wasn't around long enough to give them a chance. And some younger men were disappointed that he wasn't there to hear what they had to say on their assignments. This meeting for him was really not a conference; it was only a stage for a brief appearance.

The above paragraphs describe not any one man on any one occasion. They only describe a tendency which some have observed. When a man seems to appear only for his own part of the program, we must not judge too harshly. There are emergency calls that any man of many affairs cannot control. And some of our meetings do get pretty long. The General Conference at Kitchener, for instance, lasted six days for those who were on the General Council. That's quite a block of time to fit into a crowded schedule.

But after making all due allowance, we do feel the need of cautioning ourselves, all of us, against a certain type of egotism. There is a good deal of selfishness in any assumption that others should listen to us, but that we need not listen to others. It is still true, even for a wise and experienced church leader, that our final views are something of a composite, arrived at by listening to others as well as by our own thinking. Perhaps some sculptor ought to mold for us a new "Thinker," not meditating in solitude, but listening respectfully and thoughtfully to one who is addressing him. There is none, perhaps, who has nothing whatever to teach us; and usually the people placed on a program are the kind from whom we may expect the most help.

Maybe our conferences and other annual meetings should be made shorter. Certainly participants should be there for the beginning and stay to the end. There is a fine spirit of democracy and Christian brotherhood in the assumption that every other speech on the program is as important as mine.

—Paul Erb

Word of You

by Helen Alderfer

They brought me word of you
Across the miles, across the years.
(What did I fear to hear
Of ease of place or men's acclaim?
Of joys of earthly life
Forged well, more binding than a chain?)

"He grows mightily toward God."
It was my prayer for you.
Culp, Ark.

When the State Is God

by John Howard Yoder

The beginning of the story is that the military court of Reuilly found before it in May two very different criminals. The one, a German theological student, had killed in cold blood a captured French underground fighter; the second was Jean-Bernard Moreau, a young French pacifist, whose crime was the desire to render a civilian service more useful than military training.

The end of the story is simple enough. The German who killed was acquitted; the Frenchman whose God forbade him to kill was sentenced to a year of prison.

The explanation is clear enough; we need no long investigation to understand the contradition. For from the judges' point of view there is no contradiction. The state is simply not interested in the moral question of killing. They approached the trials from an utterly different point of view, from which there is nothing surprising about the decision to release a criminal and punish a Christian.

That point of view is, simply enough, that the state is its own god. Its ultimate good is its own existence, in the light of which decisions of right and of value are made. Its decisions are concerned not with the will of God, nor with the welfare of its citizens, nor with any other moral quantities, but solely with the obedience and submission necessary to its own existence.

It was on this basis that the German could be acquitted; for even though the superiors whose orders he obeyed were agents of the hated Nazi state, that obedience excuses him from all his moral responsibility. No matter that he knew the deed was wrong; no matter that a man in training for the service of God surrendered his moral independence which was the image of God in him; no matter that a French citizen was killed without trial: still the law of France can see no guilt in him because he submitted to the demands of the state upon his loyalties and service.

And with Moreau the case is just as clear. He concerned himself with moral values and tried to guide his life by their prescriptions. On that basis he decided that military service is no real service either to his country or to the world, and that therefore he must insist on civilian work. It is for that independence of personality, finding its basis in and centering its loyalties on values greater than the state, that the law can find no place. In vain his lawyer spoke of loyalties and laws of higher degree, of the more constructive service a CO renders; the fact remains that the law was disobeyed and must be avenged.

There is in this lived parable a striking portrayal of the essential clash between the ethical Christian and the demands of the state. It arises because the Christian can have no gods but God, no loyalties unqualified by his ultimate allegiance to his Creator and Redeemer. The conflict arises especially with the state because only the state is equipped to enforce its demands for worship and service. It is no accident that the apocalyptic writings of the Bible speak of the Antichrist, of the climax of the powers of evil in the world, in terms with political overtones. For the idol of statism today, in ever-growing degree, is capable of enlisting every evil capacity in man, to magnify itself at the expense of the society in whose service the realm of political organization was originally ordained by God.

In the accelerating process of totalitarianization the objection of a lone struggler is but a momentary hindrance, easily brushed off with a year's imprisonment and forgotten. The obedience of which the Lord says, "you have but little power, and yet you have kept my word," plays no great role in the great affairs of the evident world. And yet it is in this obedience that the strength of the obedient Christian life is found, the life whose results and rewards, whose success, are not evident to all, because "the things of the Spirit . . . are spiritually discerned." To this obedience we are called in the spirit of Him whose triumph began when He was condemned to death and Barabbas, a murderer, went free.

Valdoie, France.

1954

How one-sided is the faith that in an upper room contemplates heavenly joys and is oblivious of the degradation in the streets below him.

Of Ranchers, Thieves, and the Graveyard Shift

by Theodore Wentland

The graveyard shift, from midnight to breakfast, is a shift which few men like. Peter Trosh, machine operator, was working overtime at the shop. His hours were going into the graveyard shift, and he was angry at himself for working while the rest of the world slept.

"What's the use," he muttered to himself. "This is the only life a fellow is sure of, anyway. Might as well work. Don't know what'll happen after it's all over." He was intentionally storming loudly now. His companions at the neighboring machines could hear his devil-may-care words.

Peter, or as the night crew called him, "Pete," always went to church. Pete believed in God. Sure he did. He had confessed the name of the Lord Jesus Christ in church. He took communion regularly. He believed that Jesus died for sinners. He knew that the Bible was God's Book. He prayed often to God. Yet, he believed that no one could be sure of being saved or lost until after death.

"You gotta always be doing good, like going to church, all your life," he explained to the worker on the next machine. "Then, maybe, you'll have a chance to get inside the pearly gates of heaven after it's all over," he added. By "all over" he meant "death." Pete was serious. . . . He was sure that this was what the church taught.

Theodore Wentland: A person can lose everything, until one is all alone. But there is one thing that cannot be taken away.

He laughed at Tom on the next machine. Tom was one of those queer guys who always went around telling folks he knows he's saved. Queer guys these. After thinking these thoughts, Pete gave a final dig, saying, "Yeah, the reason you're so sure of bein' saved is because you're doing more than I am for the church. You're a Sunday-school teacher. You don't care too much about money, nor about bein' rich; and you're thinking of bein' a preacher someday." His voice grew louder. He added, provokingly, "Sure, people who give up a lot, can be more sure they're saved."

In this manner, over the hum of evening machines, was expressed a strange but common belief. If you are a Christian, you don't know whether you will be saved or lost until after you die. Often those who think thus also believe that you can make sure of heaven by doing good works.

Do you want to experiment a little, reader? Try asking at random several Christians this question: "Do you know that you are saved?" Out of ten church members that you may hap-

pen to ask, probably only one will be positive of his salvation. This happens even in Mennonite churches. Try asking it in your church. Casually, of course. Don't be crude about it. Mix it in your regular conversation somehow. You will be surprised at the answers. Maybe, maybe, even you are not quite sure that you are saved. Are you?

As in the true story of the two men working the graveyard shift, you can be a Tom, or you can be a Pete. Tom was sure of heaven, Pete was not.

What was the difference? All that made the difference was that Tom believed, without a doubt, that Jesus meant what He said. Our Lord told the first Peter and Thomas, "*Let not your heart be troubled: ye believe in God, believe also in me. In my Father's house are many mansions: if it were not so, I would have told you. I go to prepare a place for you. And if I go and prepare a place for you, I will come again, and receive you unto myself; that where I am, there ye may be also*" (John 14:1-3). . . .

From where comes the idea of working like mad to get salvation, to be sure of heaven? There was a scoundrel who never had a chance to stockpile good deeds; who never took communion; who never went to church; who never was baptized. At one time he even ridiculed Jesus. The thief had only one opportunity to learn to love Jesus. He took it. He took Jesus. What did the Crucified Lord say to him? "*To day shalt thou be with me in paradise*" (Luke 23:43b). There was nothing uncertain in these words of our Lord. The malefactor on the cross knew that he was saved. He was sure of it. The reasons: he heard it from the lips of Jesus; he believed Jesus.

In a purely earthly sense, it is true that the only things one can be certain of in this world are "death and taxes." A person can lose everything—home, family, wife (or husband), children; until one is all alone. However, there is one thing that can not be taken away from the Christian. It is this assurance of being safe in God—saved.

A rich and famous rancher became bankrupt. In one day, through war and the toll of bad weather, he lost his cattle and almost every last thing he owned. His sons met with horrible deaths. His own health was failing rapidly. Of course, he got discouraged. He regretted that he was ever born. Yet, it was this bankrupt ranch manager who said, "*I know that my redeemer liveth, and that he shall stand at the latter day upon the earth: and though after my skin worms destroy this body, yet in my flesh shall I see God: whom I shall see for myself, and mine eyes shall behold, and not another; though my reins be consumed within me*" (Job 19:25-27). Are these uncertain terms? No!

You may, as a Christian, be uncertain of much in life; but, if you believe in Jesus, you know that you are saved. You will see Him someday "face to face in all His glory." You will have a mansion. I will have a mansion. Next door will be the thief and the rancher. We will be neighbors. Neighbors all.

Chatsworth, Ill.

Christian Humanism

There is a godless humanism which makes man the source, the subject, and the end of all religion. This humanism needs no revelation from above, no divine enabling for its work. It is devoted to human happiness and welfare, but is of the earth earthy and has no regard for God's superintendence, nor for the eternal ends to be served. For the humanist social welfare is equated with salvation.

In the effort to steer clear of such a false philosophy many Christians veer to an opposite extreme. They make recognition and worship of God the whole of religion. They emphasize eternal salvation to the neglect of the alleviation of conditions which sin has brought. They are other-worldly to the extent that they are unconcerned about making a Christian impact upon their environment. Their religious expression becomes so personal that they lose all social obligation.

We must come to see that there is a Christian humanism. God's love created man in the image of God. God's care has attended man throughout the centuries of history. He has a mind to his distresses, and has in His Word revealed a way both to eternal salvation of the soul and to happiness here below. God's will comprehends both the heavenly and the mundane spheres, both time and the post-historical ages.

Only that man is truly Christian who recognizes his relation to God and to the Saviour, Jesus Christ, and who also is aware of his needy fellow man and has a loving respect for him. How can a man say he loves God if he does not love and serve his brother? How one-sided is the faith that in an upper room contemplates heavenly joys and is oblivious of the degradation in the cellars and the streets below him.

Jesus said that the command to love one's neighbor is "like unto" the command to love God. The word actually means "equal to." These commands are a matched pair, not a major and a minor. There is laid upon every Christian, every lover of God, the compulsion of a social sense. He must find ways to express loving-kindness to his family, his neighbors, his enemies, the hungry, the cold, and the lost of every culture and clime. This must not be an occasional charity, but the everyday expression of his heart. It will seem perfectly natural to him to link together the healing of the body and the healing of the soul. The hands which he clasps in prayer will also be strong to lift the burdens of those he walks among. He will not need to decide between the spiritual and the material, for he will have learned to blend the two. So, as a servant of God, he has also become a servant of man. He is a Christian humanist.

—*Paul Erb*

1955

He was a skeptic and it seemed that no argument any Christian could present would ever dissuade him. But then one evening he lifted his hand to heaven and said, "I'm his boy now."

From Skepticism to Christ

by Harold Fly

When Neighbor spied my wife's covering on the occasion of our first meeting, he said, "So you're religious people; are you Quakers, eh? For your information, I'm a skeptic!" When he discovered that we were Mennonites and not Quakers, he began to ply us with questions concerning our faith. However, he was quick to inform us that after all it was purely imagination on our part; there was absolutely nothing to Christianity. He was simply curious about our doctrines, that was all . . . .

He was an isolationist, and loved to spend his off time alone building miniature buildings and caring for his roses and gladioli. No one in the community knew him very intimately with the exception of Geza La Runda, an atheist who lived a hermit's life in a house that to all appearances looked to be very much haunted. To everyone he was "that man from Minnesota." Little did we dream that after his curt remarks at our first meeting, we would ever become friends. How it came to pass, I'll never know, except that as the strawberries in our garden were turning crimson, one evening he eyed them with fond anticipation. Mary and I coaxed him to stay for the evening meal. We had our family worship as usual with the children and Grandma gathered around the table. During the course of prayer, we remembered our friend and neighbor. Immediately

after the worship period, he excused himself and left the room, coughing violently all the while. After a short lapse, he returned and finished the meal with us. Following this experience, we had a number of informal meetings together. Sometimes it was around our old kitchen table, sometimes around his table, or in his rustic living room, around the Word of God, which he sought intently to discredit. It seemed to us that no argument any Christian could present would ever dissuade him. Without a doubt, he would live the life of a skeptic and die the tragic death of one also.

I told him of a monthly inspirational meeting held in various churches throughout our conference district. Because the meeting centers around the theme of personal work and witnessing, it has become known as "Tract Meeting." One evening he desired to accompany us to a monthly tract meeting at the Worcester Church, merely for the cultural value, he said. As I recall, the house was filled to overflowing capacity that frosty moonlit night last October. The singing was soul-searching, the testimonies heart-touching. He left the sanctuary almost immediately after the benediction, complaining about the stifling heat. Praise the Lord, I didn't realize it then, but he was being warmed by "that fire which is from above . . . ."

Several months passed and God called us to labor in a mission at another place. We packed up our belongings and left the rugged little community, moving to a city miles away. One evening, soon after we were settled in our urban home, there came a knock on the kitchen door about dusk. To our amazement and joy, before us stood our former neighbor. He told us of the fact that someone had visited him and had given him a Bible.

Time slipped by and we didn't see him for quite a while, months, in fact! Then, one evening, in need of a place to shave and wash up a bit, while en route to a meeting, the car somehow, almost knowingly, turned into his boulder-strewn driveway. To my surprise he fairly ran to the door with a skillet in one hand and a pork chop in the other. I was nearly speechless when he said, "Brother, since I last saw you, I found the Lord!"

We broke bread together that evening, but before we partook of the bounties of the earth, the former skeptic bowed his head and offered a simple prayer to the heavenly Father. I wondered, as my heart became so full of joy that some of it spilled down my face, what his former college chums would think or what old Geza La Runda, the atheist, would say if they could have heard him talk to God. Yet I realized that his sincerity would have overruled all their objections because after the prayer, he lifted his hand up to heaven and said, "I'm His boy now. Life seems so real to me; this peace is so wonderful. Why did I wait so long to find the Lord? Old Geza can't begin to understand what happened to me."

Bethlehem, Pa.

The Hydrogen Bomb and Our Peace Testimony

by Sanford G. Shetler

Considerable sentiment has been aroused in various circles, both among nonchurch and church groups, in recent months against the frightful hydrogen bomb. Every thinking person agrees that in this new devastating device of war, we have a horrible weapon of mass destruction with fearful possibilities. It seems that history is repeating itself in the spread of violence on the earth and the imaginations of man seem to be "only evil continually."

Yet it is necessary to keep our peace testimony clear even as it relates to this awful weapon. Many of the church groups, especially the peace church groups, have made declarations that the hydrogen bomb should be outlawed. It is denounced as being contrary to the Spirit of Christ, which of course it truly is.

But let us be clear in our thinking. Biblical pacifists are not opposed to *some* wars but to *all* wars, and just so they are not opposed to *some* weapons but *all* weapons of war. "The weapons of our warfare are not carnal [none of them]," says the Scripture. It is becoming almost popular to raise a cry against the atom and hydrogen bombs, not only among church groups, but also amongst nonchurch groups. Even the Communists share this view! But why not cry out against the fast-shooting machine guns recently developed, the bazookas, and flame throwers, atomic submarines, and jet-propulsion bombers which are able to strafe at the low altitude of fifty feet with a tremendously devastating effect? During the late war there was probably no means of combat any more dreaded than the flame throwers which were used by the marines and infantry. The gruesome picture of those charred bodies of Japs, shown in one of our leading pictorial magazines, still lingers in our minds. Some "Christian" American soldiers, you see, had annihilated with flame throwers some Japanese soldiers who, in their way of thinking, had taken their last courageous stand.

There is nothing about this business of war that is lovely or artistic. Even though the cause may be supposedly good, the tools to do the job are diabolic. There is no Christian way of killing a person, soldier or civilian, and the mighty blockbusters of World War II were in no sense more Christian than today's H-bomb simply because they were not as totally destructive. An innocent person caught in the path of a T.N.T. bomb or blockbuster was just as helplessly and brutally slain as the poor inhabitant of Hiroshima. In both cases the Spirit of Christ has been abrogated with the result of misery, despair, and death.

We must raise our voices against *sin* which causes men to invent such brutal tools of destruction, and which causes them to *participate* in the destruction. Let our witness be heard against all war, and all weapons, and all participation, and in fact against *all evil*, even against those flattering and deceptive and subtle forms of evil which outwardly give no evidence of destruction, but which nonetheless lead to the grosser sins (so-called) of brutality and debauchery and physical and spiritual destruction of body and soul. Let the world know that we are fighting a spiritual warfare "against the rulers of the darkness of this world," and against "every high thing that exalteth itself against the knowledge of God," and not particularly against the war lords and makers of munitions.

To do this is not popular with the world or with many church groups and pacifist action groups, but it is the correct way to present a Scriptural witness that will lead men beyond the passive position of nonviolence to the positive position of Christian love through an experience of salvation through Jesus Christ. This will bring an abiding peace which will lie deeper than any fleeting humane attitudes developed by sentimental pacifist propaganda against such mighty weapons of physical destruction as the H-bomb.

Hollsopple, Pa.

Sanford G. Shetler: Let our witness be heard against all war and all weapons, in fact against all evil.

1956

Rome was not built in a day, nor does a child become a man in a week. But 15 minutes daily can make you into a Bible scholar.

Can You Become a Bible Scholar?

by Alta Yoder Bauman

At a meeting of our parent-teacher group, the current chaplain arose to conduct a devotional period. Instead of opening a Bible to read, he declaimed Isaiah 55 with fervor and spirit. The beauty and majesty of this precious portion of Scripture was renewed in the mind of each listener. Although the speaker was an ordinary layman in the church, we were not surprised at his declamation, for he is well-known in our community for his Bible knowledge.

In conversation with this man, one could guess he could be a seminary graduate, or that he had at least majored in Bible. Surprisingly, our friend has had no formal education beyond the fifth grade. Furthermore, all his life he has been an industrious farmer, diligent in his business. Also, he reared a large family during the depression. Nor did he ever have such advantages as summer or weekday Bible school.

This busy man has the same problem the ordinary church member has—that of limited time for Bible study—yet he is a real Bible scholar. Being a Christian should be almost synonymous with being a Bible student. Yet many neglect that important factor for spiritual growth because, they say, "I simply can not find the time."

The value of Bible knowledge cannot be measured, for we should study, not only "to shew ... [ourselves] approved unto God," but so we can rightly divide the word of truth, first for ourselves, and then to others. How can we expect to teach our children or anyone else, unless we dig down deep into the Word for things that are there for the taking?

Since the intrinsic worth of Bible study is eternal and obvious, and most of us can manage only a short period daily, what can be done to make that time count? If you are not careful, you can fritter away fifteen minutes, and be not a bit wiser than before. Let us consider a few ways by which we may increase the results of a short study time.

Ask for the presence of God as you work.

Choose a time and place when and where you are unlikely to be disturbed. It may be before your family is up, or after they retire, or even part of your lunch hour. The farmer might find a spot in the field or barn; the housewife a cozy nook in the attic, when the children are napping and where she can not hear the telephone.

Have everything you need at hand (such as the Bible commentary, notebook, and pencil) so that no second is wasted there.

Decide on a definite plan beforehand. When you are not preparing a speech, or for some other specific occasion, it is important that you have a project of your own to follow.

Carry a notebook. Jot down ideas and things to look up, lest they flee away, never to return.

When studying a book of the Bible, underline a key word or phrase, as you go. A Sunday-school teacher had us to underline "wherein," as we studied Malachi. When we were done, we had an outline of the book which we could grasp at a glance.

To remember chapter content, connect its number with something special in it. This same Sunday-school teacher had us name the divisions of John in that way. For instance, the tenth is the Good Shepherd chapter.

Get a fresh view of the portion you are studying. We are apt to let the familiar become mere repetition, unless we force ourselves to look at it from a different angle. Project yourself into the time when your lesson happened. For instance, when Jesus was born, and in that country, each family had its own animals, necessary for its food and comfort. Even those that were not shepherds or

herdsmen lived among their animals, often reserving a part of their dwelling for them to sleep in. So while a stable was a humble place to be born in, there was nothing degrading or too unusual about it, for it likely happened before.

Or imagine how it would have been had Christ been born in your town now. Probably Joseph and Mary would have arrived in their 1948 Plymouth to find all the hotels and tourist cabins full. Since there would be no stables in town, the keeper would move his car out of the garage to provide temporary shelter. Then the Baby's worshipers (probably the night shift) would have found Him, wrapped in a fuzzy blue blanket, lying on an automobile cushion.

Use method when memorizing. A good way is to learn a verse a day. When the end of the chapter is reached, you will have a whole gem of beauty at the tip of your tongue.

Rome was not built in a day, nor does a child become a man in a week. You may be only a Bible student now, but well-planned, daily fifteen-minute periods can make you into a Bible scholar.

Warwick, Va.

Alta Yoder Bauman: You may be only a Bible student now, but fifteen minutes a day can make you a scholar.

1957

A Loaf of Bread

by Rosanna Yoder Hostetler

This evening Dona Arlete was at the door. Miguel opened it the minute he heard the knock. She stood there holding a steaming loaf of Brazilian bread. "All my neighbors know the recipe," she said. "I thought of you when I baked it this afternoon and was sure Americans would like this bread as well as we."

Accepting it readily, much to her pleasure, I went to the kitchen and put aside the huge embroidered napkin and saw the steaming beauty. Its fresh homemade aroma set our salivary glands to functioning. Miguel ran to get the jaboticaba jelly and set it carefully on the table.

"Jelly bread, Mommie!" Mike loved the jelly bread and so did we, but lasting longer is the warm sensation of kindness to a new neighbor from a Brazilian family like that of Dona Arlete.

A loaf of Brazilian bread! Hundreds of loaves are carried out by horse and cart through the city at the break of dawn and left on the window ledges to make bread and coffee for the wakening population. Hundreds of crisp-crusted loaves are carried under the arms of children at 4:00 p.m. on the way home from school. But this fresh fragrant loaf was brought to me today—and a token of friendship accompanied it.

Dona Arlete brought her special recipe of Brazilian bread, and naturally I will make some raised donuts in return. In return also we will be able to give the Bread of Life to Dona Arlete's family. Besides the spiritual hunger He will satisfy, our Bread will also give strength and force to live the daily life.

"I am the living bread which came down from heaven; if any man eat of this bread, he shall live for ever," Jesus said.

It was a loaf of Brazilian bread that reminded me.   *Valinhos, S.P. Brazil.*

Rosanna Yoder Hostetler: A fresh fragrant loaf of Brazilian bread—and a token of friendship.

What Address?

"Where do you live?" asked the merchant of the stranger who stopped to rest in the shade beside the building.

"I'm afraid I can't be said to live at any one place," replied the man, graciously. "Just now I'm living at this spot."

"But where is your father's house?" persued the merchant.

"My Father's house is above," said the stranger, with reverence and a touch of mystery in His voice.

"Oh, he is dead? But is your mother living?" The questioner began to feel there was some puzzle here.

"Yes, she lives with her sons in the home in Nazareth which her husband left her."

"Oh, in Nazareth. You were born there, then?"

"No, I was born in Bethlehem. But I have not been there for years."

"Do you now live in Nazareth?"

"No, I seldom go there. The people drove me away once."

"Then where is your home?"

The merchant began to ask his questions a bit sharply. It was exasperating not to be able to get information which usually came with the first question.

"I have no home," insisted the serious-faced

young man. He said it with no bitterness, but simply as a truth. And the truth evidently did not worry Him.

"But you must have a home somewhere! Everyone does—except tramps. And you don't look like a tramp. You don't travel all the time. Where do you go when you want to stay?"

"Yes, a man ought to have a home. But I haven't, except as my friends give me one. The birds of the air have nests, the foxes have dens in the ground, but the Son of man has nowhere to lay His head."

o   o   o

What an astonishing fact, that Jesus had no address! People could not have written Him a letter, for they wouldn't know where to find Him. It took personal messengers to reach Him, who could search until they found His working place for that day. The next day He would be on the way to some other place. He who came to the earth He had made never held a deed or a lease to any small plot upon it. He told His followers of eternal mansions to which He would receive them, but here He had not even a hut.

There is nothing to indicate that He expected His followers also to be homeless. Peter had a house in Capernaum, and Mary, Martha, and Lazarus had one in Bethany. He never asked them to sell these. Rather He enjoyed their hospitality.

But haven't we wandered too far from His example? We maintain a legal residence, and we are able to give our address. Our Yearbook is full of these. Any of us may need to be reached by letter or by phone. This seems legitimate. But we settle down as if we were here to stay. We get so involved in real estate and business that we forget the City where we are to move before long. We become so attached to some particular country and state and community that we just couldn't think of living anywhere else. We become so localized and provincial that our accent and our prejudices and our viewpoints quickly identify us as residents of A＿＿＿ or B＿＿＿ or C＿＿＿ Jesus grew up in Galilee, but He was not a Galilean. He belonged to Heaven, but on earth He was placeless. He was big enough to hold all the world in His heart.

A missionary on furlough was asked to write her name and address. She hesitated. "What is my address?" she asked herself. During her furlough she had stayed at several places for a few months, at least. Upon her return to the field she was uncertain where she would be stationed. She really had no address.

Foreign missionaries and, to a lesser extent perhaps, those of us at home, must learn to sit lightly, always ready to be on the move. Your editor has lived in three different states. People sometimes ask us where we like it best. The only possible Christian answer is that we would rather live where the Lord wants us to be. Windy Kansas, or cloudy Indiana, or smoky Pennsylvania is favorite country if the Lord has called us there. No earthly address partakes of the absolute or the permanent. We are a pilgrim people, not yet at home.
—*Paul Erb*

1958

In Conclusion

by Glen M. Sell

Mr. Smith, the guest speaker for the evening, had been introduced to the audience. He was told that he would have one hour in which to speak. As Mr. Smith was making his opening remarks, he said, "I'll not speak an hour." He then proceeded with his lecture.

The speaker spoke most fluently and had many things of interest to bring to our attention. The entire audience seemed to be listening very attentively. He had been lecturing approximately one-half hour when he spoke the unexpected words, "Now in conclusion." Following this statement, he spoke for twenty more minutes. By this time most of us were losing interest rapidly. The next phrase which increased the tension among the group was, "My last point is this." Mr. Smith spoke for five minutes on this and then said, "Now in closing," and continued speaking approximately eight minutes before returning to his seat. Yes, we will all agree, he killed his own lecture.

Pastors, teachers, public speakers of any kind—are you encouraging people to flee from you rather than creating interest in what you might have to say? Are you guilty of saying what you don't mean? When you say, "In closing," "In conclusion," "My last point is," "Let me summarize for you," and many other such expressions, do you do just that or does it mean you are only warming up for what is yet to come?

Avoid doing like one speaker who had been given a forty-minute topic. The moderator told him when thirty-five minutes had passed. The speaker turned to the moderator and said, "What, only five more minutes? I haven't even started on my subject."

People are not balloons and yet they are similar. You can inflate them only so far before something breaks. When speaking in public, please close shortly after the words, "In conclusion," or you may be guilty of causing your audience to go away with a bang, never to return.

Laytonsville, Md.

The New Lunacy

The word "lunacy" came into our language because of the superstitious and unscientific notion that exposure to the rays of Luna, the moon, caused mental upset. A "lunatic" was a person who had suffered mental imbalance through wandering about bareheaded when the moon was full. Such a person had become "luny."

Now the earth has, or recently had and will quite certainly have again, new satellites, or moons. These moons which whisk across our skies are man-made. They have been thrown into the outer spaces by the West's rival in the cold war, the Russian Communists. America suddenly discovered that the Russians have the technology to create earth satellites, and therefore also have power to drop nuclear missiles anywhere upon the earth.

Hysteria struck the American people. The new moons have deprived us of our sanity. This is the new lunacy.

This lunacy manifests itself in a general demand that America must at all costs recover military superiority. We must have bigger and more deadly missiles. We must again make Russia afraid of us.

In an age when terrible weapons have made war itself only the mutual extinction of lunatics, we are still supposing that missiles can protect us.

Quickly the moves which had been made to reduce military expenditure are being replaced by demands for an unprecedented military budget. Whatever the strain will be on the national economy, the American people, or a considerable portion of them, are shouting that we too must shoot satellites into the spaces. Throwing moons into the air has become the obsession of our time.

Two reports issued by groups of very influential citizens are calling for greatly increased military expenditures. Responsible senators talk about securing control of the outer spaces. (There's an awful lot of it out there, Senator!) It is suggested that we spend billions digging shelters in which to survive. Dorothy Thompson wisely asks who would want to survive a thermo-nuclear deluge. She has the courage to call hysteria this sudden demand for arms which cannot protect, this race toward mutual death.

This military preoccupation is losing America the confidence and respect of the world. In the NATO meeting the establishment of missile bases in Europe was all America had to propose, and only the insistence of the European members, who absolutely do not want to be made missile targets, brought any attention to the diplomatic alternatives. The neutral millions of the world are more and more believing the Communist claim that Russia wants peace, and America wants war. . . .

Western lunacy is seen in the sudden demand for more and better scientific education. We have no prejudice against science. It has done much for us and there are many needs waiting for its solutions. The scientists, for instance, must find a way to feed the teeming multitudes who are filling up our earth. But it is a false assumption that the science of matter can solve our problems. Our social and spiritual problems are greater than the material ones. Social science, philosophy, literature, the arts, and especially theology have more to say to our sick world than science does.

And yet the current lunacy will probably provide scholarships primarily or solely for students of science, as if the other areas of knowledge were of slight importance. Of course, in Russia science attracts the young. Only in that field are they intellectually free. And materialistic science fits into the materialism of communistic ideology. How can we be so blind as to fall into the trap of becoming like the Communists in assuming that only science is important, only science can save us?

Christians, at least, should be proof against the new lunacy. They should know that God is infinitely wiser than the makers of Sputnik. They should know that piling up munitions and tightening a cordon of missile bases along the Soviet frontier can only intensify our problem. They should know that those who trust in the Lord need not fear what men can do to them....

There is a classical proverb, that whom the gods would destroy they first make mad. All the moves to which the new lunacy impels us hurry us along the road to destruction. In the midst of a propaganda-provoked hysteria, Christians should pray and strive that they might not lose their senses.

—*Paul Erb*

1959

Feed the Flock of God

by Chester S. Martin

Pastor Miller walked briskly to the far end of the pasture. Those heifers had jumped the fence again. This was the third time in one week. Just yesterday he had stretched the fence and ran an additional wire over the top so that those heifers would be sure to stay in. But they were out again. Where were they this time? He knew—down by the stream where the grass was greener. Why couldn't they be content as the older cows were to hunt the best in their own pasture? Pastor Miller didn't know that some of those older cows did not stay because they were in love with the pasture, but rather because this had been home for such a long time; besides, it wasn't easy to cross the fence.

It had been a hot, dry summer and the pasture was short. Those heifers were hungry and wanted better pasture, but they had to be kept in. He would stretch the fence again and in this low spot where they usually crossed he would run a wire still higher. Perhaps he should put a chain around their necks and tie a short rail to it. Those heifers should be taught to stay by the barn. Maybe he would just tie them in for several days.

It was Saturday evening. The cows were milked and the milker washed and on the rack. The tractor was in the shed and the car was washed. Pastor Miller left his wife in their modern kitchen to do the supper dishes and entered his study to prepare his message.... He had thought much concerning this because of the apparent need in his congregation. This last week two families had left the church and now would worship elsewhere. He had tried to show them the value of their heritage. If they left, ... they would be out in the world and there was only one eternal abode for worldly church members—especially if they had been taught better.

Several weeks ago he had spoken on the subject, "Obedience to Church Authority." Heb. 13:17. He had tried hard to explain that the church had every right to draw the line for its members. Two weeks ago he had spoken on "the falling away of the last days" and he had really gone down the line. He had told them what little things lead to. Last week he had not really preached; he just talked about the "good old days." Dad drove a team, Mother wore a shawl, and everybody went to church on Sunday. My! how things had changed! The devil with his modern inventions certainly had got a foothold in the church.

His mind came back to the message he had chosen for the next morning. He looked at the title, "The Voice of the Church." After all, did the church need to, and did it have the authority to, insist on a higher standard of separation from the world? He was sure he had the answer, a definite YES. To raise the standard was the only way to keep the young people in the church.

The fence—oh, yes, those heifers. Why did those heifers always jump the fence? He had raised it; now they would stay in. The church standard to keep members. A fence to keep heifers. Why did those two families leave the church after last Sunday's service and say they would now seek fellowship elsewhere? They had an idea that all we need is the Holy Spirit for our guide and the Bible for our rule book. Dissatisfied heifers; dissatisfied church members. Why did those heifers want out so badly?

Pastor Miller's thoughts chased each other in a confusing manner. Slowly his mind came back to his message. He had to prepare that sermon. The text he had chosen was somewhat out of the context, but it did fit for his message. He read it again, "But if he neglect to hear the church." The last few weeks his text had not exactly fit either; at least that was what one member told him. He leafed absent-mindedly in his Bible for a better text. His mind wandered. Restless heifers; restless church members. His eyes fell on 1 Pet. 5:2, "Feed the flock." Oh, yes, maybe he should give those heifers some hay. The pasture was short this year. Could it be that they were simply hungry?

He started to read again, "Feed the flock of God." Those restless members—he still had some. Could it be that they were hungry? He read on, "... which is among you, taking the oversight thereof, not by constraint, but willingly; not for filthy lucre, but of a ready mind; neither as being lords over God's heritage, but being ensamples to the flock."

Pastor Miller buried his head in his hands in deep thought. Hungry heifers leaving the pasture; hungry sheep leaving the flock. Could it be? Was his spiritual flock's pasture too short? Had he not fed them properly? Tears filled his eyes. "O God," he prayed, "show me the way." "Feed the flock," the verse came back. If he had fed those heifers, the fence would have been high enough maybe he would not have needed to pay attention to the fence at all. Those families who had so recently left— was the fence at fault or the pasture? "O God," he prayed, "forgive me for my fence building and help me to feed the flock."

It was 11:00 p.m. In the wastebasket lay some torn paper. On the pastor's desk lay some new notes. The heifers in the barn were eagerly watching Pastor Miller opening the bales of hay. Two families would get unexpected company tomorrow. The heifers would get their fill; the flock would be fed in the morning.

Sumner, Ill.

If They Strike You—

by J. Paul Sauder

It happened on the Welsh Mountains where so many things happened. Father was a good storyteller and had interesting stories to tell. He had spent seven serviceable years among those beloved people of a darker skin and different ways. He had gone there at the bidding of his Lord. His dying wife had said, "Promise me that you will do whatever the Lord asks you to do." He had given his willing promise and so here he was two years later, working at his industrial mission. He loved his work in spite of trials of one sort or another during arduous days of unsalaried toil. You see, he was working for the Lord, not for wages.

Many of the mountain people got their mail from the mission box. When the mail came in, there was quite a knot of folks standing around in those days more than half a century ago. One day the mail was handed out to each by my father and when it was apparent that the remainder was for mission personnel, a woman whom we shall call Jane came up and demanded her letter. She was huge and her manner was beligerent as she towered above Father, who was shorter than average, though very strong and agile. Now Jane barked, "Give me my letter." Father replied calmly enough, "There isn't any letter for you today, Jane." "There is so," she fairly shouted and slapped Father's cheek hard with her open palm, sending his glasses flying and almost throwing him off balance. Then doubling up her fist she shoved it under his nose and threatened, "I'll pound your face into jelly, too."

Now Father professed a desire to practice the Sermon on the Mount and that sermon by the Master contains specific instructions about just such a situation. Letting his arms hang loosely he calmly said, "When your letter comes, you shall have it."

Muttering to herself Jane walked away. Father went into the house from the presence of the spectators, including the mailman, who had tarried. Then the crisis came. Hot temper surged within him. I knew him as a man of spirit to whom nothing of import could happen without reaction of some sort. In the telling of this story, and he retold it, he always credited the Lord with a restraining hand in that the teachings of the Master, which teachings he professed to love, were not compromised by unchristian conduct while he had been under test and observation. Hereafter if "Mr. Levi" taught the Sermon on the Mount, those bystanders could testify that a missionary had been that sermon on display at testing time.

Next day a considerably humbled Jane came around, apologized and asked forgiveness. Considerable pressure had been applied from her own conscience and from without. Had she not struck "Mr. Levi," who not only had been undeserving but had been Christlike

through it all? But to her credit be it said that she "could eat humble-pie" and that promptly.

Oh yes, I must not forget to tell you—her expected letter came later.

Elkridge, Md.

1960

Questions of Social Concern for Christians

by Guy F. Hershberger

Have modern Mennonites had any experience with the death penalty? Yes. In July, 1957, Paul Coblentz, an Amish Mennonite of Holmes County, Ohio, was shot and fatally wounded by Cleo Eugene Peters. The jury found Peters guilty, the court sentenced him to the electric chair, and his execution was set for Nov. 7, 1958.

Had it not been for the unusual response of the Amish Mennonite community, Peters would have been executed along with the 48 who did die on the gallows, the chair, or the gas chamber in the United States in 1958. What then was the attitude of these people? And what did they do that influenced Governor C. William O'Neill to commute the death sentence to life imprisonment seven hours before the scheduled execution?

1. The prevailing attitude of the Amish Mennonite community was one of penitence and forgiveness. The people did not show hostility or demand vengeance. They confessed that they had been negligent in their own Christian witness and they believed that God was speaking to them through this tragedy.

2. At the trail 28 persons of the county were rejected for jury service because of their conscientious objection to the death penalty.

Guy F. Hershberger: Here is an example of what the New Testament means.

Among those rejected were many Amish or Mennonites.

3. While the trial was in progress, Peters' parents, whose home was in Iowa, were invited to take dinner with Amish families in Holmes County, although the invitation was declined.

4. After Peters was sentenced, petitions were signed and more than 100 letters from members of the Amish Mennonite community were written asking the governor to spare his life.

5. Letters were also written to Peters himself, expressing an interest and a concern for his welfare. One of these came from Dora Coblentz, the widow of Paul Coblentz.

6. After the commutation was granted, two ministers, Paul Hummel and Urie Shetler, were delegated to visit Peters in the Ohio State Penitentiary.

7. A letter from the Amish people which the visiting ministers carried with them included the following: "... we come to you at this time, having made a last effort that mercy might be shown you by Governor O'Neill and now to assure you that we do this out of Christian love. It is through Jesus Christ, God's Son, that we are brethren and we wish to share this relationship with you. Will you accept Jesus Christ as your Lord and Saviour?... Accept our forgiveness.... Read the Bible.... Trust Him and be saved."

8. To this Peters replied: "I guess God had to allow all this to finally get me saved. Only a few weeks before I was to die I finally found the Lord and real peace.... I get a letter every week that has done me a lot of good. It's from Harvey Bender ... from Kalona, Iowa."

Here is an example of what the New Testament means when it says: "Love your enemies, bless them that curse you ... pray for them which despitefully use you." "Do not be overcome by evil, but overcome evil with good."

Had the people of the Amish Mennonite community in Holmes County, Ohio, believed in capital punishment, had they demanded "justice" of the one who had murdered their brother, they could not have been obedient to this command of love. And they could not have served as ambassadors of God's great salvation to Cleo Eugene Peters.

Goshen, Ind.

That Pocketbook Nerve!

by Boyd Nelson

Stewardship is a spiritual matter, but spiritual matters often hinge on the practical aspects of our lives. The tithe, the personal service, the small, small sacrifice (which at first seemed large), the loving gift or service, or the onerous task are all just steppingstones to strong spiritual lives. Until we see them clearly for what they are in their ultimate spiritual and eternal meanings, however, they may remain the stumbling blocks which keep us bruised and sore, hobbling along instead of climbing victoriously and joyously upward toward the fullness of Christ, our joy and crown.

Just this week I sat in the barber chair while the barber chattered away in his amusing manner. For six weeks his wife's dryer had been out of order. For six weeks she had asked him to look at it. But he was too busy to get it done. Finally she called Sears to find out what a service call would cost. Six dollars for a half hour was the answer.

"Shall I call the serviceman, dear, or do you want to look at it?" she asked in sweet reasonableness. Confronted with the prospect of a serviceman taking from him in a half hour what would require him two hours to earn, he felt suddenly alive. All business, he went to work and in a few moments discovered that all that ailed the dryer was a broken electrical connection.

"When somebody says money," he said, "I become alert at once. I'm really wide-awake then."

He understood himself rather well, I thought to myself, with a pang of self-recognition. Christians are not always so understanding of themselves, nor are they prepared to be quite so frank about it. Perhaps that is where some of our problem lies.

The analogy may be somewhat like a toothache. After a few visits to the dentist we discover that toothaches are not always pleasant. A slight twinge in our tooth may worry us. Hot, cold, sweet, sour, or pressure may bring momentary discomfort. Probably should have it checked, we tell ourselves, but somehow there is too much to do . . . .

And then one day comes the awakening. The root of the tooth is exposed. It throbs and pains. We try aspirin or other home medication, but we end up in the dentist's chair with more pain, more expense, and possibly one less tooth. But we are awake. Too late, perhaps, but awake . . . .

An active layman in our area is a successful businessman. He insists that any stewardship teaching and practice which does not *begin* with our pocketbooks will miss the point in our churches and in our society. Until we touch that "pocketbook nerve," he maintains, we will not be successful in our stewardship. Perhaps the urgent fund appeals from conferences, mission boards, schools, and other aspects of our Christian program constitute the inordinate desire for power or bigness or American success, we rationalize. But perhaps they are to be even more simply understood as another twinge of the "pocketbook nerve." Until we more nearly reach the tithe as a church and can at least begin on the offerings as part of our response to the Lord, we cannot regard these appeals for finances in any other way than twinges of the "pocketbook nerve."

1961

A testimony of how it came about that he is a Mennonite preacher.

I Chose to Be a Preacher

by Richard J. Yordy

Among my little boy dreams of an important job to do there was the dream of becoming a minister in the church among the people of God. One can hardly tell the factors that changed that dream into reality.

Why did it not go the way of those other dreams—like the dream to be a livestock farmer on the prairies and timbered hills of Illinois; a conservationist or agricultural agent; a social worker in the inner city of a metropolis; a public-school teacher; an administrator of a municipal utility; a manager of a factory service garage?

My home was a factor, Christ and the church were central in our life. In our home, ministers and missionaries were regular visitors and friends. Church-wide meetings were in the family plans. We went to church not only on Sunday morning, but attended the evening service as well, even though the number of worshipers was small and sometimes the program followed a drab routine. There was concern about vitality and commitment in total church life. My home was influenced by my grandfathers and two uncles who served among the ordained ministry of the church.

However, no member of my family ever suggested the Christian ministry as the kind of vocation for which one should be prepared. By influence and example they indicated that church vocations are important and worthy. In the best moments of my growing years, there was the consciousness that, should God and the church call, I would be ready to serve as a minister among the people of God.

Factors outside my home gave the decisive impetus to prepare for Christian service. When that decision was finally made, it was with the consciousness that my further life plans remained subject to the leading of the Lord and the call of the church.

My pastor was a most important factor. In a community junior college, I heard the appeal of a secular world view that was idealistically humanitarian. Several of the most challenging professors were antagonistic to organized Christianity. I knew of none who were conservative evangelical Christians. In the ensuing struggle to develop my own world view, my pastor was a sympathetic counselor. My doubts did not shock him. He understood how deep the struggle was for me. He constantly held open the option of church vocation and the Christian ministry as service to man's ultimate need. He made it clear to me that the church needs youth who will prepare to give themselves in specific Christian service. At a most crucial period in my experience, my pastor held open the possibility of such Christian service under the grace of God.

The Mennonite Church was a factor, through a wholesome congregational life that met many needs of youth living in a large city, and through ministers in our area who expressed confidence in youth and provided challenging inter-congregational youth activity. At one of these youth meetings, my answer to an appeal for public consecration lifted my sights to Christian service at a strategic time. This act of consecration or dedication, although somewhat vague, caused me to give greater consideration to the will of God in my life plans. The church also had a developing program of training for Christian service. If this program had not been available and expanding, the course of my life could hardly have been the same.

Perhaps the most decisive external factor was outside the planned direction of any person. One evening two weeks before enrollment for my second year at our local junior college, a member of our congregation called. "Hey, Rich, do you want a good job? It pays $25.00 per week." (I had received $16.00 per week all summer.) The next night, after an interview, it was decided that I would drop out of school for a year and save money to go to our church school. None of us realized then how much that brother in the church may have been serving as a tool of the Holy Spirit in leading my life. In the ensuing year the decision was made to begin preparation for specific Christian service, as the Lord would lead.

Even more than these external factors, I look back with the conviction that it was God who used these and others to extend His call through my total life experience. My service in the church today brings the fulfillment of God's call in my life. Step by step in the last fifteen years, the church has called to tasks that challenge all that is in me and more. When I have failed, others stood with me before God that my gifts might be improved. The service of any mortal in the church can only be by the constant renewing grace of God. The ministry I carry today is not my own, but belongs to the church. I am called to be a channel of His grace, a gift of the Spirit in this generation, and a servant of Christ in His church.

Arthur, Ill.

Richard J. Yordy: I look back with the conviction that it was God who extended his call.

Seething with Apathy

In an article on civilian defense published by the American Chemical Society a Bostonian is quoted as saying, "On the subject of civilian defense, I seethe with apathy."

The development of a civilian defense program in the United States, we understand, has a hard time in getting on its feet, not so much because of opposition as because of apathy. People just aren't interested in civilian defense. It can hardly be that the public is unaware of the dangers in our world to the whole population. It is more likely that they are skeptical about the adequacy of any proposed defense if the horrors of modern war should come upon us. They are not interested even in discussing futility.

This editorial is not about civilian defense. But it occurred to us that on many other matters there is a vast unconcern. The attitude of even Christian people constantly seems to be saying, "I couldn't care less."

The world boils with hatred and unrest. New nations scramble toward the top of the international pile, and the nations which have long had the place of dominance hold them back. The rising sea of color is flooding the Caucasian coast. The hungry of the world scream for food and shelter. But many church people wonder what all the excitement is about.

The sins of our age mark their gains on every side. Alcoholism increases. Crime rates grow. Juvenile delinquency runs rampant. Obscenity floods the newsstand. Dishonesty undermines the national character. But many of us "seeth with apathy." "What do you expect us to do about it?"

Militarism holds a smoldering bomb over our earth. Most of our national spending goes into armament, much of which is obsolete by the time it comes from the makers. The nations throw their billions into an insane arms race. Those who are in power argue for a "balance of terror." And the multitudes somehow believe "it can't happen here."

The home, our basic human institution, is under attack from every side. Modern inventions batter its moral integrity. Continued industrialization defies its schedules. School, and even church, invade its prerogatives. Worldly philosophies of success dissolve its standards. But who cares enough to even try to do anything about it?

The world's population increases explosively. The proportion of Christians decreases. The world is farther from complete evangelization than ever before in the Christian era. False religions are becoming aggressive and effective. Hell enlarges herself. But the mission of the Christian Church struggles to maintain the *status quo*. Our giving says to our mission boards, "Don't increase the budget." Our apathy votes for retreat from satanic attacks.

The Old Testament prophet lashed out against those who were at ease in Zion. It was not the ease of those who had nothing to be concerned about. Evil was rife in the land, and foes threatened without and within. But it was the ease of sloth, of spiritual blindness. Of indifference to the call of God and the needs of men. It was the ease that led to death.

"Awake thou that sleepest," said the apostle. Amplify that call from all our classrooms and pulpits. Sound it in all our homes and churches. How can we be apathetic as the world and all it holds rushes toward judgment?

—*Paul Erb*

We Can't Go Back

"What did you think during your first weeks in the Chaco?" we asked the cooperative leader at Filadelfia.

"That if we could go back, we would," was his reply.

They could not go back. There would be the sixty miles to the end of the railroad through the wildest of brushland. They had suffered enough doing that road once. There would be the ridiculous train back to the river port. There would be the days and days on a river boat back down the Paraguay, the Parana, and the Plate. They would have to find another boat to take back across the Atlantic. They would have to struggle again to cross international borders to get back to Russia. And in Russia—still the communist threats to life and faith. No, they could not go back.

And so they stayed. There was no way but forward. They must disregard fear and homesickness and poverty. They must dig wells and build houses. They must clear brush and plow the ground and plant seed. They must feed their families and sell some produce, who knows what and where, for the cash they need for clothes. They must start the long search for crops that will grow, for products that will sell, for industries that will succeed, for adequate communication and transportation. By this time they have come so far that, though life in the Chaco is still hard, it is more than ever impossible to think of going back.

Clocks do not run backward. Calendars do not restore the torn-off pages. The knitting of the years is not unraveled.

We may regret the passing of time, the march of events, but we cannot stop it. We may yearn for the yesterdays, but we cannot restore them. We may deplore the changes that come, but we cannot prevent them.

This is not to be fatalistic. It does not mean that we are swept along without any direction. Reformation and restitution are possible. Lost virtues may be recovered. But whatever good out of the past is recovered, it is held in a new context. The total situation is never an exact duplicate. Old truth has new meanings; old values have new appraisals.

Therefore it is a counsel of folly simply to hold what has been, to go back to what was. Jesus said that a man who puts his hand to the plow and then looks back is not fit for the kingdom. Paul counted himself not to have attained, but was determined to press forward to the mark set for him.

We do well to preserve those elements in the past of individual or community or congregation or denomination that have permanent relevance. There are many such elements, and we lose them to our peril. But we also do well to study every situation to see what new facts are involved, what new needs are to be served, what new resources we have to use, what new ends are to be served. Our God is the God, not only of yesterday, or today, but also of tomorrow. The unchangeable God wants to preside over all our changes, to make them serve His purposes.

—*Paul Erb*

1962-1973

THE PREACHER

He had listed seven good reasons why he should not be editor, but none of them held up.

1962-1973

John M. Drescher

The Preacher

I hung up the phone and said to Betty, my wife, "Someone called the wrong number." I was still in something of a daze as I explained that A. J. Metzler, publishing agent for Mennonite Publishing House, had called stating that he would like to stop by our home in several days to talk with us about my becoming the next editor of *Gospel Herald*. "But" I said, "I could not imagine myself doing something like that." Betty responded, "Perhaps you should not say 'No' too quickly." That statement stuck with me.

By the time A. J. Metzler arrived I had listed what I thought were seven good reasons why I could not be editor of *Gospel Herald*. I was a pastor enjoying my work. I sensed inadequacy in myself for the task of editor. I could think of others much more qualified if suggestions were invited.

Rather than accepting my reasoning I was encouraged not to make a quick decision. In addition I was urged to pray about the invitation and to write to numerous leaders in the church who knew me well and consult other persons who could give guidance.

I did this, and to my great surprise all encouraged me to accept the invitation to become editor. After considerable time of prayer, searching, and seeking counsel the decision was made and our family moved to Scottdale, Pennsylvania, in the spring of 1962.

As part of the preparation for my becoming editor, an article of introduction was written by the publisher. He asked me for a photo of myself. I sent a recent photo but it was returned promptly, asking if I could send another because I looked too young to be

Gospel Herald editor. (I was 34.) I had another photo taken and reported that I looked as old as possible on this one.

Paul Erb, my predecessor, was Mr. Mennonite to the church. He was well known as a churchman, preacher, professor, and editor. I knew I could not fill his shoes but that, as God led, he would also enable me to help meet the needs of the hour in the life of the church.

My eleven years as editor were some of the most demanding and delightful years of my life. I learned to know the Mennonite church at large as well as to relate to leaders of other denominations. The editor of the denominational weekly was also to be in the church half the time ministering in many different ways. Not only was I expected to attend district and church-wide conferences and be present at church-wide board meetings, but to take responsibility on numerous programs, planning committees and boards of the denomination. In addition I was called upon to speak for all kinds of occasions up to twenty times a week.

Without the deep commitment and able assistance of Bertha Nitzsche to handle the details of *Gospel Herald* for the first years and Elva Yoder during the last years, I could not have carried the work as editor.

In reflecting on the sixties and early seventies I view those years as a time of turbulence and trouble for both the nation and the church. For both it was a time of much action and reaction.

In Vietnam, the longest war in United States history dragged on with growing disillusionment. It was a day of draft-dodgers and civil disobedience. Wide distrust for authority revealed itself in outspoken opposition. Creeping corruption in politics seemed to consummate in Watergate. Many persons marched for concerns such as peace, racial equality, and poverty or in reaction against war and specific political positions. Campuses were filled with so-called "radicals" and antagonism was intense between the generations.

Youth, reacting against every kind of "establishment," were especially critical of the church which many considered uninvolved, irrelevant, and dead. Youth had their support from some church leaders who predicted that preaching was a passing thing and the church, as we knew it, was done. A new theology and a new morality were promoted by the religious and irreligious.

Ecumenism was in the air. At all levels church unity was discussed and debated. Great stress was put on unity of organization. Fragmentation and denominationalism were described by some as the greatest curse upon the church. Some large and smaller bodies did unite and much time and expense went into ecumenical discussions and reorganization. Under the pressure for unity, numerous new groups formed by splitting off and dividing. Some attacked the ecumenical talk and church unions as the heights of heresy and sure marks of apostasy.

During these years several things became clearer to me. One was that to a remarkable degree the church took on the character of the world. The attacking, restless, divisive, antagonistic, and reactionary spirit so apparent in society had a corresponding spirit and parallel in the church.

Along with the shake-ups in society were the shake-ups in religious circles. The cleavage between younger and older in the nation was felt in the families of the church. The great drive to reorganize at many levels in secular society was present, perhaps even superceded, in the reorganization of religious structures.

So also the seventies, in which people settled down in a spirit of self-satisfaction, found a corresponding spirit in the church. Entering the indulgent eighties finds the church in much the same mood and primarily concerned with itself.

Overall, the satisfied seventies and indulgent eighties are probably a greater threat to real spiritual life than the shaking, insecure, and sniping sixties. The sixties, in spite of severe differences, showed that people were concerned about issues which mattered.

During the sixties God reminded me many times that he was allowing the shaking so the things which cannot be shaken might become more clear. And, in many ways, issues such as the true nature and task of the church and the true nature of the world were sharper than in a time of ease.

During the sixties and seventies people were searching for answers to hungers and hurts of the human family. Also many Christians searched for new life and grappled with the meaning of church.

As part of that search the charismatic movement added a much needed emphasis to balance the more formal, outward activistic expressions of religious life. While the "charismatic" and "born again" emphases are always in danger of being too individualistic and internalized, they have probably done more than we know to keep faith, hope, and love alive individually and corporately.

One of the requirements to edit a denominational organ is to be as aware as possible of the central issues before the church and to help interpret these in a way which will build up the people of God. The prayer I prayed most during my years as editor was that God would give me discernment for the day; to know what God's people should be and do during a time of great upheaval and change in the church and world. I remember clearly there were certain things I sought to keep central and today they still seem important.

First is the fact that Christ must be the center of our faith. "Other foundation can no man lay except that which is laid in Jesus Christ." People again and again asked questions such as, "If we lose this distinctive or that practice what thing will hold us together?" I did not tire of saying that no "thing" will hold us together. We can usually tell what holds us together by the thing that divides us. And if Christ is at the center, if we are united in him and to him, we cannot be divided. If we are held together by anything less than Christ himself, it will only be a matter of time until we will lose what we have.

Second, the church will not be destroyed. Christ said, "I will build my church and the gates of hell will not prevail against it." It is not our church; it is Christ's church! Rome goes down in ruins; the church goes on! Theological controversy may extinguish creeds but not Christ. And when communism and all the other isms die the church of

Jesus Christ will still be around. Further, if the church of one land or time is not faithful, Christ will raise up a faithful people elsewhere.

Third, the Scripture must be central in the life of the church and in the individual believer's life. At times of rapid change and reaction it is necessary to hold on to that which has proved true through the centuries. Here are the truths which have stood the test of a thousand fads, the winds of new doctrines, and meanderings of men's minds in every age.

During the years I've found firmness and balance by going to the Scriptures and to students of Scripture in the past, along with the present. It is necessary to be open to the new. But safety is in sticking to those truths which have stood the test of time.

Fourth, I have believed that the place and importance of the Holy Spirit in the life of the church must be taught and experienced. If not, people drift in all directions and are divinely led in none. So during the time of my editorship there was a great and encouraging renewal of interest in the work of the Holy Spirit, particularly with a stress on the gifts of the Spirit. To bring what I believed was a needed balance I wrote articles and a book on the fruit of the Spirit.°

Fifth, one of the themes always before me was the offensive the church must have in the area of evangelism. We struggled with the meaning and practice of evangelism and discipleship as if we thought evangelism and discipleship were exclusive of each other. They shall always be two sides of the same coin. The church needs both and must do both to be faithful. I despise a discipleship which does not lead to evangelism as I deplore an evangelism which does not lead to discipleship. As the individual does not walk straight by looking at his or her own feet, but by looking to objects ahead, so the church walks straightest when its face is turned from itself to Christ and the world in need.

Sixth, the church must keep a historical perspective, but it must also keep looking to what God is doing and desires to do today and in the days ahead. Our history is important, but it is not enough to laud our ancestors and think we are faithful simply because we have Menno Simons for our father. God is able to raise up children to Menno from the stones. Mennonites, at times, are in danger of ancestor worship.

Too often we have remained only a clique and talked about Anabaptism until those who don't have Anabaptist biological background feel ostracized and unwanted. We still have a long way to go to absorb persons without Mennonite background in our established congregations. This has been and will be one of the tests of the church in the years ahead.

—*John M. Drescher.*

° *Spirit Fruit* (Herald Press, 1974).

1962

The Value of Involvement

by Elizabeth Showalter

When the Bamboo Curtain fell, I was sure I ought to pray for the Chinese Christians behind it. But I seldom did. Often I did not think of it, for to paraphrase the old saying, "Out of print, out of mind." I wasn't even sure how my prayer could help a nameless Chinese who existed only by hearsay, a statistic from "the last report coming out."

Now when an African student from a country closing to Christianity writes, "Pray for us and what we are doing," the case is different. I have known him. He is real. His country and its problems are real. I see my prayers and the prayers of all Christians leaping geographical barriers of ocean, mountain, and desert. I rejoice that no government can by edict or intrigue stop prayer at its boundaries. The Gospel seed is already contained within its borders, planted in human hearts. Our prayers shall keep it growing.

My concern for known Africans carries over to the unknown ones. I find it much easier to pray for the Christians (black and white) caught in the web of *apartheid* than I did those Chinese with whom I did not feel involved. Not everyone will get to know a national on his native soil. But I now believe that everyone can become more personally involved if he wishes to. In this age of swift communication and travel there are many opportunities to make contact with individuals and institutions.

I know a certain missionary who needs a transistor tape recorder for village work. I'm pretty sure there are persons among us who are tempted to get a tape recorder more or less as a hobby. Why not send the hobby overseas and follow it with prayers?

A certain man, endowed with imagination, collects old telephones from the telephone company for which he works and repairs them for missions. Our own hospital compound in Ethiopia is thus equipped, saving the personnel much time and energy.

One of our older churchmen has begun writing to two overseas pastors. It is never too late to share encouragement, books, and the like with such persons.

Many people near universities are entertaining foreign students. Few ways of sharing can be more significant, for such students may otherwise leave our country without experiencing genuine hospitality or seeing Christian home life.

Sometime, failing all else, I'd like to hear of someone who spins a globe (after a prayer), places his finger on a spot, and begins his mission right there. Travel books abound that tell you about the people of almost every spot on earth. I truly believe that it is possible to learn to love them vicariously.

The big thing is—get involved. The Lord can provide the ways and means.

Elizabeth Showalter: Sometime I'd like to hear of someone who spins a globe, places his finger on a spot, and begins his mission there.

Missions but . . .

A foreign mission worker whom I know was showing slides, picturing his home church building in the States, to the people to whom he ministered. In speaking about it, he said that he suddenly became conscious that the people were not looking at the church building at all but were gasping at the many automobiles flashing in the sunlight around the church building. While his stick was pointing out the church building, their eyes were seeing the cars.

They tell us that the United States has enough automobiles to take everyone for a ride at the same time, with no one in the back seat. In America we must have our cars. And we must see that they keep going.

Some time ago I heard a missionary speak on the great need today in missions. He told us that probably the greatest reason for the lack of meeting this need was unconsecrated money in the hands of Christians. Then he threw a question at us. He asked, "What do you do when you need an automobile? Do you wait six months or a year and then consider if you are more able to purchase one? No, you probably get one." He went on further, "What do you do when you need a tire for your car? Do you say, 'I just can't pay out for a tire right now; so I'll leave the car in the garage or by the side of the road for six months'? No! You probably purchase a tire."

Such questions could be asked concerning many different articles or areas of one's life. What do you do when you are in need of a coat, a pair of rubbers, an extra bed in the house, or a tractor tire? Do you discuss it or begin looking for ways and means of purchasing the needed article?

Although I do not remember where, I do remember of hearing about a meeting of a congregation which was held to discuss the possibility of meeting financial needs. Finally one brother suggested that each one sell his automobile and give the proceeds to the church. He felt very sure that by next week each one would have another automobile.

The lesson is very simple. An automobile is necessary today. Very few can do without one. But the church and the work of the church is necessary for our spiritual welfare. We cannot do without it. Yet there are many who have a hundred dollars to pay out on a car who cannot possibly dig out that much for a church project in a year's time. There are those who can purchase an automobile tire immediately who think that $20.00 for a mission program per year is going to "bust" things up.

To him that hath much, from him also much is required. In a somewhat different sense than the opening illustration, when the call comes to give to the work of the church and we begin to feel it's too much, we need to take a fresh look at the cars parked around the church. It may help us. At least, think it over!

—*John M. Drescher*

Never Go Back

by Lorie C. Gooding

Never go back to that green childhood hill,
that mountain-rising hill that stood so tall
that you could see the world spread out
beneath.
It will not be the same. It will be small,
a little elevation in a field
from whose round, grassy summit you can see
a stretch of meadow-pasture and a stream,
a corner of the wheatfield, and a tree.

Go back and you will find your dream grown
less,
and lifelong you will pay with secret pain;
because, in finding that your hill is small,
you will not walk so tall upon the plain.
Never go back. Remember and go on,
seeking another mountain each new dawn.
Killbuck, Ohio.

1963

At Such a Time

The assassination of our president, John F. Kennedy, thirty-fifth president of the United States, shook the world. It darkened the horizon. It did more. It called our nation to prayer and to the Bible like few events in history. There was the continual call to prayer vigils and services of memorial and mourning. Many churches and synagogues were crowded midnight Nov. 23 and the days following. Attendance was the heaviest since the end of World War II.

It is a time of sorrow and tragedy. The world sorrows. Our own hearts are shaken with grief. This century will go down in history as the century of assassinations. We sorrow for the Kennedy family, the Tippit family, the Oswald family, for our nation, and for the world. We sorrow as a church for the failure to reach such as Lee Harvey Oswald with the saving Gospel of Christ.

It is a time of heart searching. What makes such a deed possible? It seems impossible until we remember the bomb in Birmingham, the murder in Mississippi, the hate-filled hearts and violence we read of daily in our papers. It seems impossible until we think of the hate engendered by war, the shooting and killing on TV, and the lust for violence and retaliation.

These days of mourning ought to be days of heart searching. We listen too readily to the preachers of hate. We listen too eagerly to those who agitate against our leaders. We too often join such in failing to honor those in authority. We fail to pray for all in authority. This incident should teach us to turn our ears from listening to those so-called religious or political leaders who stir up hate and stoop to name calling. It should turn our lives to the practice of love....

It is a time for dedication. Even this dark day can determine a new direction if we will come with true dedication. "If my people, which are called by my name, shall humble themselves, and pray, and seek my face, and turn from their wicked ways; then will I hear from heaven, and will forgive their sin, and will heal their land."

—*John M. Drescher*

On Clocks and Worship

by Charles B. Longenecker

"But why does the clock occupy such a central position in your church?"

These words were tossed back at me as we walked out of the little Mennonite church. I had just begun to introduce some tourists to the faith and practice of the Mennonites. He continued, "Is there a reason that a clock should take the place of the cross in the furnishing of your church?"

In a rapid one-two punch fashion, his wife added, "And it isn't even very pretty—just a common IBM clock."

I explained that we do not emphasize the cross as a mere symbol but rather Jesus who gives the cross its significance. But my tourist friends caught me off balance when they very honestly asked about the centrality of the clock.

The question continues to gnaw at me as I think more about it. I try to justify myself by thinking that we are just being functional. But that fails to satisfy. Are we unthinkingly promoting time-consciousness rather than God-consciousness in our worship services? Have the mundane elements of time and matter so thoroughly saturated our being that the clock has acquired symbolic status?

In our attempt at simplicity and absence of forms and props in our worship, could it be that a vacuum has been created which subsequently has pulled into itself something of higher priority—an instrument to measure time rather than a medium to help focus our short attention span on the One who transcends time?

While living in the framework of time, we need to observe schedules. This is not our greatest need, however, when we enter into worship. The clock on the front wall will not likely tell the verbose speaker that his time is spent, but it will vie for the listener's attention. When it has done this, it will also have severed the I—Thou relationship in worship.

Do you mix worship with clock watching?
New Holland, Pa.

clothed, for anyone that is interested in materialism knows that this is important and surely you know that you have need of these things. So seek after these things, and if you have a few minutes left, add it to the fifteen minutes that you already have donated to the kingdom of God.
Elkhart, Ind.

Matthew 6:25-33 A Modern Translation

by Robert J. Baker

Therefore I say unto you, Take out plenty of insurance upon your life, considering with care the cholesterol content of your food, remembering, please, that it does not hurt to count even the calories in what you drink. Take care also of what you wear, forgetting not that a well-tailored outfit gives one a certain air of distinction. After all, isn't life rather important, and the good opinion of one's friends concerning raiment worn, doth it not add to the wearer's feeling of security?

Now consider the birds of the air. It is true that they sow not, nor gather into barns, but is it our fault that they do not have double-stalled garages? Nay, they are but birds, and you are much better than they.

Incidentally, I would remind you, that by wearing elevator shoes one can add several inches to his stature. Surely this is a mark of great accomplishment and a true measure of man's maturity.

And to continue, why shouldn't you be well dressed? The lilies of the field are pleasantly clothed and surely you deserve better than they, for you can both toil and spin, especially if you have one of the new portable sewing machines that does zigzag stitching. It is true that God looks out for the grass, but it wears only green, and you know how poorly you look in green. Don't you think it wiser to follow the dictates of the fashion world, O you of little humility?

Wherefore consider with care what you eat and drink and the clothing with which you are

1964

Fruitful Leisure

The work week is decreasing. In 1800 it averaged 84 hours; in 1909 it averaged 52 hours; today it averages slightly under 40 hours. Labor unions are pressing now for a 35-hour week. In light of automation we are told to prepare for the two-hour day. Joseph Pendegast of the National Recreation Association predicts that within a century the work week will consist of seven hours.

Today the average workingman has 22 years more leisure time than his grandfather. He has also a longer life span, shorter work week, and more vacation time. It appears that we have almost arrived at the longed-for day when life is filled with leisure. Now we find the truth that we are tested by our leisure time. Herbert Hoover said many years ago, "This civilization is not going to depend on what we do while we work, but on what we do in our time off." What can be done to keep leisure from becoming mere idleness which demoralizes and bores?

Life must have practical purpose—be this in work or leisure. So leisure can add enrichment to life or can become a serious psychiatric problem. We can have the brains to save time without the wisdom to use time. Some simply sit as spectators. Others engage in harmful activity. The call is for creative activity which builds and blesses.

The question we face as Christians is, What

are we doing with our leisure time? Some are turning to entertainment, boats, weekends on the beach, and such like. Will we turn our time to selfish pursuits or redeem the time for God? As families and individuals we ought to form clear guides for the use of leisure. "Whatsoever ye do, do all to the glory of God" (1 Cor. 10:31).

Then, too, our increased leisure time should make more voluntary service possible as the church. Maybe churches ought to do more to organize and train people in giving voluntary service in the community, in helping local pockets of poverty, in giving time to the building of better relationships, in visiting the sick in hospitals and homes, and in assisting pastors in doing the work of the church in the community.

Yes, increased leisure time can be a great asset in helping to fulfill our role as Christians.

—*John M. Drescher*

Challenging God

One of the saddest commentaries on much of current Christianity is the treatment of Mrs. Madalyn Murray and her son, of Baltimore, Md. According to numerous reports Mrs. Murray is waging a war against God. She was successful in winning the Supreme Court's "school-prayer decision." Now she wants to test the constitutionality of tax exemption for churches. She feels that should taxes be levied on churches, they would wilt and die. . . .

Mrs. Murray wants to see no symbol of God in any public place. Chaplains in the Capitol, with armed forces, in hospitals and prisons she hopes will disappear. The phrase, "In God We Trust," she says should be removed from U.S. money. Everything supernatural is merely superstition.

The saddest thing in all of this is that so-called Christians have demonstrated anything but Christianity to Mrs. Murray and her son. She has received hundreds of letters filled with vile epithets and even threats on her life. She and her son have been ill-treated, to the extent that they have needed to flee for their lives to Hawaii. Telephone calls and threats of all kinds keep coming.

Certainly in a free country Mrs. Murray has the right to speak her mind and beliefs—just as much as we have a right to freedom of speech. Without a doubt she is more ready to state her beliefs and suffer for it than many who claim to believe the opposite.

And certainly Christians with calm confidence in God's Word need not fear the onslaughts of atheists. Such fear exposes lack of trust in God. God's church will go on. His Word is still true. God is the Ruler yet. And perhaps Mrs. Murray is fighting her last-ditch battle against a God who she inwardly knows is calling her. God has been assailed before. He has never lost nor will He.

Perhaps those who in the conflict demonstrated by their feelings, actions, and words against her the exact opposite of the Christian spirit may be the more guilty. It is still true that it isn't hard to believe in a God of love if it is just seen in the life of one who says he believes in such a God.

What would have been the reaction of Mrs. Murray if, instead of cursings and threats from those who say they believe in God, prayer, and the church, she would have received hundreds of letters telling her of prayer and love for her? What would have been her reaction if multitudes had written her giving testimony to the reality of prayer and the marvelous works of God in our lives?

Mrs. Murray should be the object of our prayers and love. She should not be scorned or hated. And as God brought about the conversion of the blasphemer, persecutor, and injurious Saul, so He can again change the life of this woman. She too can be saved by putting her faith in Jesus Christ. But it will now be doubly difficult because so many have demonstrated scorn and hatred rather than prayer and love. Christians too by this wrong have also challenged God and His power to accomplish His will.

Yes, Christ died for Mrs. Murray and her family just as much as for any other. And Christians are called to pray, love, and long for her good as much as for anyone else.

—*John M. Drescher*

1965

The Prayers of Luke Warm

In this issue we begin a series, "The Prayers of Luke Warm." You will immediately see that these are written in satire or irony. Satire is a literary style of writing devoted to point out, censure, and reprove some prevailing vice or wrong. In order to show the wrong more clearly the writer states things the opposite of what he really means. Both Christ and Paul at times used satire or irony in order to sharpen and strengthen the point driven home.

Behind the smooth, polished, and often stereotyped prayers that we all offer to God, there are other prayers which outshout them. These are the prayers that are demonstrated by our lives and actions. They are the prayers that we unconsciously put in words by our thoughts which we assume God does not know. These prayers are the real prayer which tell God our spiritual temperature.

The prayers of "Luke Warm" are prayers of complete honesty which should probe our lives. They are written in irony or satire because actually the lukewarmness of much of our discipleship, when seen in the light of God's greatness and all-knowingness and God's demands, is ironical. How ridiculous many of our actions must appear to God.

So, today, we start a series of letters from Luke, written by a writer somewhere in Mennonite Land, America. Try these and see if perhaps they may not, at times, probe some of the instinctive actions of the old man. Before you criticize, either Luke Warm or the editor for printing these letters, let them search your life and try your thoughts. Human nature is usually quick to rise in criticism of the very thing which threatens its sin and the *status quo* and it can find many reasons for not liking something which speaks to areas of deep need. Luke Warm in these letters does just this.

—*John M. Drescher*

Dear God:

This morning we made our triumphal entry at church in our new Buick. I wish, dear God, you could have seen it. Twenty years ago we'd never have dreamed that such a car would be ours, but you've blessed us so wonderfully. (Thanks again for the prosperity.)

Anyway, everyone was visibly impressed except our pastor. I know his old car is rusting through, but certainly he took that into account in choosing his occupation.

I gather that our pastor feels that you would question the way we spend our money, too. But, Lord, when your Son chose His transportation, it was no secondhand donkey. According to my exegesis, it was the latest model and white, just like our Buick.

All the driving we do in our travels, we need a good car! We get better mileage than most, and since we're not so young anymore, we need the comfort. Also, in case of accidents, the heavier car has the advantage. Well, I could go on, but I think you understand. I must run now. We're driving over to the lake this afternoon. So until next Sunday . . . .

Yours as always,
Luke Warm

Wind of Winter

by Lorie C. Gooding

The wind of winter sweeps away the leaves,
Dry, rustling leaves. It tears them from the
   trees
Whereon they cling with futile desperation,
And drives them all before like frightened
   sheep.
It leaves the woodland bare and beautiful,
Stripping away the useless and outworn;
Revealing the essential line and curve;
Cleansing, refreshing, preparing for new
   growth.

I need a wind of winter in my mind,
A cold, clean wind to tear away old thoughts,
To pull loose from their moorings old opinions
Half formed or misformed; and to drive away
Incoherent and unrecognized ambitions,

Incidental and extraneous desires
From the dark woodland-places of my mind;
Leaving the bare bones of intellect,
Essential line and angle of belief,
High-arched and indispensable curve of faith,
Cleansed and refreshed, renewed in height
　　and depth
For newer, bolder thoughts to grow upon.
Killbuck, Ohio.

1966

The gospel is never really ours until we have given it to another person.

What Does the Church Say?

by Nelson E. Kauffman

On a plane to Washington recently in conversation with a soldier, I asked, "What do you think the church is saying to the world?" He said he did not know. He had been at home for a month and had gone to a Baptist Church three out of four Sundays.

I asked if he heard people talk about the Gospel. He said he had, but he could not tell me anything about it. I asked if he thought the church made any difference in the lives of people. After some thinking he said he thought not. I asked if he knew any real Christians. At first he thought not. Then he said possibly his grandparents and an aunt and uncle.

In a Buffalo, N.Y., workshop I sat with a young Jewish boy and asked what he heard the church say. He told me he would have to reply from the synagogue. As we talked, he said, "Judaism has no message."

In a little town in central Nebraska, I asked

a regular churchgoing Lutheran barber, "What is your church trying to say to the world?" He said I would have to ask someone who knew more than he. I suggest the reader use this question and find out what answer he receives in his community. No doubt many Mennonites would be little better able to say what their church is trying to say.

Why do churchgoers not know what the church is saying, or trying to say in its existence and activities? Why, as the soldier reported, is there so little difference to be observed?

At first he said he could tell by observing people which were Christians, but when I asked how, he said he didn't believe he could tell Christians from non-Christians. Would knowing Mennonites help him any? We say we let our lives tell people our faith.

Why No One Hears
I would like to suggest some reasons (they may not be the right ones) why our message is not heard.

1. We are not clear in our concept of the Gospel, our "good news." It gets lost in all we say about Bible teaching and moralizing.

2. We tell what we have to say mechanically without relating its meaning to where people are, here and now. We can say words, good words, such as grace, salvation, faith, etc., but what we really mean is not explained in non-theological weekday language.

3. People in the pews or Sunday-school class don't really listen or don't really hear what we say, or don't really understand. They come to think that the Gospel is "church talk." We give and accept easy answers, and neither we nor they ask "Why?" or "What do you really mean?" as we talk on spiritual matters. Possibly this is because we are afraid of being exposed as ignorant, or we are hypocrites doing Sunday talk only.

4. It may also be that what we are trying to say, our good words, are just parroting. Perhaps they do not issue from experience of the real Gospel. Then the words kill, because there is no living spirit there to produce life. We speak from the stance of a microphone or loudspeaker saying words, and not from the stance of a living person who speaks from per-

sonal experience. Our words are heard mechanically and without a "heartburn."

Now, if there may be some valid reasons for the world not knowing what the church is saying, what can we do to cause our message to be heard, known, understood, and accepted? The following may help:

Translate into Everyday

1. As preachers we can try to put Gospel truth in simple, current, and not religiously stilted words. As, Hertz "puts you in the driver's seat," Avis "tries harder," "things go better with Coke," and "keyed-up executives unwind at the Sheraton," so the church could be saying, "God cares for bad guys" (1 Tim. 1:15); "Look, Jesus is boss" (Rom. 10:9); "Things go better with Christ" (2 Cor. 2:14); and "You can relax with Christ in control" (Phil. 4:13).

We could give a piece of paper to every person in the pew next Sunday and ask listeners to respond—yes, no, or uncertain—to statements we make. We could thus see if what we say is heard and believed by those inside our church buildings.

2. We could use our adult Sunday-school classes for a few weeks to ask each other what the Gospel is. Each person could be asked to explain what has been received and experienced and in words that would be understood by people on the job.

After a week or two while every member has examined and become familiar with a Scripture (possibly 2 Cor. 5:10-21) describing the Gospel, has experienced it, explained it to the class, and defended it against possible critics, each could ask three to five persons of various backgrounds during the next week, "What is the church trying to say to the world?" These answers could be reported.

These conversations will invariably open the door to opportunities to give the Gospel away. The Gospel is never really ours until we have given it away to another person.

People in our neighborhoods should be saying, "At least it is clear what the Gospel is according to the Mennonites." Other Bible-believing churches shouldn't be able to say it any better than we, but surely we evangelical churches all should be saying it clearly in our time.

If a church is really clear in what it thinks it is trying to say, it will surely have less difficulty in being heard accurately. We can hardly expect people to respond to a church if its message is unclear.

We also must learn to say more truth with fewer words. As Mennonites we are not merely second, like Avis, but possibly thirty-second. Therefore we must be better people by Holy Spirit power, and let Christ lead us to "try harder" (Phil. 3:13, 14).

1967

In the 200 Block

by J. Paul Sauder

We live in the 200 block of West Woodlawn Avenue, just a short block and a half east of the 400 block. We of the 200 block are still making mistakes, along with having some successes, to be sure. The occupants of the 400 block make no mistakes. That's because they don't even try. They speak no encouraging words either. For the 400, 500, and 600 blocks of West Woodlawn are part and parcel of Woodlawn Cemetery. No mistakes are made there, nor is there gossip, nor encouraging talk. You and I, who "live in the 200 block yet," may be annoyed temporarily by the mistakes we make, the opportunities we let slip through our fingers, or by what have you, but it is the Lord's own blessing that we are still His tools, trying at least, for the Master's sake. When either of us here at "Sometimes Inn" makes a mistake, the other is apt to say, "Well, you're not in the 400 block yet," and then the mistake-maker goes the more cheerfully on to doing something right, like

—Writing a letter to a dear sister who occupies a wheelchair, because, as she smilingly said, "My legs won't obey me anymore." We tell what we are doing, or have done lately. We don't pity her, for she is too happy to pity. So we don't put any pity in the letter—just news, and thanks for her prayers and letters.

—Watching the antics of the birds on the lawn. It's great to describe their doings in the next family letter written to the grandchildren.

—Visiting the sick man in the hospital. He is champion listener at the preaching services held once a month at the retirement home. Incidentally, he said, "I was really concerned about your health. Now I'm glad to see you looking so well." And he said, "I knew you would come and look me up." Now how did he know that? Hospital visitation with a purpose is one thing you can do if "you are not in the 400 block," or disabled.

Let us suggest that you who read these lines while living in your own "200 block," wherever you be, can do a very simple thing. Hold a fragrant rose to your nose for sixty seconds (one full minute) and meditate, giving memory free rein. Or some meadow tea, or catnip, or a ripe apple or banana. Some good odor is readily available; so soak up a minute's worth of that sector of God's world. Then follow that impulse to do that good deed that comes to your mind as you inhale.

Just because you are alive, write your pastor a letter of appreciation for something he did, or is, or preached. He may wonder, "What's up?" when he gets your letter, but he'll get over the shock of the novelty of hearing from you.

A Christian was picking up colorful feathers in a park where gaily colored tropical birds wander free. To a kind-faced lady standing by he explained what he did with these feathers, for he gave them away, with Scripture verses. She proved that she was a Christian by saying, "Isn't it wonderful what we can do if we use our imagination for the Lord!"

Of course, it's wonderful to use your imagination for the Lord. Indeed that's one of the reasons "you aren't in the 400 block yet." True it is that we are still making mistakes— the mistakes of *omitting to do the good* and the mistakes we *commit*, one way or another. But your mistakes are not the meat of life for you. "I must walk today, and tomorrow, and

the day following," said the Master. And so He "kept His eye peeled," as the saying goes, for He saw opportunities and performed the available response thereto. So can we, "while it is day; [for] the night cometh, when no man can work." Till then, you are "not in the 400 block yet," but are still remembering, let us hope, what the Christian lady said in the park, "It is wonderful to use the imagination for the Lord!" It is for just such opportunities that the Lord preserves you, "While it is [yet] day." He preserves you all the way through your mistakes, successes, omissions, pleasures, sorrows, and what have you. You may wish you had been what you are not, or had the chance that was another's, wealth instead of what you call poverty, a sounder body—you name it. But you are "not in the 400 block yet"; so give thanks and get going.

J. Paul Sauder: If you live in the 200 block, you still make mistakes, but you can also do some good.

Truth or Treason?

by Robert Hartzler

The cool brightness of the second day of fall was superb. Committee meeting had finished a half hour early, giving me twenty minutes before the eighty-mile drive home. The park by the Mississippi waterfront was an ideal spot.

A well-dressed stranger approached the railing, his attention caught by The Thunderbird—the excursion boat tied up 50 feet out. Looking around he noticed me and asked,

"You mean they still operate excursion boats out of Davenport?"

"Oh, yes," I replied, "we took about ninety of our youngsters on a moonlight cruise in July."

"Is that so? You must be a teacher."

"You might call it that; I'm a preacher."

"Really, of what faith?"

"Mennonite."

"Oh, yes, the Mennonites. I'm a Presbyterian. Say, when you Mennonites turn out a nurse, she IS A NURSE! I'm from Illinois and know some of your people around Bloomington."

"Thank you! I wish everyone had the same impression."

"Tell me a little of your church's background."

"Well, our church began in Switzerland in the sixteenth century. One of our earliest leaders was Conrad Grebel. Later we took our name from a converted priest—Menno Simons. We were the radical left wing of the Reformation. Luther didn't push his reform far enough, especially on the question of believer's baptism."

"Now is that real history or is that only *your* version? I have some friends of another denomination who attempt to trace their history back that far too."

"No," I replied, "any competent church historian will trace the Mennonites back to the Anabaptists of 1525."

"Well, if what you say is true—if Mennonites actually were the left wing of the Protestant Reformation, you surely have betrayed your original position. Because if I

know your people today, you are on the extreme right of Protestant Christianity."

"There is my ride," I observed; "it's been good talking with you."

I thought about it the whole way home. A month later I'm still bothered by the man's evaluation. From extreme left to extreme right. What has happened? Have we betrayed the Anabaptist vision or has mainstream Protestant Christianity passed us by on the left? I'm not sure.

1968

Master Missionary: Milton Vogt

by Paul G. Kniss

"I have always thought of Milton Vogt as the ideal missionary," said a missionary-nurse to a friend a few months ago. Now Milton is gone. As we recall how he lived, we are inspired to pray, "Lord, make me that kind of man." His qualities of openness, simplicity, diligence, fearlessness, never-failing cheerfulness, and his deep devotion and sense of purpose combined to make him not a flashy personality, but a person loved and respected by all who knew him. He carried many responsibilities, and his colleagues are wondering just how they can do without him.

Milton Christian Vogt was born on Aug. 14, 1901, near Moundridge, Kan., the first child of Christ and Barbara Vogt. From a congenial home-farm atmosphere, he entered the first grade of school knowing not English, but German. Later the family moved to another farm near Hesston, Kan. From early boyhood Milton showed mechanical skill. His father entrusted farm machinery maintenance to him. Milton then trained his next brother who took over the responsibility until he in turn taught the next.

After completing high school at Hesston Academy, Milton taught school for one year. His own brothers (he had five brothers and three sisters) were among his pupils.

Education at Hesston

Following his year of teaching, Milton enrolled at Hesston College. Among his classmates were J. B. Martin, Tilman Smith, Fred Brenneman, and M. A. Yoder. Esther Kulp, the only member of the class Milton did not know, had come for her high school senior year when Milton had been teaching school. Milton and Esther became members of a small group of friends. Milton shared his keen interest in foreign missions, and in India particularly, and the group frequently prayed together for these concerns.

During their sophomore year Milton and Esther started their courtship and the next year were engaged. For his senior year he matriculated at Goshen College. He received his BA degree in 1927 after which he went to the General Mission Board meeting at Milford, Neb. There he, along with Esther Kulp, was appointed to serve in India. The Milford congregation undertook Milton's field support throughout his career.

After Mission Board meeting Milton returned to the farm until the harvesting was done; then, after being ordained to the ministry at Hesston, he was married to Esther Kulp by D. H. Bender, then president of Hesston College.

Esther came from a singing family and wished that Milton would sing more. He enjoyed music and wanted to sing along with Esther; so he took voice lessons at Goshen. Although he never excelled in singing, he always participated in it. His favorite hymn, which is so descriptive of his life and his aspirations, was "O How Happy Are They."

When Milton and Esther arrived in India in the fall of 1927, they went to Ghatula where they lived with George Lapps and studied Hindi. When the Lapps returned home on furlough, Milton and Esther were the only missionaries at Ghatula and were responsible for an industrial school, evangelistic work, and a medical dispensary. The Vogts were stationed at Ghatula from 1927 until 1941 except for one year in Balodgahan. There they replaced the George Beares who were on furlough. During this time three sons and a daughter were born to them. The year 1937 held some especially severe trials for them. When baby Bernard was two months old, his mother suffered a stroke which paralyzed her left side. Seven months later a diphtheria epidemic claimed the life of baby Bernard, along with many others.

Call to Kodarma

In 1941 the Vogts were chosen by their fellow missionaries to go to a new field at Kodarma, Bihar, to work with S. Jay and Ida Hostetler. They were in this area until 1946. During this time, in 1943-44, Esther and the children remained in Bihar while Milton went to Calcutta to assist in famine relief.

Passage abroad in 1946 was difficult to arrange, but the Vogts' furlough was overdue. They went to sultry Calcutta to remain "at the ready" in order to board ship at short notice. The family lived on the second floor of one building and had to go to another building for meals, on the colonial schedule, four times a day. During this time Milton and his two sons worked at an army surplus disposal, sorting and selling vehicles, clothing, and other equipment to missionaries and organizations. After waiting three months, they suddenly received word that they could board a ship leaving the next morning. There were several hours of frantically trying to get documents in order, as it was a holiday, but they made it.

During this stay in Calcutta, Milton purchased a Harley-Davidson, army-surplus motorcycle. This heavy old motorcycle became a familiar sight in the Mennonite Church area, for it carried Milton many times over rough terrain, through riverbeds and streams, and often on longer trips to the cities of Daltonganj and Ranchi. He was riding this same motorcycle Jan. 5, 1968, when he seemingly suffered a stroke that led to his death.

In 1949 the Vogts returned to Bihar but to a new field—Palamau District. They left their three older children in school in the States and brought their two young daughters to India. Milton was appointed secretary-treasurer of the mission, a position he held for the next 18 years. He enjoyed bookkeeping and figures. He said that when he got a headache, he began working on accounts to eradicate the pain.

The years in Palamau District were fruitful and satisfying. Although for several years Milton was greatly weakened by paratyphoid and a siege of amoebic dysentery, he continued his work. The village churches were small and scattered, but Milton would visit a congregation of only two families for a week-day prayer meeting as well as Sunday services although it meant miles of driving coupled with a few miles of walking. But he enjoyed "roughing it."

Many-Faceted Mission

Milton's responsibilities were many. The last number of years he went to Satbarwa Hospital three days a week (about 60 miles) to oversee a hospital. He served on a number of church committees, and often did not get home until after midnight. Up again at 4:00 a.m., he would take a brisk walk in the dark, spend some time in worship (reading by kerosene lamp), and then do some bookkeeping or other office work before 6:30.

Milton's experience as farm mechanic was useful in later years. Living far from any garage, he serviced his car himself. When the springs of the '49 jeep station wagon were flat or bowed the wrong way because of overloading, Milton took them off and hammered them back into shape with a sledge hammer. Overloading was a constant problem because of his accommodating many people. Many times there were 20 or more persons in the car and a loaded luggage trailer behind.

When Milton died, the shock was great for all who knew him. He was so full of life and so strong that it did not seem credible. The people of Bathet turned out in force—every able-bodied man—to dig his grave. Many people came for the funeral from the entire Mennonite Church area. Everyone was impressed with the courage and hope expressed by his wife, Esther, who testified at his funeral and helped to sing his favorite hymn, "O How Happy Are They."

An evangelist and co-worker said, "Brother Vogt taught me by precept and example the meaning of the Christian life." A non-Christian villager said, "He'd do anything anytime for anyone." This included taking along a shopping list when he was on a busy trip to the city or taking a sick person to the hospital 75 miles away in the middle of the night. His youngest daughter, at Goshen College, wrote her mother that her daddy always had time to fix a toy no matter how busy he was.

In all of Milton's life, his main concern was building the church. Every prayer in his last years, even a short prayer of thanks before a meal, included, "Lord, bless Your church, that she may grow and be strong." This was not idle repetition but the consuming passion of his life.

At his funeral Mrs. Vogt said she thanked God for the privilege of living with Milton for 40 years and five months. We, his colleagues and the church in which he gave himself so wholeheartedly, thank God for the years of living and working with Milton. We will miss his jovial laugh, his sympathetic concern, his penetrating question, and his mature counsel. But with Esther we rejoice in the sure hope we have in Christ and have only praise to offer our God.

Milton Vogt: When the springs of the '49 jeep station wagon were flat or bowed, he took them off and hammered them back into shape.

1969

I was elevated and humbled, thrilled and stilled, on the night an outstanding leader asked if we might wash feet together.

The Rich Experience

by Robert J. Baker

The most impressive act I ever witnessed in the fellowship of the believers occurred at the Prairie Street Mennonite Church when I was a teenage boy. That is over thirty-five years ago. And yet the experience is as fresh in my mind as if it were happening this moment in this very room.

It involved two people, one now deceased, the other living today far away from this city of Elkhart, Indiana., where the original memorable event took place. In another sense, however, it involved us all in that church that day. It was hidden from none; it was open to all. What I saw has outlived any sermon I ever heard.

I was sitting near the rear of the church when the tall man came down the aisle. He stopped several benches ahead of me, signaled to a particular man, leaned over and whispered a few words. I was close, but I could not hear the words. Yet I knew what he said. The expression on his face was one of great tenderness and love. I thought he was about to cry. Later he did cry. Knowing what was taking place in that church during that particular service, I did not have to hear the actual words he spoke. I could read his slightly moving lips; I knew why he was there. And my boyish heart was strangely stirred. Thirty-five years have passed and I have never observed a more significant or more meaningful event in any church service that I ever attended. And I have attended a lot of them.

A Noble Christian Act

When I was a boy, kind brethren in the church who knew of the poverty of our family, arranged for me to work on Saturdays and after school at a local store that employed only Mennonites at that time. I had not been at that place of employment very long before I realized that two of the brethren did not get along. They had periodic misunderstandings. Voices would be raised and anger was present. As a new Christian I could not understand these differences, the harsh words. I was puzzled, disturbed, hurt.

That Sunday at the Prairie Street Mennonite Church some four pews ahead of me the two men faced one another. The words the tall man said to the older brother on the church bench, the words I could lip-read, were the whispered words, "May I wash your feet?" I still feel tender as I recall the event.

As I write, my eyes are wet; I am unashamed of my emotions. It was a moving, meaningful scene. I watched those two brethren walk to the front of the church. The tall one took a towel from the bench and gently motioned the other to be seated. Both of them were barefoot.

The tall one knelt down, girded himself with the towel, and tenderly washed his brother's feet. Then they exchanged places and the act was repeated. They both arose, the towel was laid aside, and they stood facing one another in front of that church. The clock stood still; time was frozen for a microsecond; it was like a beautiful painting.

Their faces glistened with tears. Then action once more, gentle, gentle action. They pressed their lips to one another's cheeks. Then it was over, yet it was never over. By that brief act of washing one another's feet they dissolved all the puzzlement, disturbance, hurt that swirled within a young boy's heart.

Some people will know of whom I speak. The one participant is now with our Lord in heaven, the other, the one who initiated that act of love and forgiveness, lives for the same Lord here below. He will not care if I share the incident. It was a symbol for all to see, and he wanted us to know. He publicly admitted his part in the misunderstanding; he sought his brother's forgiveness, the forgiveness of the church, the forgiveness of God. It was such a good thing that he did, far more noble than some things I have seen done in the church.

I Need This Practice

To me, the act of feet washing is one of the most helpful and meaningful ordinances in the church. I believe in it. If you are voting on whether to keep it, count me a loud "Yes" in favor. Keep it because I need it, desperately I need it.

The washing of the saints' feet has endeared itself to me because it symbolizes the cleansing within my own heart. As the water is laved over my feet, I remember how Jesus washed me of my sins those many years ago. I recall how my heartache was eased, how the cleansing flood made that which was scarlet as white as snow. Feet washing to me symbolizes inner cleansing.

I wash my brother's feet to indicate my readiness to serve anyone in that church. I bend my knees, I bow my head, I cup my hands, raise the streaming water, and let it tumble gently over my brother's feet. I take the towel and with tenderness dry those feet, the top, the bottom, the front, the back. And by it I cry, "Let me be your servant; let me minister to you; call upon me when your loved ones are afflicted, when the sorrow of death touches your family, when you have need. I will come."

And as I wash my brother's feet I become involved in an act of worship. My Jesus said that this was a practice I was to keep. I never participate in this ordinance without recalling that last night that Jesus was with His disciples. From that upper room He went to the Garden of Gethsemane. And there He prayed for me. Through this act of feet washing I relive with Him those last trying, testing hours. And always I come away richer for the experience. It was one of His dying wishes, that I continue in it. He said, "If I then, your Lord and Master, have washed your feet; ye also ought to wash one another's feet." And so I have. Surely there will always be someone in the brotherhood to share with me this act of worship.

A Great Leveler

Feet washing is a great leveler. I was elevated and humbled, thrilled and stilled, the night one of the outstanding men in the Mennonite Church asked if we might wash feet together. I know he did not think of the difference between us; he just saw me as a brother that he loved. And so this man of God, pastor, bishop, evangelist, writer, educator, personal worker, church leader washed my feet. He did it graciously, lovingly. At the basin we found ourselves one, no barrier between, no wall of superiority.

I have shared the experience of the two brethren who found release in the act of feet washing, that significant experience that blessed me as a boy. When I shared it with my daughter, she shared one in return. She said her most memorable and meaningful involvement with this act came under the leadership of the late Christmas Carol Kauffman. At that time Carol was in charge of a group of teenage girls, leading them in a devotional exercise. She asked each girl in the circle to turn to the girl on her left and state one thing that they appreciated about that particular girl friend. Their participation and sharing in this way took place just before they engaged in the act of feet washing among themselves in the MYF room. Feet washing is a time for appreciating the brotherhood, the sisterhood too.

Pride is an ugly thing. Frankly, it has been a thorn in this flesh of mine. When I wash my brother's feet, my pride dissolves in the water I pour upon his feet. To wash the feet of the saints is a good reducing exercise. It makes you smaller, puts you in proper perspective.

Oftentimes in church we wash feet with one of our special friends. There is nothing wrong with this, but there are times when I should go to a brother and ask him if I may wash his feet because he and I have had differences in the church. Let the church see me go forward with him. I care not. I want to kneel in front of him; I want to wash his feet, to have me become a part of him, him a part of me, both of us a part of Christ. It is a soul-stirring experience for me, a catharsis of the spirit, a renewing of Christian love within. It's brotherhood.

When a church looks at the feet-washing

activity out of the corner of its collective eye, when members of that body feel that the ceremony is a carry-over of the days when we were a people of the farm, when they are embarrassed to mention it as a practice of the church to which they belong, then this simple, meaningful command of Jesus will slip away from us. We will have a new "revelation" of John 13, a revised interpretation for Jesus' order. And, personally, we will be sorry that we explained away this rich experience.

Robert J. Baker: As I wash my brother's feet, I become involved in an act of worship.

1970

Women, Equality, and the Church

by Dorothy Swartzentruber

Something new has dawned on the horizon of church thought: the realization that women do not have equal standing with men in the work of the kingdom.

"Church work has always been a men's monopoly. They sit on the church councils, build the buildings, counsel the minister, decide the policy, set the budget, and keep the church program moving. Women, at least in the past, never got inside the inner circle of control." So states an editorial in the April 22, 1969, *Canadian Mennonite*. The thirteen Ontario Mennonite congregations who responded to a survey substantiate this fact with added comment that "that's the way it ought to stay!"

Segregation is built right into our church structure. An appearance of a dual church—one for men and one for women—is frequently given when men meet to counsel, plan and project programs while the women do the same thing for a separate program in a separate location. By continuing to tolerate the segregation of the work of the church by sexes, the two-church myth is perpetuated.

Many Mennonite women have become professional people. The church is the loser if it does not capitalize on the contributions such women can make to its total program. While the "ghetto philosophy" keeps some women safely and snugly tied to a quilt in a Mennonite church basement, those women whose experience and training has geared them to a sense of responsibility for broader community and world needs will find ways to serve in nonchurch programs if they are not used in a church context. Many thinking women *want* to get involved in the mainstream of the church's program. Whether the church is prepared to appoint some of these women to its committees and boards remains to be seen.

The degree of acceptance which women will find in such positions will depend largely on the women themselves. However, it is also true that women who have for centuries been relegated to the Sunday school, the choir, the church kitchen, and the sewing circle will need to be "nurtured" into positions of church responsibility even if qualified to accept such positions.

On the other hand, women who serve on committees and boards should be sensitive to attitudes which cannot be changed overnight. Aggressive women or those with personal aspirations are not appealing. Women who wish to "take over" or "run the church" are few and, I might add, those most qualified are also the least likely to desire such positions. Nor should women be appointed simply because they are women; this is demeaning. Election to any position must be on the basis of qualification, not sex.

The body is made up of many parts, each part contributing to the whole. When the resources of Mennonite women are fully utilized in the work of the church, richness and wholeness will be added to the body.

Tongues—Sign of the Spirit?

As one who is much interested in the charismatic movement of today I am saddened when unscriptural statements are made which build a basis of reproach for a movement which has much to offer the church.

If there is one thing clearly obvious, it is that the Christian church needs an outpouring of the Holy Spirit. The dynamic which only the Holy Spirit can give is desperately needed. The gifts of the Spirit are needed by the church. We have seen enough of the frenzied, foolish striving in the strength of the flesh. The frozen wastelands of formalism can be thawed only by the melting work of the Holy Spirit. Ritualistic religion will not do for those who seek a personal God who lives today. And, thank God, there are many signs that God's Spirit is being poured out in these last days.

However, an idea which persists by word and inference many times is that the gift of tongues is a requirement, a test or mark of the Holy Spirit. This turns some off immediately because a remark or inference that speaking in tongues is the necessary evidence of the filling of the Holy Spirit is in direct opposition to Scripture.

While it is God's will that all be filled with the Spirit, the Scripture clearly states that not all are given the gift of tongues. 1 Cor. 12:11, 30. Tongues is no more a test of the Spirit than teaching or preaching. Paul says we are not to deny this gift or magnify it above others. In fact, he says, "I would rather speak five words with my mind, in order to instruct others, than ten thousand words in a tongue." This he says, not to disparage the gift of tongues but to point out its comparative significance in the body. It might be significant that through the centuries of the Christian faith the great spiritual giants do not testify to the possession of the gift of tongues.

Genuine religion has always been harassed by imitators. So we need the attitude of candor and caution in order to be receptive to all God's blessings and to avoid false doctrine. Perhaps no other gift of the Spirit can so easily be imitated as tongues. On the other hand some have found not only a fresh but entirely new spiritual meaning and warmth in the exercise of this gift.

Scripture points out certain spiritual restrictions in regard to tongues. First only three people are permitted to speak in tongues. 1 Cor. 14:27. God does not desire confusion and disorder. Second, no more than one should speak at one time. 1 Cor. 14:27. A multiple display of tongues in public is contrary to Scripture. Third, where there is any public speaking in tongues there is to be an interpretation. 1 Cor. 14:28. And fourth, it appears women are excluded from speaking in tongues in a public service. 1 Cor. 14:34. Note that Paul's statement "Let your women keep silence in the churches" is in the context of tongues. It is not in contradiction to woman's vocal participation in the church in 1 Corinthians 11.

A careful study of 1 Corinthians, and the Book of Acts, gives no support to the idea that speaking in an unknown tongue is either the evidence of the baptism of the Holy Spirit or is a gift of the Holy Spirit to be coveted or sought above any other.

What is the test of the possession of the Holy Spirit? The sign of the Spirit is not one or two spectacular gifts but the exercise of the fruit of the Spirit; love, joy, peace, patience, kindness, goodness, faithfulness, gentleness, and self-control. The gift of tongues is confined to approximately three chapters of the New Testament. The tongues of Pentecost is different from the ecstatic utterance in 1 Corinthians. It is mentioned in 1 Corinthians because of the misunderstanding of the gift, while the fruit of the Spirit is stressed throughout the Scripture.

So the power of baptism of the Holy Spirit is not attested primarily or necessarily by spectacular gifts but by the portrayal of inviolate character. Is one Christlike?

According to the Scripture the primary work of the Holy Spirit is to magnify Christ and make us Christlike. When we seek anything but Christ Himself we become confused by side issues and will finally fall. A big part of the trouble with the Corinthian church was that they had turned their eyes from Jesus Christ. So Paul came determined to know nothing except Jesus Christ and Him crucified. He tells them Christ, not tongues, must be the center of their striving and affection.

Thus, we do not forbid to speak in tongues. Wherever God's Spirit is at work there this gift will likely be given to some persons just as the other gifts will be given to other persons. We do say, however, that when speaking in tongues becomes a test of the baptism of the Spirit there is false doctrine expressed.

Therefore it is good to remember that the test of the Holy Spirit's control and baptism is not so much in the gifts of the Spirit but in the fruit of the Spirit. We are inclined to laud the former because they are spectacular. We need to long for the latter because they are spiritual.

—*John M. Drescher*

1971

The beginning of a column written by someone who had to be wiser than his use of the English language suggested.

Seth's Korner

This reporter will be making komments from time to time in our church papur. I will be riting about things happening to me and others at my church, if any. You will be lurning from me what I think about sertan things and I hope you will read my kolum each time our editor prints it. If no one reads it he will not print it. Or if it is to bad he will not print it.

I am vary happy that sumone like me who has nevur went to Goshen Collige kan rite for this papur. Maybe you kan lurn from me and us at our church unless your church is so big and fancy you know everything. If it is, then this kolumn wont do you any good and you kan just keep on reading the Nashunal Geografik which takes you places this kolumnist kant and besides prints piktures in kolor which this papur dont.

What do we need most at the Mennonite Church where I go and I go twice on Sunday and sumtimes during the weak but not to often since we don't have prayer meetin anymore? I wuld ansur this in my furst kolum which is this one. We need more peepul, most at my church, who will say yes instead of no. Sum here are xperts at sayin no in English and Pennsylvania Dutch yet. Maybe our preechur can even say no in Greek but I dobt it for our preechur is a buzy man who says yes when he shuld say no. But sum peepul here have more xcuses than Mr. Carter has liver pills. Sum cannot take a church job because they are going to have a baby or there wife is going to have a baby. Sum are to buzy being Lions or going on the Rotary. Sum peepul at my church work vary hard so they kan earn more money so they kan buy more things so they kan work vary hard to pay for them. They are to tired to say yes to anything but weather they want anuther peace of pie.

Peepul at our church may say no without thinking. Like one purson was asked to teach but he said no he could not teach. He did not know how. Our Sunday skool leaders would be purty dum to ask sumone to teach who kannot teach. I do not beleeve our Sunday skool leaders are dum. They may not be vary brite, but they are not dum.

So like I say, what we need is more peepul to say yes to what the church koncil asks them to do. And they shuld say yes to what God asks them to do. If they got in the habit of saying yes to the church, maybe they wuld lurn how to say yes to God. But it may be the othur way round. This riter does not know everything.

This kolumnist is no xception. What I say for you, I say for me. If I ball you out, I ball myself out which sumtimes I need all though my Sunday skool teachur does very well at it and my wife does to.

Truly Yours,
Brother Seth

The Morning Sermon

For some reason, if I sense the thinking of some Christians, the sermon is falling into disrepute for the Sunday morning worship service. I have been trying to learn just what has taken place that this kind of trend should develop.

For me the Sunday morning sermon has always been perhaps the highest point of my worship experience so far as corporate worship is concerned. In the sermon I expect from the minister a word from the Lord. I don't necessarily expect it to be a one-way communication just because I'm not speaking but only listening. There is a silent language, too, going on in my inner self as the minister speaks from the Word of God.

From this sermon I expect to hear God

speak to me through His servant as he understands the Word of God and as the Holy Spirit has spoken to him. If he has prepared his sermon and has yielded to the Holy Spirit, I know that God will not forget me in my needs in this sermon even though the pastor may not know at all he is speaking to me. His words may comfort me where I'm troubled or trouble me where I feel too comfortable. He may speak words of conviction, strength, challenge, encouragement, inspiration, and so on. These words prepare me in my own individual need for the tasks that I will meet when I face my work for the coming week.

In addition to listening to the regular Sunday morning sermon in my own congregation I also listen to several others on a Sunday which are sermons preached to a congregation or a radio sermon. It is remarkable how one can find people who are really hungry spiritually and who are in dire need to be fed the living bread and water from the Word so that they can face the work and frustrations in the home, office, community, and even in the church itself.

—E.Z. (Ellrose Zook, Executive Editor).

1972

Delivered by God: Brazil's German Mennonites

by R. Herbert Minnich

More than 1,250 German Mennonites left Russia and migrated to Brazil forty years ago. Their stories of miraculous deliverance and God's amazing grace on their journeys to their adopted homeland stir fellow believers to praise God.

Gerhard Heinrichs and his story are fixed forever in my memory. A farmer by occupation, Gerhard is also a deacon and longtime youth leader in the General Conference Church in Witmarsum Colony, forty-five miles west of Curitiba. Returning from an international youth retreat, I watched him relax in the bus by removing his shoes and socks. One foot was partially amputated.

"I imagine there is an interesting story behind that injury," I said, as he rubbed the cutoff end of his foot. As we bounced along the dirt highway, he described how it happened.

It was the night his family fled their Mennonite village in eastern Russia. Rumors had been circulating that his father, a minister, was to be sent into Siberian exile. Quietly the father turned all his liquid assets into cash and his mother sewed the rubles into her ankle-length dress.

One cold winter night a Chinese smuggler appeared at their door dressed in white fur from head to foot. His parents, and a few close relatives who were making a convenient visit that evening, quickly loaded three wagons with their most prized possessions and Gerhard was instructed to do as he was told.

They left their cows in the barn and fled through the night behind the smuggler who unrelentingly ran across the fields on snowshoes. The group followed him blindly, hoping and praying that he could fulfill his promise to get them past Russian border guards and across the Amur River into China.

Gerhard drove one of the teams which forced him to sit quietly in the below-zero night air. He was wearing boots too large for him and blowing snow seeped into one of them and melted. The cold water soaked his woolen socks and he whimpered in pain as his foot got colder. His uncle, not realizing the gravity of the boy's problem, told him to be quiet and be a man.

Finally they reached the river bluff. Their guide informed them he would sneak to the last remaining blockhouse and attempt to kill the guard who watched the section of bank they would have to descend in order to get to the frozen river. "He told us if the guard emerged alive from the blockhouse we were on our own! We could bolt for the river or turn back."

Then he lay down on the ground and weasled his way through the snow toward the watchtower, completely camouflaged by his fur clothing. After waiting for a long time in the gathering dawn, they peeked over the low hill.

The smuggler suddenly got to his feet at the base of the tower and waved for them to come ahead. The extreme cold had driven the guard out of the watchtower and he apparently had returned to the border town a mile downstream. Gerhard and his family escaped from communist Russia without the shedding of blood!

By this time the boy was almost beside himself because of pain in his foot. He lost control of the horses as they slid down the bank to the ice and one of the wagon wheels broke. The smuggler, in desperation, lifted the loaded wagon and acted as a wheel as he urged Gerhard and the others to whip the horses to gallop across the river.

Chinese soldiers met them when they arrived on the other side, and Gerhard's father was obliged to give them all the cash remaining in his mother's dress in order to get Chinese identification papers. The smuggler had already been paid $3,000 for his daring night's work and, Gerhard observed, "He earned every ruble of it. When we saw him several days later he was puffed up and purple from that night of superhuman effort. My mother wept when she saw him and we recognized him only by his voice."

After successfully crossing the Amur River, Gerhard's family was able to pay attention to his personal tragedy. While his father negotiated with the border guards, his uncle tried to get the boot off his pain-wracked foot. When this proved impossible, he used a knife.

"When my uncle finally cut the boot off my foot and saw my toes frozen in a chunk of ice, it was his turn to cry. I had so much pain for the next two weeks that I could neither sleep nor eat. I had to keep moving at first and gangrene set in. One of the Mennonite nurses in our expanded group of refugees took a butcher knife and chopped my toes off. We had no pain-killers. Finally we got to a city where I was put in the hospital. The infection had already spread into my foot and the doctors finally amputated the front part to avoid more trouble."

After spending several years in Harbin, China, Gerhard and his family came with other Mennonites to Germany. From there they migrated to southern Brazil and ever since have been part of the courageous story of ethnic Mennonites in Latin America's largest nation.

During the ocean voyage, Gerhard's baby brother, Frank, contracted measles and was permanently blinded. That child survived the rigors of pioneer life in the mountains of Santa Catarina and accompanied his family to Parana. Today Frank Heinrichs is a blind evangelist in the Mennonite Brethren Church.

Gerhard, along with his wife and children, recently entered an MCC-sponsored voluntary service program in northeast Brazil. I suppose part of his motivation for this service is related to his own deliverance, for he once told me, "When I think of the Mennonites' escape from Russia, I remember how God delivered the Israelites from Egypt. He finally led them to the Promised Land."

Hundreds of German Mennonites in Brazil have similar experiences of divine deliverance; God directed them to Brazil with a mighty hand. The hosts of World Conference this July are veteran pilgrims, but after forty years in Brazil, they are no longer strangers here. Their agricultural progress and dedication to hard work are well known. They are losing their traditional shyness about sharing their faith, and many young people now attend universities and professional schools. Those who attend World Conference this July will quickly feel at home in their fellowship (if they know a little German) and their deep gratitude for God's deliverance is contagious.

1973

If anyone doubted that the actions of government can become demonic overnight no one can deny it any longer in light of the Christmas season bombings in Vietnam.

Bombing, Law and Order, and the Press

If anyone doubted that the actions of government leaders can become demonic overnight no one can continue to doubt it or deny it any longer in light of the Christmas season bombings in Vietnam. The arrogance and pride of a country, such as ours, which will destroy and commit such atrocities must smell to high heaven. It reminds one of Herod's slaughter when Christ's birth was rumored. Herod felt that his political position was threatened.

Apparently the president has put tremendous pride in his recent election triumph. Apparently he feels no need to listen to anyone but persists in the adolescent approach of "if you don't give me what I want I'll wipe you off the map." Apparently the president feels the vote gave him absolute freedom to ignore the Congress, the concerns of citizens, and the concerns of every other country in the world.

Let us put it down. The United States will suffer for its barbaric atrocities. Any nation which allows its leaders to delve into such devastation on others cannot last very long. Our nation is not very old and such arrogance will not allow it to get old.

One of the strangest things is that a president who speaks of law and order is the world leader who demonstrates, at least in an open way, his lack of respect for law and order.

And how does one make a just and honorable peace by doing unjust and dishonorable things? In spite of all the evil and wrong of one's enemies, it cannot be said the actions of the United States can be justified.

The *Reformed Journal* says it right when it calls upon people to take issue with the idea of a "just and honorable peace." It suggests this is like an adulterous man going to Billy Graham, telling him of all his adulterous acts and the trouble they have gotten him into at home and elsewhere. Then he tells Graham that he wants out, but in a just and honorable way. Says the *Journal*, Billy would be the first to tell him to repent and to change his ways. So also the nation.

In addition to the usurping of power in pounding Vietnam to death, there is the continuing pressure to stifle news reporting. Perhaps few of us know what the president's news blackout involves. But the little we do know means that great danger is present.

A guarantee of our country is freedom of the press, and, of course, freedom of the press is one of the first things a ruler denies when he grasps for personal power. Maybe Harry Truman's admonition should be heeded, "If you can't stand the heat, get out of the kitchen." There is no doubt in my mind that Jeremiah would be in the dungeon today were he alive.

—*John M. Drescher*

readers say

Submissions to Readers Say column should comment on printed articles.

Your prophetic word in your editorial of the Jan. 16 issue of the *Gospel Herald* is deeply appreciated. You came through to me like an Old Testament prophet. It almost seemed as though John the Baptist were risen from the dead. Thank you for having the courage to speak out in this way. It means so much coming from you. I know it is authentic and out of genuine conviction.

Thank you for the tremendous service you have given to the church through your editorial pen. I trust that even though you will be discontinuing as editor you will not discontinue your prophetic voice and written word.

As I read your editorial I felt I heard the judgment rolling down as waters which Amos had predicted.

God's continuing grace and blessing to you, John, and your good work.—Howard J. Zehr, Elkhart, Ind.

We have never subscribed for the *Gospel Herald*, as we have been receiving it through our church. We would like to have our subscription canceled.

Your recent editorial calling President Nixon's actions as demonic for bombing military installations in Vietnam, while urging us to heed Truman's admonition, who was responsible for the bombing of Hiroshima, clearly indicates your political bias, as well as many other articles have.

When your paper once again becomes a "*Gospel*" *Herald* instead of a political magazine, we will again subscribe to it.—Mrs. Ralph Ulrich, Eureka, Ill.

I want to express my gratitude that you, a man of God, have said what needed to be said about the incredible Christmas bombing campaign of President Nixon. You give us hope that the church has not lost its soul.

You will be soundly criticized for being straightforward. You will be accused of meddling in politics, of speaking of things about which you lack information, of laying hands on God's appointed ruler, etc. etc. But when it is all said and done, God's truth revealed in Jesus Christ will support you and that is enough.

May God bless you and sustain you.—John K. Stoner, Harrisburg, Pa.

I am sorry to see your editorial at the top of page 64 (Jan. 16, 1973). I hate to see the Mennonite Publishing House used as a base for anti-United States political editorials. It seems that some of the Mennonite intelligentsia feel that they should teach the United States government to be nonresistant, like a good church is supposed to be. Perhaps you also have this same idea. I don't think this can be expected of world governments today.

I notice that you refer to our government as demonic, arrogant, proud, adolescent, barbaric, dishonorable. (Incidentally, I wonder how our government would fare if you were in charge.) I haven't seen you point to the evils, the dangers, the intentions, and the total commitment of the other side.

If we could bring about a nonresistant U.S. another country might be controlling your little printing press and then you wouldn't dare print such an editorial.

We all hate this war. We all know it's a very complicated problem. (Not one for church editors to solve by stirring up hatred for their own country.) We should appreciate that in this country our nonresistant churches are protected and honored by the government. That cannot be said of the governments that are committed to our downfall.—B. F. Weber, Lititz, Pa.

Surprised Both Ways

I've observed that most difficulty arises in the interpretation of Scripture where doctrine turns into practice.

Samuel Butler suggested that religiously respectable people are "equally horrified to hear the Christian religion doubted or to see it practiced."

In our profession of Christianity it is possible to be flawless and precise. It is possible to demand that the preacher pronounce the exact clichés of the past or we question his orthodoxy. But in the practice of Christianity it is possible to remain atheists and have few notice. It is possible to be a church member in good standing and never commit ourselves to the way of Christ in any practical way.

So we love to prove our theological positions by strong declaration of what we believe and by denunciation of those who differ. But Christianity has never been proved or propagated by pure declaration or denunciation.

We are shocked when someone comes along who denounces the faith. Maybe the kind of faith we put forth should be denounced. A Christian leader, confronted by a skeptic replied, "Tell me about the Jesus you have in mind. Perhaps I don't believe in him either."

We are equally shocked when someone comes along who practices Christianity and we cannot see the similarity of the radicalness of such with Christ and his early disciples. . . .

Why is it that we have less trouble with the doctrinal portion of the epistles than the practical? Romans, chapters one through eleven, are generally well interpreted. But Romans 12 to 16 causes considerable difficulty. Why? Because practical Christianity is most shocking.

We are soon shocked when someone begins to apply what Christian commitment means to our present problems of affluence, the poor, to business practices, to war, and governmental sin. . . .

We will always be shocked when we see Christianity practiced until we are committed to follow Christ at all cost ourselves.

—*John M. Drescher*

Hooked on Hair

All of us have shared in or heard those conversations about long hair and beards. Usually I've noticed the spirit of the discussion is worse than what is considered the problem. There is more heat than light, more hate than love, and more feeling than fact.

One part which comes up in such discussions now and again goes something like this: "I know a school where long hair and beards are not tolerated. Every student must sign a statement and believe me it is enforced. We need more discipline like that."

Now it is true that some persons are scurrying the countryside sounding off concerning certain schools which they promise will clean young people of such practices. "If you send your young people to our school" such boast, "we'll guarantee you they will not have long hair [and note this] and they will return loyal, patriotic young people." Such also, although they never considered 1 Corinthians 11 relevant for women, suddenly see this passage as a proof text against boys with longer than they desire hair.

While one may have many reservations regarding long hair, sideburns, and beards, particularly the question of following a style set, in the main, by antigod youth some years ago, yet I've noticed some of the strongest reactors are those who many times set their standards by the antigod forces of mammon and the military.

So, since I have a choice, I prefer a school which does not spend time debating the length of a boy's hair but teaches the way of Christ in contrast to that patriotism which promotes a blind following of legal standards and military mind-set. Length of hair has been relative. But the Christian engaging in warfare is not relative.

We must be careful lest we allow our judgments to run with those who sympathize with an emotional reaction at one point while promoting an entire way of life contrary to the Spirit and teaching of Christ.

—*John M. Drescher*

1973-

THE PRESENT STAFF

What is expected of the *Gospel Herald* staff today? Not to have the last word as it might have been 75 years ago. But they may be measured by the role assigned to the Preacher-Philosopher of Ecclesiastes who "tried to find comforting words, but the words he wrote were honest" (Eccl. 12:10, TEV).

1973 -

Elva Yoder, secretary; Daniel Hertzler, editor;
David E. Hostetler, news editor

The Present Staff

Gospel Herald uses no color, no glossy paper, and few splashy visual effects. It has a small circulation by typical publishing standards—about 23,000 in the U.S. and Canada.

Yet within the Mennonite Church, the *Herald*'s block-letter nameplate and two-column layout are as recognizable as *Newsweek* or *The New York Times.* Readers from Archbold to Phoenix, and from Edmonton to Miami, use *Gospel Herald* as a source of church news—from ordinations and baptisms to reports of meetings, marches, and programs. It also provides personal news—births, obituaries, and marriages. And many people find inspiration, stimulation—and even anger—in reading the feature articles, letters, and "Hear, hear!" column.

At certain times and places, *Gospel Herald* has even functioned as a means by which Mennonites can identify one another. What better item to carry in the Pittsburgh airport, for example, when trying to make connections with out-of-town visitors one has not met before?

"*Gospel Herald* is the one medium which addresses virtually all aspects of Mennonite Church life, faith, and strategy," says Eugene Seals of Southfield, Michigan, vice-chairperson of Mennonite Board of Missions (Elkhart, Indiana). "Writers come from a broad cross section of theologians, farmers, musicians, administrators, sociologists, medical practitioners, and free-lancers."

Ruth Guengerich of Harrisonburg, Virginia, sees *Gospel Herald* as keeping "the East Coast in touch with the West Coast and the liberals with the conservatives." Reading the magazine is "a very good way to find out what are the strong movements in the church." The letters "tell us how diverse a body we have."

"One of the pluses of a relatively small denomination is the possibility of knowing personally many of the people involved in church life," says Abe Hallman of Akron, Pennsylvania. "The *Gospel Herald* keeps us informed" of what people in the church are doing.

According to a 1982 survey conducted by the magazine, Robert Baker's "I'm Listening, Lord, Keep Talking" column, the editorials, and the "Readers Say" letters column are the most-read parts of the *Herald*. Readers who responded also expressed strong interest in the feature articles, Church News section, Newsgrams, Mennoscope, Items and Comments, and "Hear, hear!"

Since late 1973, Daniel Hertzler has been responsible for general direction of the magazine. He normally prepares the longer articles and the "Items and Comments" section along with writing the editorials. Dan is an ordained minister and has served as moderator of Allegheny Conference and a member of the Mennonite Church General Board. A graduate of Eastern Mennonite College and Goshen Biblical Seminary, he holds a doctorate in religious education.

News editor David Hostetler joined the *Gospel Herald* staff in 1971. In addition to his half-time work with the *Herald* (editing the news section, second half of the magazine), he spends half-time as editor of *Purpose* magazine.

He is a graduate of Goshen College and Goshen Biblical Seminary. He also holds a master's degree in journalism from and has completed a residency in mass communications at Syracuse University, Syracuse, New York. Goshen College alumni, Dave and his wife, Rose, spent 1955-1969 as workers in Brazil under Mennonite Board of Missions.

The longest-term member of the *Herald*'s staff is neither Hertzler nor Hostetler, but Elva Yoder, who has worked as the magazine's secretary for nearly 17 years. She describes her job as "working between the editors and the production office and keeping things moving." She also handles correspondence and general secretarial work.

Having worked under Hertzler's two immediate predecessors, Elva is in a good position to observe changes made in the magazine. Largely due to increased postage and other costs, there are currently more 16-page issues and fewer 24-page issues than John Drescher published, she says. She also observes that Dan solicits most of his articles, especially lead articles, and has made increasing use of photo and art covers rather than starting articles on the front page. In content and style, Elva believes that the *Herald* is "geared a little more to the educated than maybe it used to be."

As for Dan and Dave themselves, "I appreciate working with both of them, because I feel that they're trying to be sensitive to the feelings of people throughout the church," Elva says. "I think they're dedicated to their work and to the church as a whole."

As editors of the Mennonite Church's official magazine, Hertzler and Hostetler see themselves "as keepers of the Mennonite tradition," Dan says. At the same time, "I don't view tradition as static. We're trying to keep the best."

Dan and he are "reshapers of tradition in a changing world," Dave says. As such, they need to allow different positions within the Mennonite tradition to be heard, he says. According to Hertzler, "our problem comes in discerning" when a view is so "aberrant" that it falls outside that tradition.

In making decisions about what to print, Dan uses different limits for different kinds of articles. Unlike editorials, which are written as an attempt "to interpret personally" what Mennonites believe, "letters are published not to define any doctrines or speak for the church. My understanding is that the letter-writer speaks for himself, generally."

Because of their nature, "letters are the most free" in what Dan will allow the writer to say. Hertzler does refrain from printing letters that appear to be libelous or seem wildly irrational. He also limits the number of letters he will print on one subject. Generally, though, "if a letter-writer wants to hang himself I figure that the readers can discern."

In feature articles, the limits are tighter. In these pieces, such controversial topics as homosexuality need to be handled carefully, Hertzler believes, because of their tendency to bring out "irrationality" in people. Some hot topics, such as the payment of war taxes, are best handled by printing an article side-by-side with responses from people with other viewpoints, Dave believes.

Neither of the editors wants to see disagreement banished from the *Herald*. Reporting controversial issues or "awkward situations" can often contribute to healing, by encouraging discussion, Hostetler believes. He cites *Gospel Herald's* coverage of the July 1979 consultation at Smoketown, Pennsylvania, as an example.

One goal of journalism is, if possible, "to make everybody think," Hertzler says. "If everybody felt somewhat condemned and somewhat reinforced by everything in the magazine, that would be ideal."

In some ways separate from the rest of the *Herald*—and outside Hertzler's continuum of expression—is the Church News section. While Dan carries final responsibility for everything *Gospel Herald* prints, Dave is primarily responsible for the choice and treatment of news articles.

The first news editor in the magazine's history, Hostetler was hired "in response to a request from church agencies that not enough news was being published," Hertzler says. "There was a feeling that we needed more professional coverage of the work of the church."

Dave views the news section as having both a mirroring and a "bulletin board" function. Mennoscope items and other news shorts provide necessary but less exciting information. They also provide an ongoing historical record.

More compelling by usual definitions of news are the reports and news features. The purpose of these is to reflect back to the church "what its boards, agencies, congregations, and people are doing," Hostetler says. If edited well, the news section over the course of a year should give the average reader "a fairly good understanding of what the church is doing."

In spite of the origins of his position, Dave believes he has a responsibility through the news section to "offer some critical look at our institutions. The reporting is not to sell the institutions, but rather to tell their story as objectively as possible."

At the same time, Dave recognizes the difficulty of doing that as a half-time editor. Of necessity, the majority of news articles that appear in the *Herald* are based on news releases from church schools, mission boards, and Mennonite Central Committee—institutions that have large communications staffs (at least in comparison to Hostetler and his few part-time reporters scattered across North America).

Despite such limitations, Hostetler believes the news section—and *Gospel Herald* as a whole—is playing an important historical role. "What we're doing is trying to record the work of God," he says. "There's a sense in which the book of Acts is a model."

The *Herald* focuses on a particular segment of God's people—in the magazine's case, the Mennonite Church. Indeed, the best phrase to describe *Gospel Herald* as it enters its 76th year may be "a people's paper." More than many publications, the *Herald* has readers who feel that the magazine is theirs and who have a stake in what it covers.

Because they care so deeply, *Gospel Herald* readers can be quick to criticize the magazine. Some people call it " 'social gospel' oriented" and humanistic; others say that it is "narrow" and irrelevant to the concerns of the larger world.

Some readers believe the magazine's emphasis on things Mennonite is a weakness as well as a strength. Lorna Beth Shantz Shenk of Harrisonburg likes the way the *Herald*'s personal news helps "keep us aware of what who's doing," but wonders "if it doesn't function just as much as a way for us to maintain our clannishness."

"One impression I have in reading *Gospel Herald* is that only what happens in the Mennonite Church counts and that everything outside it is bad," says Edward Taylor, director of home missions of Mennonite Board of Missions. "I have problems with that."

In response to critics, Hertzler often cites James 3:1-2, substituting "editors" for "teachers" and noting in verse 2 that "we all make many mistakes." He also "takes some comfort" from the saying that "editing is a cross between 'playing the horses' and practicing psychiatry without a license."

If editing is the imprecise task Hertzler says it is, *Gospel Herald* readers would do well to remember that the modern world—and the Mennonite Church of the 1980s—is at least as complex and difficult to define. To the casual observer, the Mennonite Church can often look like a crazy quilt or a haphazardly woven piece of cloth.

The mission of *Gospel Herald* is to help people take a closer look. At its best, the *Herald* sheds a corner of light on the Mennonite fabric—enabling readers to discover rich textures, frayed edges, and the common threads that hold it together, almost in spite of itself.

—*Dave Graybill.*

1974

If we truly want to take the local congregation seriously we will need to find ways to be with them and not simply in contact with them.

Send Us an Apostle!

by James M. Lapp

It's not that I don't appreciate the efforts of our leaders from Goshen, Elkhart, Scottdale, and Lombard. I very much do! In fact, when my Oregon brothers and sisters speak suspiciously of the leadership "back East," I feel a defensive spirit arise within me. It was only two years ago that I lived "back East." And I have worked closely enough with the churchwide program to value it highly and to know that there are sincere, dedicated persons working with integrity at the issues facing the Mennonite Church in North America. The statement of purpose in the Bylaws, that "the Mennonite Church is organized ... to enable and assist the congregations to fulfill their function and mission," I believe is right on target. The question that all of us wrestle with is how that enabling and assisting is best done.

Sometimes as a pastor, I feel as if our congregation does not need any more resources to evaluate, or programs to consider, or goals to work at, or issues to study. Not that we haven't been receiving solid and creative help from the churchwide boards and institutions. It is simply that I sometimes wish the larger church would send us an "apostle," rather than a booklet to read or an article to study. Of course, we benefit from those 24- or 48-hour consultations and contacts we have from time to time with churchwide leaders.

But consultations tend to result in more refined resources and better articulated goals

and more issues to study. I am coming to feel we would benefit more if the "consultant" could stay with us long enough to help us to develop some of our own resources and goals and programs that would arise from the body of believers in the local community, rather than provide us with materials from a Board of experts. In other words, at this stage in our life, persons would help us more than papers.

It may not only have been due to the slower and less efficient transportation in the first century that the apostles ministered for long periods of time in a given city. It may be this was considered necessary for a significant ministry of encouragement and assistance to the local believers. Might not this type of assistance to local congregations or communities of believers be valid for our day?

For years we have been sending deputations to foreign mission fields to encourage and support our missionaries in wrestling with the issues they face in establishing the church in new cultures. When are deputations sent to local communities of believers in North America, not to raise funds or to find out our needs and leave again, but to encourage us

James M. Lapp: The early church was not united so much by organization or mass meetings as by apostolic visits and letters.

and assist us in being the faithful people of God in our own cultural setting? In years past, I suspect that traveling evangelists, who would come to a congregation for a week or two, fulfilled to some degree this type of ministry of spiritual stimulation and support to pastors and local believers.

Might there not be a valid "apostolic" ministry for our day, when spiritual leaders would come and spend extended periods of time in a local area to enable the believers there to reflect on who they are and where they are going, to work on problems that tend to get neglected, to give objective feedback and counsel on life in the congregation(s) as they see it, and provide fresh teaching and spiritual insight to the church?

I believe there are a variety of persons across the church who would have the gifts to fulfill such a ministry, and may be able to take a "sabbatical" from the pastorate or institutional job every few years to fulfill this kind of assignment. It may be some of our denominational staff money should be put into persons who would move to another community for two or three months (or longer or shorter as it seemed most appropriate), rather than into persons who make briefer executive type of visits.

Such an itinerant or "apostolic" ministry might well be coordinated by the Mennonite Board of Congregational Ministries. Surely there would be a limited number of persons qualified or prepared for such an assignment. Traveling and short-term moves like this are difficult with a family. Maybe persons with families would need to take three months in a summer for a task like this. Perhaps we could use persons whose children are grown for a ministry such as this. Maybe we need to consider again the suggestion of Jesus and Paul that some persons should refrain from marriage or from bearing children for the sake of the kingdom.

I believe if we truly want to take the local congregations seriously we will need to find ways to be with them and not simply in contact with them. Just as frightening as individualism in America is the prospect of congregational independence and isolation. I sense the early church was not united so much by organization or common programs or annual mass meetings as it was by apostolic visits and letters.

It is interesting (and perhaps instructive), that when God came to visit the earth He stayed for 33 years in one relatively small area. The Apostle Paul seemed to feel it was not a waste of time to devote 18 months to making tents and ministering in the city of Corinth (Acts 18). It is fine to send Howard Charles to be a teacher among the believers in Ghana for a year. What might be the result if a few of God's choice people were freed for longer term ministries in the various communities of Mennonite believers in North America? It may be exciting to find out.

To Aaron Decter and Max Schenk

Dear Friends:

You included me in a recent tour of Israel conducted especially for editors of Christian magazines. I am grateful, for you have helped me get back my heritage. For 40 years I have been reading the Bible and comprehending its geography in a measure. Now I read it with new eyes, for I have personally witnessed the land where its most important events transpired. Nine days is too short a time to travel around the country from Dan to Beersheba, but it is something.

It is not that I have a crush on holy places. I do not believe that God is more present one place than another. In fact I am more comfortable this way, for the devotee of holy places opens himself to distress in Israel. It seems there are often either two or more places supposed to be the one where the event happened or two or more groups insisting that they should have its custody. But there is a kind of definiteness which comes from having traveled from Nazareth to Capernaum. Now I can feel the significance of *down* in Luke 4:31: "And he went down to Capernaum."

There is also the strange magic of Jerusalem. At first reaction, it seems a city of rocky hills (who would want them?) but the personality of the city grows on even the visitor. Militarily unsafe, as Major Horowitz told us, because of the higher mountains around it, Jerusalem has excited the imaginations and passions of friend and foe for generations. Having been there only two weekends, I begin to sense why this is so without being really able to explain it.

A part of this excitement must be related to the claims on Jerusalem by three different religions: Judaism, Christianity, and Islam. Since men can never quite separate religion from real estate and politics, these counterclaims have complicated the lives of its people.

Recently I saw a map of Jerusalem from thirty years ago which showed the city divided into four quarters: Christian, Armenian, Muslim, and Jewish. As we all know, more recently the city was parts of two countries. Now it is again politically one, but with divided loyalties. In fact, Jerusalem and the state of Israel serve as living parables of the dilemma of mankind. The world, like Jerusalem and Israel, is really a very small place. We must learn to live together somehow or we may all be destroyed. Yet there are enmities of short and long standing which drive people away from each other. To weep over the plight of Jerusalem and Israel is to cry for the world. Reconciliation to God is needed so that we may be reconciled to each other.

I was emotionally moved in Jerusalem by a visit to a memorial for six million Jews slaughtered in World War II. But I was encouraged to see beside it a Garden of the Righteous with 1,500 carob trees planted in honor of people who helped to save Jews from death during that troubled time. Carob trees were chosen, we were told, because they are evergreen and represent the psalmist's description of a righteous man whose "leaf does not wither" (Ps. 1:3).

At various times during the tour I was led to reflect on the incredible atrocities committed against Jews in the name of Christ. In Shakespeare's play, *The Merchant of Venice*, for example, conversion to Christianity is used as punishment for a Jew. What stretching of imagination and perversion of justice does it take to come to this? As members of a "non-establishment" church, we Mennonites also have had experiences when people could not bring themselves to accept us because we refused to fit their categories. Those memories are mainly behind us today, at least in North America, where we are seen as quite inoffensive and harmless people.

As Jewish rabbis, you organized the tour from a specific point of view. But your credibility was enhanced by including contacts with persons representing more than one opinion on Israel. Thus it is hard to come to a comfortable view about Israel. Indeed no comfortable view is possible, for as I mentioned above, it bears within itself many of the common problems of mankind.

Being a cautious Christian, I am not inclined to make rash statements. I am particularly slow to pronounce on modern Israel and its relationship to its neighbors. Perhaps, however, I may draw on the thinking of Frank Epp who holds that the movement of prophecy in the Bible is toward an increasingly larger view of God and His people. "The promised land," he says, "is extended rather than narrowed. Its people are increasingly known for their moral righteousness rather than for their military might. 'Jerusalem' becomes the eternal city of God and of man rather than the temporal city of a nation or tribe" (*Whose Land Is Palestine?* pp. 241, 242).

The biblical vision is always larger than we are able to follow. But it stands there as both judgment and blessing on what we attempt to do. When I get to this point as I often do, I wonder, where next? And the only answer that comes to me is to live with peace and service.

Through this short trip, the people of Israel and the Middle East are more in my mind and prayers than before. Shalom!

—*Daniel Hertzler*

1975

At the age of 50 one looks both ways. The past persists in memories and as a foundation for the life that one hopes is yet to come.

On Passing the Age of 50

In many respects one day is like another. From the beginning of life to the end of it, they follow in unbroken succession. Yet, no doubt, a part of the image of God in mankind is the ability, in fact the need, to organize the days into weeks, months, years, centuries, millennia.

And there is the urge to celebrate the passing of time. As individuals and groups go through life, they note occasionally that a major time block has passed. They pause to reflect on the meaning of what has gone before, what is, and what may follow.

The end of a year is a regular time for reflection. Decades, quarter centuries, and longer units are often seen as significant. And so with birthdays. Until about the age of two, the child has a birthday every month. Then it is yearly and as these are added, each seems less significant until about 75 or 80 after which each added unit is borrowed time and thus significant.

The young person generally aspires to be older until about 21 to 25 when adult privileges have been bestowed and aging is suddenly less desirable. After the age of 30, age differences blur somewhat. From here on it may be expected that in business the younger may command the older without resentment. And so the individual days and years pass with little notice. But one pauses a little more thoughtfully at the decade lines.

Those who went before have said that it is somehow different after forty. They tend to speak in parables which are not entirely clear, but the impression comes through to the younger of a bittersweet reality based on the realization that there is less of life than formerly, but more personal resources with which to enjoy it.

And what of life after 50? Here are a few thoughts written by one less than a week into his sixth decade. As noted above, there is no jolt as of crossing a barrier. As with the boundary between two friendly countries, the scenery on one side is much the same as that on the other. Except for the record on one's birth certificate and accompanying documents, one would not know that he had passed from one to another.

But with this evidence, the passing of the 50 line brings some new awareness. One observes, for example, that life must surely be at least half over. Though a number of near relatives have gone beyond 90 and a doctor with a straight face predicted that I would live to be 100, the knowledge is pressed home that life on this earth is not perpetual. Thirty years ago one knew this more abstractly. At 50 it begins to seem real.

Not that one would wish to go back, for life is a pilgrimage or race which has its own fulfillment. To use another figure, for 50 years life has been a slowly opening flower. The time may come when the flower begins to close, but that time is not yet. Though one has great admiration for 20-year-olds, particularly those of his own family, there is no desire to go back and join them.

At 50 years there are more than 40 years of happy-sad memories. And some memories of foolish things done which one would be glad to forget. One reviews the decades with certain notable events: the death of his mother at age 10, seeing the world from a cattle boat at age 20, heavy family responsibility at age 30, graduate program at age 40 (will he never get done going to school?).

At the age of 50 one looks both ways. The past persists in memories and as a foundation for the life that one hopes is yet to come. One begins to consider more carefully the possibilities ahead. What should one aim yet to be and do by the help of God? If there is to be only a decade and a half of professional life, how can this time be used most fruitfully? Is one now an elder statesman old enough to be taken seriously or already too old to count in a youth-oriented culture?

I believe in God and I have known the love of the church. At the same time I recognize that many aspects of life are puzzling, and death is in some ways the most puzzling of all. So as I accept the pleasures and pains of upper middle age I remind myself of Abraham, the biblical model of a forward-looking pilgrim. According to Hebrews, "he looked forward to the city which has foundations, whose builder and maker is God" (Heb. 11:10).

Age 50 is a time for renewal. In fact, is there not the need and potential for renewal at any age? For even as the process of death begins with birth, so must renewal. And this renewal, if it is directed by the Spirit of God is "into his likeness from one degree of glory to another" (2 Cor. 3:18). So be it.

—*Daniel Hertzler*

Not Liberated and I Love It

by Cena King

From what I heard about the woman being liberated—I guess I'm not! I should have been rebellious from the day I was born because my parents wanted their fifth child to be a son after having four daughters, and my older sisters wanted a brother and definitely not another sister. I wasn't—but I never wanted to be a boy. Farm life gave me the privilege of holding newly hatched chicks, milking cows, and helping make hay, even if I was a female. I could also bake, iron, sew, and play baseball.

I'll admit that in my courtship days women's liberation wasn't in the news, so I could, with undivided opinions, bask in the happy thought that I was a young lady being sought after and courted—by far the more desirable role! When a truly noble young man of sterling character asked me to share life with him, I was blissfully happy! I felt a real thrill of pride to write Mrs. before my husband's name. It gave me equal status and in no way did I feel that I was losing my identity—I still had my own name and his too. After our wedding day I continued teaching school. Some students called me by my maiden name and some by my married name—I was the same person—the same me.

Because I so deeply loved this man with whom I was sharing my life, I was most happy when over a year later I felt the faint stirring of a new life within my womb. I experienced a surge of ecstasy when I realized that my husband, the man who loved and cherished me, had fathered the unborn infant and it was my body so wonderfully made, that cradled his child. I feel a little sorry that man can never know this exhilaration of a new life—it belongs to women alone!

The women's liberation movement speaks much about jobs and earning ability. When our children were small and the family was growing up I met the challenge of homemaker while my husband met the challenge of provider. Neither of us counted hours to see who put in the longest day. Neither one of us felt the money belonged more to the one than the other. Never was I made to feel that my position was an inferior one because there was no pay envelope with it. We have a joint bank account and trust each other. Because my husband cares for me he bought household conveniences to make my work lighter and because I care for him I tried to make a cheerful, happy place for him to hurry home to.

Sharing life has multiplied some of our interests. We both enjoy wildlife, birds, music, and reading, but while my husband likes to hunt and fish, I enjoy writing and sewing. And he lets me be me and makes it possible for me to take courses and pursue my interests.

When I think again about being liberated, I can't think of anything to be liberated from! What should I ask for? I guess I'm not liberated—and I love it!

1976

To Hans Herr

There is an old house in Lancaster County, Pennsylvania, which bears your name in literature, though indeed the initials above the door are those of your son Christian. For some years I have heard about this Hans Herr house, but only recently did I take time to visit it.

It was a little hard for me to generate enthusiasm for an old house as a museum piece. I reasoned that a house is for residence, and if we cannot live in it, it would seem to have little value. But they were getting up a group of Mennonite editors to tour the house and I went along. Earl Groff took us through and he seemed not only well versed in the subject, but also most respectful of the Herr family and others of your time.

He told us that this is the oldest house in Lancaster County (the date of building was 1719) and that it was abandoned as a residence for many years. Instead, farmers had been using it as a tool shed, and a picture of the house before restoration shows that "moth and rust" had well nigh had their way with it. But money was found to restore it and now for a small fee we can get a glimpse of the context of family life in the early 18th century.

I guess what impressed us most was the evidence of how you coped with your environment. The house and most of its furnishings were made from the native wood and stone. Though it seemed small on the outside, the house was actually quite roomy and constructed for relative comfort and efficiency. For example, Earl pointed out that the fireplace was large enough for two fires, it had a built-in oven, the back of it extended into the next room for radiant heating, and the room upstairs drew heat from the chimney. Such efficiency has been quite foreign to us in recent years, for many have had poorly insulated houses which have been most prodigal with the fossil fuels used to heat them. But we are

getting the message that we cannot go on like this and so your example is instructive.

We were impressed also by a story of Indians coming into the house to warm by your fire during the coldest weather. We were told, in fact, that Indians and Mennonites always got along well in Lancaster County. (Being from the Amish tradition myself and remembering that some of our people were killed by Indians farther out on the frontier, I wondered if you knew something we did not. More likely it was that our people found themselves between the conflicting groups and were mistaken for the enemy.)

Of more concern to me than the shape of your house is the shape of the faith which has been passed on for almost three centuries. We have continued the concern for peace and love which your people cherished. Though some of your descendants doubtless became weary and left for other faiths or no faith, others have been brought in and so the people of your tradition continue until this day.

We have found, however, that a variety of theological forces has influenced us during the years so that the faith which the present generations received is not exactly what yours passed on. We find also that we do not completely agree among ourselves, but we keep going back to the Bible in an attempt to understand how its story and teachings should inform our life.

One of the sources of confusion among us is change. Though for the first two centuries after your time there was little change in way of life, it has recently been very rapid. For example, nearly all American Mennonites were farmers until my generation. Suddenly there has been a rush away from farming combined with a pressing in by the outside world. In the area where you once lived, this pressing in has come particularly in the form of tourism. In other parts of North America, a similar pressure has been exerted, though tourists are less in evidence.

We were not adequately prepared for this sudden change and some have made decisions that in the long run may be found unwise. Many, for example, have sold their farmland for commerce and housing when the voice of

166

the highest bidder was heard in the land. It is only land, they reasoned, and why should we not profit from its market value?

The Old Order Amish have resisted this tendency, for it is a matter of faith for them to try to keep the family down on the farm. We are tempted to consider them backward, for we have not seen in the Bible a direct commandment that one must farm for a living or that he may not sell his land to the highest bidder.

But recently some of our Bible students have dug a little deeper and noted that according to the faith in ancient Israel, land belonged to God and was used only by His permission and for His glory. Have we been shortsighted in our easygoing sale of land to the developer with the big money?

Earl Groff stressed that in building you planned for the future. The result of this planning is evident not only in the sturdy old house, but in the faith of those who seek to follow the way of peace today. Some of us believe, however, that we are today in a time of testing to find out whether people who have become prodigal with our land and other natural resources can preserve a faith worth passing on.

—*Daniel Hertzler*

The Hans Herr house near Lancaster, Pennsylvania: We are in a time of testing to see whether we can have a faith worth passing on.

What Makes Church News?

From time to time we ask ourselves what kinds of information you like to read in *Gospel Herald*. We are serious enough about the question to have conducted two reader-interest surveys in the past five years—one this year, 1976, and one in 1971.

Through these we have a fair idea of your higher and lower areas of interest, as well as an average grade you gave us for the job we are doing. You have told us, for instance, you often turn first to "church news."

So, we are forced to ask ourselves what makes church news. . . .

Ideally, church news should be the recording of God's action among us and our response to that action. In a sense, church news would be chapters added to the Book of Acts.

Since it is not always easy to determine what God is doing through his people in the world, it becomes difficult to report according to the above criterion. Furthermore, we assume God works in the most minute details of life. Thus the question of significance becomes important. You are probably not interested in routine matters such as church business meetings, baptisms, and the like unless they affect you or your family and friends.

Where do we begin, then? Well, our research has confirmed our hunch that you still see yourself as a part of a church family. Births, marriages, and obituaries are important to you.

Theoretically, we agree the congregation is where the real action takes place. In practice, however, we have not been entirely successful in obtaining news from congregations.

What kinds of stories might interest the reader in Oregon as much as the one in Florida or New York?

How about innovative approaches to any of the routine activities in your congregation such as in the areas of worship, Christian education, or evangelization? Significant celebrations? Or maybe you have brothers and sisters in the faith who are making important contributions to your community?

There are also catastrophes, such as the one suffered by five members of the Springs (Pa.) congregation who were killed in an automobile accident. When your congregation suffers, the broader church suffers.

Then we call news that which reports on the work of our church boards and agencies in missions, education, mutual aid. Names like the General Board, the Board of Congregational Ministries, the Board of Education, the Board of Missions, and Mennonite Central Committee may or may not sound familiar. But the bulk of our reporting comes from these agencies and their projects. We may have a disproportionate amount of information from these organizations in comparison with that from congregations or districts. Check back issues of the *Herald*.

There is also a heavier side to the news. We have worked hard at bringing you the "good" news from every source. But this has led some perceptive readers to question whether nothing bad ever happens in the church.

Generally speaking, church boards and agencies, including Mennonite Publishing House, depend on your confidence and support to keep doing the things you want done. Therefore, it is not likely that anyone who is dependent on your good will wants to do anything to offend you or to cause you to lose confidence. Thus, stories of poor decisions or failures are sometimes omitted for this reason and to avoid hurting those involved. This does not mean there are cover-ups. It simply means there are questions as to how much bad news you really want to hear.

We believe it is our duty to pursue the whole story whenever that is necessary. We believe that withholding negative information, though seeming to be a good thing in the short run, is self-defeating in the end.

It is our goal to carry all the news necessary for your understanding of how the church is functioning, whether good or bad. We know that since our cause in Christ will be victorious, good will eventually overcome evil.

We will continue to go after all the information that's worth printing and to do what we can to carry the news with excellence.

—*David E. Hostetler*

1977

Mennonites have faltered in facing up to the high cost of following Christ in the painful detail of day-to-day living, and yet their dream lives and moves their spirits.

The Mennonite Dream

by David Augsburger

Mennonites are a people with a dream. A dream that has kept them alive for centuries, four and one-half centuries.

"It is an impossible dream," say some who hear it, "and small wonder that it has had less than success!"

"It is a possible dream," Mennonites reply. "It has not been tried and found a failure; it has been tried and found hard—and then men hesitated to pay the cost."

Yet the dream has endured. Surviving its enemies who tried to stamp it out, surviving its friends who tried to soften it up.

The dream is yet alive, leaping generation gaps, bridging theological gulfs, and linking east with west, right to left, liberal to conservative.

Mennonites have a dream.

A dream that it is reasonable to follow Jesus Christ daily, radically, totally in life.

A dream that it is practical to obey the Sermon on the Mount, and the whole New Testament, literally, honestly, sacrificially.

A dream that it is thinkable to practice the way of reconciling love in human conflicts and warfare, nondefensively and nonresistantly.

A dream that it is possible to confess Jesus as Lord above all nationalism, racism, or materialism.

A dream that it is feasible to build a brotherhood church that is voluntary, disciplined, and mutually committed to each other in Christ.

A dream that life can be lived simply, following the Jesus-way in lifestyle, in possessions, in service to man.

Who are these Mennonites?

They appeared first in the early years of the Reformation as a third way. Neither establishment Catholic, nor reformation Protestant, they called for a new revolution—a restitution of early Christian patterns, a restoration of primitive principle and practice as taught by Jesus.

As the first free (non-state-aligned) church, they called for a whole new approach to Christian faith—the new approach demanded by simple obedience to the teachings of Christ without accommodations to any culture or caesar.

They confessed Jesus as Lord voluntarily.

Symbolized it in voluntary adult baptism.

Crystalized it into a voluntary

brotherhood church.

They confessed Jesus as Lord radically.

Demonstrated it by following Jesus simply and sacrificially.

Certified it by obeying Jesus nonresistantly in love, even unto death.

They confessed Jesus as Lord universally.

Professed it by separation of church from state.

Practiced it by refusing nationalism and warfare.

From its beginning, January 21, 1525, in a meeting of men at prayer, it spread from Zurich, Switzerland, across Europe as a people's movement, a revival of personal faith in Christ.

Persecution and martyrdom followed from Christians on right and left. In the first decade there were over five thousand identified executions.

Men, women, children died at the stake, the rack, on the block.

Almost the dream died with them. But the flame, once caught, flamed out again . . . and again until, uncontrolled, it blazed through Christian groups of many churches, voluntary churches.

These gradually crystallized into denominations of many persuasions.

What persecution could not kill, adoption by the broad streams of Protestantism almost did.

And yet the dream lives.

It's a dream that dies hard.

Again and again it springs back to life, - probing like a conscience, attracting like an unforgettable love that lives on in the heart. Yet when the moment comes to turn dream to reality, all too many men falter, rationalize, and come up with some blend that is, as they say—"more responsible with things as they are" or "more sensible in light of complex modern problems."

Yet when the dream does appear in reality it takes shape in tangible, practical, concrete ways.

First—the dream appears in a radical conviction that the way of Christ can be followed unconditionally in day-in, day-out family-business-social life. It affirms that Christianity is not primarily something to believe and know, but Someone to experience and follow.

"No man can know Christ truly except he follow Him daily in life," wrote Hans Denk, an early martyr. There is no true faith in Christ, without discipleship to Christ. The Sermon on the Mount is an operator's manual for living . . . .

There can be no gap between faith and life—if we follow the Christ.

Christ can be followed—unconditionally—in life. It is no idle dream. It becomes reality.

Second—the dream appears as a radical commitment to the way of Christ in reconciling conflict through love. Nonviolent love. Even suffering love. It accepts the obvious truth that Christ called His followers to nondefensive love that seeks to bring understanding, forgiveness, and oneness wherever possible and to suffer nonresistantly where it is not.

Thus they refuse warfare, or violence in any form. Not because it is too dangerous, but because it is too weak, too shortsighted, and inevitably self-defeating. But the Christ-way of suffering love is the way of eternal victory. . . .

There can be no gap between love of God and love of man—if we follow the Christ.

Christ can be followed—unconditionally—

in nonviolent, loving forgiveness. It is no elusive dream. It becomes reality.

Third—the dream appears as a radical dedication to making each fellowship of Christ's followers a brotherhood of transformed people, joined together voluntarily to Christ and to each other in loyalty. Such a people knit together by love, share in witness, in common service, in responsible discipline, and in mutual aid. They stand together, suffer together, worship and work in cooperation with each other.

They become a family—with all the diversified uniqueness of many parts and with the richness that the gifts of all contribute.

There can be no gap between witness and service, between faith and action, between evangelistic concern and social concern—if we follow the Christ.

Christ can be followed—unconditionally—in forming an accepting, witnessing, serving, redemptive brotherhood. It is not an unreachable dream. It, too, becomes reality.

For four and a half centuries . . . men have struggled with this hope of unconditional discipleship. They have been unable to resist this vision of radical discipleship.

They have been misunderstood by nationalists who identify love of Christ with love of country.

They have been discriminated against by men who place final trust in violence and not in the way of Christ.

They have faltered in facing up to the high cost of following Christ in the painful detail of day-to-day living, and yet their dream lives and moves their spirits.

So they seek to make it reality in flesh and blood relationships.

So they live that Jesus may be Lord amid the sweat and tears of living.

So they give themselves that the way of Jesus may be seen and known here and now in the twentieth-century tangles and complexities of life.

Is that not the call of the Christ?

Know Him truly.

Follow Him daily.

This is Life.

1978

We Decided to Forgive Them

by Simon Schrock

This time they were caught in the act. Some young people were failing to respect the property of others. There had been some problems earlier, but it was hard to find out who really was doing the dirty work. One blamed the other and the other "didn't know" who it was. However, this time they were caught in the very act.

On this hot Sunday afternoon they strayed into our yard and picked some precious Golden Delicious apples from the tree. Since the apples weren't ripe, they didn't pick them to eat. They took them to the next door neighbors to throw at the huge hornets' nest near the peak of the roof of the garage. Of course the hornets' nest was damaged and the ventilator was bent from being hit with hard green apples.

We confronted several of the offenders and asked them to round up the others who were involved. Soon they were all on the street to tell their story. What is wrong with picking a few apples? they wanted to know. They even volunteered to pay for the apples. They suggested buying some at the store to replace what they pulled off the tree.

At this point, I felt the issue was not so much the value of the apples as it was respecting the property of others. I felt they needed to learn this respect while they were young. They needed to realize that taking an apple is wrong and that the wrongness is not in the size of the offense. Therefore, I wouldn't settle for just a replacement of apples.

Here were my terms. Since our Choice Books headquarters is located at the entrance of our street, I requested that each one meet me there the following morning. The penalty was going to be stiff. It would be two hours of work. Part of it was going to be cutting and trimming weeds around the building. There was another alternative. They could return to see me with their parents. In the event their parents would not support this action they would be relieved from the penalty. So they had the choice—work for two hours, or see me with their parents.

Since this happened in the afternoon, I had some time to think through the incident and how I responded to it. I wondered whether my action was a proper response for a Christian to take. Since I am not the owner of things, but a steward, how would God want His children to respond to destruction of His property?

I thought of the young people. They need to be loved, they need companionship and acceptance. The parents worked, which left them alone much of the time during the day. Is there another way to show love and at the same time teach respect for others and their property?

After serious thought and discussion with several other Christians who heard the incident I changed my mind and decided to forgive them with no strings attached. (That is what forgiveness means.) We will let them show up the next morning at the agreed time. Instead of requiring them to work we will take time to explain forgiveness and show them from the Scriptures God's plan of salvation. We will explain what the forgiveness we received from Christ meant to us. That His forgiveness sets us free and releases us from paying the penalty ourselves. This would be an opportunity to illustrate to them what forgiveness really means.

We prepared for the arrival of the group. I outlined Scripture verses and made enough copies for each to have one. My partner who had witnessed the ordeal picked up a box of donuts. The young people arrived, anxious to see what their penalty would be. We sat around a table, passed the donuts, and discussed the incident. Most of them showed signs of regret and saw the point of respecting the property of others.

We had a good discussion on stealing and principles for living. Then we looked at the Scripture verses together. After telling them

that Christ has forgiven us, we explained that because of His forgiveness to us—we decided to forgive them. Forgiveness means they can now go free. They may go home without working. They are released from the penalty.

Forgiveness opened other doors. To maintain relationships with them, we invited them to our house for a game of volleyball that evening. We had a good game, followed by devotions and refreshments. On another night the young people stayed around and asked questions about God, hell, and other important subjects that opened the door to sharing God's way of life.

Because we decided to forgive, they went free and later I pulled the weeds and trimmed the grass. Forgiveness to another means he is released from further demands. That is what Christ did for us. He paid our price for sin so we could go free.

I think it was the right thing to do. It healed relationships and opened doors to further friendship and discussion of God's Word. I trust God's Spirit will lead them to seeking God's forgiveness through our Lord Jesus Christ.

Simon Schrock: Forgiveness to another means he is released from further demands.

The Man Who Started Packing

Our congregation invited Peter Dyck to tell the story of the 1947 deliverance of some 1,300 Russian Mennonites from Berlin. It is a story fictionalized by Barbara Smucker in *Henry's Red Sea* (Herald Press, 1955).

The story is rather long and Peter, who was one of the chief actors, took plenty of time to tell it. First he gave a verbal presentation. Then he followed with movies which he himself had taken. The whole took close to three hours, but most of the audience remained until the end.

He described the lengthy process of seeking the help of the United States Army to get the Mennonites out of Berlin. Permission to leave was negotiated, but then it became clear that it would not be safe to take these people through the Russian zone without Russian permission. But no one knew how to get Russian permission when all other Russian refugees were being sent back to Russia whether they wished it or not.

So although a ship had been chartered to take them to Paraguay, Peter had to tell the Mennonites in Berlin that they could not go on the ship to Paraguay. The refugees took the news calmly, for they lived with many disappointments. But someone began to pray for a miracle.

After the meeting, Peter reported, they went to bed, but then one man began to pack his belongings. In a crowded refugee house one person does not make a move without others knowing, and soon many were packing. In reflection on this episode, the man who started packing stands out as a key actor. For when word came that they were permitted to leave, the refugees were ready and waiting.

In simpler times one would give thanks to God and go on from there. But today as we give thanks we also wonder about the explanation. How did it really happen that these Russian Mennonites got permission to come to the West? The answer is that an American general challenged a Russian general to make a decision. So the Russian did—he signed papers giving permission for the refugees to leave—and the process began immediately. The man who started packing had helped to get them ready and within hours they left.

There seems not to be quite so rational an explanation of how the train crossed the border without being checked by border guards. As Peter Dyck tells the story, while he and the engineer were chatting, the railroad signals suddenly changed to "go" and the train simply crossed the line.

Immediately, questions come to our orderly minds. Why should these 1,300 Mennonites be delivered and thousands, perhaps millions of persons, be sent back? Did God have a special concern for 1,300 Mennonites? Like Job's comforters, the conventional wisdom cannot answer questions like these. Nor can we. But we can still applaud the man who started packing. Who knows whether the deliverance might not have collapsed without his prompt and decisive action? He seems in the tradition of Abraham, who, according to the Scriptures, left home not knowing where he was going.

Now it is appropriate to maintain an open and tentative spirit in our relations with God. There is mystery here and to deny it is either to close our eyes or to frustrate ourselves. In *The Christian Belief in God* (Westminster Press, 1963), Daniel Jenkins complained of some groups who give the impression they know all about God. On the one hand, he identifies Christian groups who are piously confident that God is on their side. On the other, he places "most naturalistic philosophers" who assume that God is not at work in the world.

In contrast to these rigid attitudes is the humility that accompanies faith. It is open to God and open to experience, but does not demand that either God or experience must conform to predetermined categories.

Just the same, as experience develops, there comes a time to move in faith. For Noah building the ark, Abraham starting for Canaan, or Jesus on the way to Jerusalem, destiny was tied into decision-making and action. So, for the unnamed Mennonite refugee in Berlin, it was time to begin packing.

—*Daniel Hertzler*

1979

A Love-Hate Affair with the Automobile

Americans, it has been said, have a love affair with the automobile. Though I have not heard the same expression used with Canadians, it would appear that the same principle applies.

Both are countries with large areas having relatively thin population. Both have been highly committed to road building. Both have had large petroleum deposits. Both have been rich enough to pay the bill to develop, market, and service the family car. So the auto has become a basic piece of furniture on the North American scene. Hardly anyone raises questions about the automobile. Maybe someone should. This is to raise a few questions about the automobile.

Certain types of autos have been likened to a mistress. The analogy has some meaning. Not for Henry Ford's Tin Lizzie, which would more logically have been likened to a maid of all work. But the modern passenger car in many cases seems more attuned to frivolity than utility.

I was smitten by the automobile early, but my father stood in the way. A bad investment, he said, sounding like a surly stock broker. You can do nothing but lose. He was so right his words should have been framed, though I did not enjoy hearing them any more than the next teenager. The situation was made worse because my teenage years coincided with a war and car prices were inflated. So I held off for some years and then raised the question again. By this time the opposition had collapsed and I have been involved with autos ever since. In 30 years I have held title to 10 cars and poured into them more money than I would care to think about.

A personal car is a convenience, for it is on call at any time to go wherever one wishes. But the auto as personal transportation has several flaws. For one, it spends too much time idle. An auto driven 12,000 miles a year at an average of 40 miles an hour would be in use 300 out of a total of 8,760 hours, or 3.42 percent of the time. During the other 96.58 percent the auto is simply depreciating away its value. And how it does depreciate!

In addition to a poor use of time, the auto makes poor use of space. Thus it is particularly inefficient in the city or wherever a lot of people need to be moved at the same time. The heavier the traffic, the more it gets in the way. Yet our independent nature drives many of us to travel one person to a car, even in heavy traffic. Buses or trains would be a much more efficient way to travel.

A more urgent problem of auto travel is the danger to human life. No other form of transportation except general aviation is nearly so dangerous. According to *Accident Facts*, the 1975-1977 average U.S. passenger death rates per 100 million passenger miles were as follows: autos, 1.36; buses, .15 (inter-city buses .02); trains, .07; domestic scheduled air transport planes, .04. In 1977 the total number of deaths related to motor vehicles in the U.S. was 49,500, nearly 1,000 a week.

Indeed from 1900 through 1975 the total number of persons killed in the U.S. by motor vehicles was about 2,100,000. This compares to 1,156,000 U.S. military deaths in nine wars from 1775-1975. In another grim table it is revealed that Canada and the U.S. are fifth and eleventh highest respectively among 44 nations in motor vehicle deaths per 100,000 population.

Can nothing be done about this senseless slaughter? Yes, there are things which can be done. Because they do not seem dramatic or definitive, they may be overlooked.

Drinking alcohol is reported to be involved in at least half the fatal accidents with motor vehicles. In spite of this, a large majority of Americans drink alcohol. They are ignoring a clearcut safety factor.

Another specific safety device is safety belts. According to *Accident Facts*, the use of belts by all auto passengers in the U.S. would save at least 12,000 from death each year. Thus it appears that drinking and the failure to fasten safety belts account for two thirds of the annual U.S. vehicle deaths.

A more general solution promoted by the U.S. National Safety Council is *defensive driving*. The emphasis is on alertness, carefulness, and courtesy. If other drivers are careless or insulting, we need not be. In driving defensively, we may save both their lives and ours.

The implication is that if we conclude we must drive cars we ought to seek to drive safely. A short story written and told by John Ropp while a student at Eastern Mennonite College presented a conscientious objector who was stopped for reckless driving. The officer in the story exhorted him with words somewhat as follows: "Son, they are just as dead if you hit 'em with a car as if you shoot 'em with a gun!" Amen.
—*Daniel Hertzler*

It Does Matter How You Earn and Spend Your Money

by José M. Ortiz

Puerto Rico had three main cash crops: coffee, sugarcane, and tobacco. Staple foods like rice, beans, potatoes, and meat were imported from the United States. It was a typical case of colonial agriculture: the importer and exporter made the moves and also the money with the produce. As a tobacco raiser, my father had access to seed, fertilizer, insecticides, and funds for planting and harvesting. Planting tobacco was a family affair and all members were able to participate. Once the tobacco plants were removed, corn was planted, taking advantage of the fertilizer left by the tobacco.

On becoming a Christian my father became aware that tobacco was "hazardous to the health." The neighbors could not understand why he began to plant vegetables and grain rather than tobacco, the "cash crop." It meant no fertilizer, no seed, no subsidies, no sure markets, yet he went ahead because now he was a Christian, and Christians should not engage in producing those things that are harmful to others such as tobacco.

At that time I was graduating from high school. The agreement with my father was for me to finish school and help on the farm, or get a job and help him provide for the rest of the family of nine children. Other youngsters would quit at sixth grade, get married by the time they reached eighteen years of age, and have five to seven children by the age of thirty.

However, for me it turned out differently. At a youth camp I accepted the Lord and later on I wanted to go to Bible school. My father could have stopped me from going, and I would have respected and honored his decision, but he permitted me to leave home, making the family load heavier for him. Maybe he was true to the Hispanic tradition, that families reserved a son for the military and another for the priesthood. One would serve God, the other the king.

My father's favorite sport had been cockfights which is a pocketbook version of Spain's bloody bullfights. He used to put his time, skills, and money into the game. The money left from the cockfights sometimes went into "bolita," an illegal lottery. It is a pathetic picture to see the poor gambling among the poor. On becoming a Christian he found a new way of entertainment and a new way of looking at money.

Our congregation, the Coamo Arriba church, had won an attendance contest and the prize was $25. My father was present at the meeting and tipped the scales in favor of using it for a "Fondo de Ayuda Mutua" (Mutual Aid Fund). Later he was one of the founding members of the "Cooperativa de Crédito Menonita," a conference-sponsored credit union. Neighbors would stop at our house to borrow some money for buying food, and he would assist or send a "vale," a note to the grocery saying "charge to my account." He would not water the pigs before the sale nor pack the tomatoes with empty spaces between them.

Twenty years later he is still living with limited income as a worker in an egg processing plant and taking care of chickens at his own ranch which he rents to another farmer. At evening gatherings, he sits and talks with the neighbors about the Bible and politics. He is still a strong believer in the Popular Party. Politics in Puerto Rico is a pastime.

Faith is sometimes an expensive endeavor— it could mean a change of job, releasing the eldest son, sacrificing sports, moving from gambling to mutual aid, and sharing not of the surplus, but what is needed. The faith of my father is an expression of the power of the gospel to transform and live in the promise of Malachi 3:10: "Bring the full tithes into the storehouse, that there may be food in my house; and thereby put me to the test, says the Lord of hosts, if I will not open the windows of heaven for you and pour down for you an overflowing blessing."

1980

The radicals. The extremists. We who are 40 are on the lookout for them, with fear and trembling . . . and great expectation.

The Radicals

by J. Daniel Hess

Imagine, if you will, that the class of 1980 were the most radical of all graduating classes in the modern era. Not just a little radical, but radical radical. Not just the signing of a petition, or walking in a demonstration, or joining a revolutionary organization. I'm talking about being extremist in all of life. If we were to give these radicals a decade on the loose, we may learn ten years from now

—that they left their teachers and their teachers' assignments, and the next day they gave to themselves even more difficult assignments;

—that they volunteered for Mennonite Central Committee work in Akron, Louisiana, and Haiti;

—that some went to graduate school where they didn't forget who their parents were;

—that upon obtaining their first employment, they gave an average of 10 percent of their income to the work of the church, despite their college debts of $10,000;

—that they put in a full day's work and stayed till the floor was swept;

—that they trucked in honest weights and full bushels, accurate labels and authentic ingredients, fair prices and exact change;

—that they became rich, not from a glut of money, but from a lack of care and cumber;

—that they didn't covet their neighbor's house, nor the neighbor's attractive spouse, nor the sports car, the microwave, the oriental rug, the Jotul wood stove, the sound system, the job, nor anything else that was the neighbor's;

—that their men walked humbly and didn't confuse courage with arrogance, that those men were not rugged individuals from Marlboro Country, but servants who knew empathy and tenderness;

—that their women, grateful for their femininity, didn't opt to come a long way, baby, but chose to honor themselves, their men, and their God by giving their bodies to be temples of the Holy Spirit, their minds to be intellectual oases in the wasteland, and their emotions to the apprehension of all things beautiful;

—that their women and their men gave birth with love, teaching their children to laugh, to ask forgiveness, and to sing;

—that they put away their dead with the same reverence as they raked leaves in the fall;

—that they disliked artificial flowers, but cultivated roses;

—that they didn't need, for their sense of well-being, the year's Paris fashions, nor the latest intellectual *tour de force;*

—that they enjoyed good food, but retained a weight of two times their height in inches;

—that they baked bread on Saturday, and ate it with friends on Sunday;

—that the leftover food they respected no less than the firstfruits;

J. Daniel Hess: We who are 40 are on the lookout for the radicals, with fear and trembling and great anticipation.

—that they left the garden soil better than the year before;

—that they gave fruit as gifts, and cherished the well-sent smile;

—that they feared less for their own sanity than for that of the unemployed neighbor;

—that they learned to give a compliment without flattering, and to receive instruction without pouting;

—that they found the importunity of Emily Dickinson more compelling than the hyperbole of Howard Cosell;

—that they sought out good music as they sought good books—and they brought that same keen discrimination to dramas, movies, and of course TV;

—that although they had been to Central America, Poland, or China, they didn't have to travel far to live well;

—that they respected their allies and loved their enemies;

—that they supported militarism neither with guns nor dollars nor diplomatic shrewdness;

—that they believed in God, not to escape hell, nor to enter heaven, but because God is the great I AM;

—that they made chi-square tests but also believed in miracles;

—that they accepted neither unquestioned inspiration, undocumented argument, nor undisciplined workmanship;

—that, when asked if they were saved, answered on behalf of the shalom of the entire congregation;

—that they lived without guilt, yet did not pray for easy grace;

—that in church they worked in the toddlers' room, directed an MYF play, and volunteered support of the Board of Missions, Publication Board, and their church's schools and colleges;

—that they were not drunk with wine, but filled with the Holy Spirit;

—that their word was as good as their bond;

—that they feared the Lord and served humankind.

The radicals. The extremists. We who are 40 are on the lookout for them, with fear and trembling . . . and great expectation.

Foolishness?

"But anyone who says, 'You fool!' will be in danger of the fire of hell" (Mt. 5:22, NIV).

No one enjoys being made a fool. When I was a boy in grade school, I had high insteps. This had the curious effect of causing my toes to be slightly raised, which, in turn, made my shoes curve slightly upwards at the tips. This unfortunate circumstance provided an opportunity for a few of my schoolmates to call me "sled runners." Though I'm sure now this observation was innocent—not malicious—the impression made on me was indelible. I felt foolish because of a minor physical problem, which in time corrected itself.

Since then, I have experienced, on many occasions, a certain discomfiture because of a verbal or physical slip. Feeling foolish is not pleasant for anyone.

Sometimes we play jokes on each other with the calculated, but friendly, intent to produce a minor sense of embarrassment. Maybe we detect small traces of pride, or even arrogance, in a friend and our response is to help that person become aware of the problem, even though this purpose is never stated. We may be testing to see how a friend will respond to a practical joke. Or joking with each other, in this way, may merely be the result of a playful mood.

When I was younger, many of my friends enjoyed playing April Fools' jokes on each other and on me. I, too, liked to participate. But something in my background would not permit me to do this freely. In our home, it was understood that to call someone a fool was anathema. So that even the innocent joshing which occurred with an April Fools' joke was not encouraged. There was a certain soberness about our piety in such matters.

Apart from the fun that often goes with April Fools' Day, there is something strongly negative about being considered a fool. I suspect that behind Jesus' teaching, in Matthew 5:22, there is a profound sense of respect for the individual. Before God, each person is of great worth. Therefore, to hate or show contempt through derisive statements is cause for concern and stiff punishment. I am not saying that there is no room for levity in our relationships or that we should not participate in April Fools' jokes. But the importance of the people around us should never be underestimated.

Though I have delivered more than my share of anger, criticism, and backbiting, I have always felt unhappy and repentant, whenever this happens. I know that such activity can be extremely harmful not only with regard to the objects of my sin but also to myself. And I pray daily for the ability to rise above my own feelings about others to a level of understanding and love that forgives both my own shortcomings and those of the people around me.

Such effort is required every day, hour by hour, and sometimes moment by moment. Though I never actually call any of my acquaintances "fools," I, nevertheless, have acted as if they were, on occasion. I'm sure that others have felt, or do feel, the same way about me in the decisions I make and the way I live.

Thus, I feel that Christian love demands that we all work toward respect for, and the enhancing of, dignity in every person we meet.

On the other hand there is a foolishness we are asked to bear: the foolishness of the cross. We may not become so engrossed in cultivating our own wisdom and salvaging our own dignity that we lose sight of a wisdom that is "foolishness" to those who do not understand the upside-down nature of God's kingdom. This "foolishness" absolutely prohibits that we label another person a fool.

Today, April 1, is a good occasion for reflecting on these matters.

—*David E. Hostetler*

1981

Don't Ever Give to Beggars

by Jonathan G. Yoder

Trains are the worst. The beggars clamor around your window at almost every stop. White faces seem to attract them most. Some of them scoot along the ground, because they cannot extend their legs to walk. Some protrude their bandaged and ulcerated hands into your face, and the ulcerations are less than aromatic. Some hobble along on sticks with an arm or a leg missing. A lot of them are children or very old people who appear famished, and are very obviously not able to work.

But if you ever give to one of them, you are in trouble. The others become just that much more insistent. Besides we have been warned over and over again against pauperizing people, and we have been told about the "rich" professional beggars.

They surely know their profession well. They always bother you most when the train stops at a station where you are eating your lunch. The way they keep gesturing and patting their hollow stomachs, while you are filling your own, does really bother the digestion. We long ago learned that it is best to lock our compartment door and pull down the window blinds when we are at the station eating. Then we can eat in peace.

I am writing this on my typewriter here in my home at Dhamtari. Outside the window the women keep filing past in rows carrying dirt to build a road for our new hospital. When they line up with the loads of dirt in basins on their heads they look very graceful and the work does not look all that hard. And they duplicate what our massive earth moving machinery does in America. They build massive dams, miles and miles of roads and canals. All it takes is hundreds and hundreds and hundreds and hundreds of basins of dirt—and the roads are built.

They are paid 40 or 50 cents a day to do this, and they are glad for a chance to get the work. But whenever we white people walk past, they ask, "Kiya time hi?" (what time is it) and the question becomes more urgent about the time the work is supposed to stop for lunch.

I really prefer pounding the typewriter to carrying basins of dirt all day for 50 cents. Maybe we should double their pay. But then all the downtown merchants would complain about how the foreigners splash their money around, and about the way they upset the whole Indian economy. So I cannot do that. Then, maybe I should grab a pick myself, and give Fyrne one of our basins to help carry dirt. That way we could "identify" with the people whom we are trying to help. But somehow I just continue sitting here at the typewriter and I keep writing about building bridges. Also I keep pulling down the window blinds when I eat on the train.

I have a lot of old friends around Dhamtari. They come to our home for tea, and they invite me to their homes. They stop me in the bazaar and show me the scars of past surgery I did for them. They are so friendly and they are most grateful. So we do know that we have built some bridges. But we are still far apart.

Sometimes I remember St. Francis who totally renounced his princely wealth, and became a beggar with the beggars. I remember what Jesus said about helping the least of these "my brethren." And then I am awed by the dedication of Mother Teresa who lives in total poverty and keeps giving everything for her own poverty-stricken people. They say her whole order of poverty-dedicated nuns exudes happiness. But Fyrne and I could never have lived like that. We had children that we had to rear and to educate in America. St. Francis and Mother Teresa had no children. So I draw down the window blinds again.

I will have this conflict settled shortly. I expect to return to America in four weeks. After I pass through customs and immigration I will not have to draw the blinds any longer. Customs and immigration restrictions will do that for me and the blinds will stay down. Inside the boundaries of the U.S. I can relax and enjoy it all.

Inside America people do not stand outside the windows and pat their stomachs while I am eating. But I guess we folks in America had better stop looking at the TV news. And I guess our newspapers should not keep publishing pictures about "underdeveloped" countries. There is no use getting behind the blinds, if you still mean to keep peeking out. Besides, it does bother my digestion.

My Personal Journey Through the Mennonite Church

by Anne Allen

This is a journey for me that travels back 27 years, considerably over half my life. I have experienced joy, encouragement, and fulfillment, as well as pain, frustration, and disappointment. As your mind travels with me I want you to know it is because of this journey that I am who I am today.

During the time that I was growing up in the small village of Lincoln University, I cannot remember going to any church except the Sunday school at the University at the age of 8 and 9 and that consisted only of play activity.

One hot summer day, the Mennonites from a nearby Mennonite church in southern Lancaster County were canvassing the village and invited my sister and brothers and me to Bible school. Being only a fifth-grader, this meant a new adventure for me

A year or so later, my family moved near the church where I was still attending on a regular basis. I had accepted Christ as my Savior and had gone through instruction class and was now a member of the Mennonite Church. I was not aware then of what impact this would have on my life.

My Sunday school teacher took a great deal of interest in me and influenced me enormously. She was very conservative and "plain." Being plain in this congregation 21 years ago meant hair parted in the middle, prayer veiling with a band of 1 and ¾ inches, veiling, ribbons, cape dress without a collar, long sleeves, black stockings, brown cotton stockings for the younger girls, and black shoes. I became a carbon copy of her in attire and thinking. I vividly remember being very proud as a 12-year-old in my "plain" garb.

My mother was not very pleased with my appearance and even more shocked that my regular clothes had very quickly become obsolete, as far as I was concerned. With my new instructions of how my life as a Christian should be different and separate from the world, she could not possibly persuade me to wear anything but my "plain" garb to junior high school or to go with the family to activities and occasional parties that played worldly music, such as jazz or rock 'n roll, or where anyone was engaging in any form of dance.

This created tension between my family and me. Then, I did not understand fully what being different from the world meant. To me being so-called "plain" was my savior.

The laughingstock

My little world of "conservatism" came crashing down on me during my junior high school years. I became the laughingstock of the school. No one else, especially among the few blacks in the school, looked like me. Mennonites were not known very well at that time

in the area where the school was located. The next year I enrolled at Lancaster Mennonite High School and I fit right into the mode of attire there and that problem was solved.

Thinking back over my years at Lancaster Mennonite High School, I think of it as the place where most of my Christian principles were formulated. The community of Christian teachers and students did leave a great impact on me in various ways. I lost my black identity. I wished to be like them in all aspects. Yet I knew deep within that I could never become a white ethnic Mennonite no matter how hard I tried.

Being so conservatively influenced in church and school, my high school years were so restricted that during my teenage years I missed many good activities a teenager should have been involved in such as seeing good films—Christian and non-Christian—roller skating, bowling, the beach, or amusement parks. My only social event was attending Christian Youth Retreat at Camp Hebron one week every summer. But I struggled through racist attitudes and slurs at Lancaster Mennonite High School and managed to graduate as the only black in the upper half of my class of 115.

As a Christian young person of 18 I suddenly realized that I had never really thought out or questioned anything that I had been taught. My secret idea I kept in the back of my mind was that I would leave this church when I graduated from high school and go out entirely on my own. This never happened because I realized later that the church had become my whole life. But I had to settle some of this teaching and Mennonite tradition in my own mind. Being so carefully taught that Mennonites are a quiet, humble, peacekeeping people (which are all good qualities), one thought long and hard before starting any confrontation with anyone who was teaching and leading. If one had any urge to do so, it was quickly suppressed.

In 1959 I received a call from Luke Stoltzfus asking if I would like to work in Philadelphia. So being a country girl I suddenly found myself at the age of 18 journeying to the large city of Philadelphia into another Mennonite setting which was almost identical to the conservative environment I had just left, although this has changed through the years. The main exception in this Mennonite setting was its situation right in the middle of a large black ghetto-type residential area.

Quite An Adjustment

Thus far, all my associations had been with white Mennonites except my immediate family. I left home at age 14 to go to Lancaster Mennonite High School, a boarding school, and never spent very much time living at home after that. So living in a totally black community and working in a totally black office was quite an adjustment for me.

Many things began to happen inside of me as I really began thinking for myself. I began to really question some of the Mennonite rules and traditions that I had been taught so well over the years. For example, why was it wrong for a Mennonite to marry a Christian from another denomination? It appeared to be a sin because a public confession had to be made. However, I can see both the advantages and disadvantages of this. I also struggled with the question, Why is it wrong for me to appear in public without my prayer veiling? Or why is it right for a Mennonite Church to be located in the middle of another culture and neglect to incorporate any of that culture into their worship services or use any of the gifts of the church members who are a part of that cultural setting?

As I began slowly to find my identity as a black person in a black environment, I had to break away from some of these traditions and rules. As a result, I fought an ongoing battle within myself for several years.

Regained My Identity

Over the past 21 years I have had my membership at Diamond Street Mennonite Church. I have had some good experiences there, but I have taken advantage of various opportunities to become aware of as much as possible about the total Mennonite Church. I have made efforts to get to know my black brothers and sisters in the Mennonite Church, and the Black Caucus has been the main chan-

nel for this. I have also made special effort to get to know Christians from other denominations. They have a lot to offer too. I am still learning, but through my experiences thus far I have regained my identity and the self-awareness that I need. I have settled to a great extent in my mind what I believe God is saying that we as the church and as Christians should be doing.

I have a deep appreciation for the Mennonite Church and what it stands for. It is because of the Christian principles that were taught to me in the early years of my life that I am what I am today.

1982

The Day I Went Public with My Faith

by Martin W. Lehman

Three months ago I read *The Company of Strangers* by Parker J. Palmer (Crossroad, 1981). According to Palmer I've kept my faith a private matter. True, I'm an ordained preacher (proclaimer) but my preaching has been in a church, and mostly to my friends. I've preached to few strangers.

I decided it was time for me to go public with my faith. In little ways, I did. But what I did in Sarasota at the June 12 Rally for a Nuclear Freeze Now surprised me.

The surprise began twelve days before the rally. Mr. Moss, rally coordinator, called the Southeast Mennonite Convention office to promote the rally among Mennonites. In response to questions he told me of the religious organizations supporting the rally. He said that the religious leaders of the community would be asked to speak from 3 to 5 minutes. Persons speaking would represent the United Methodists, the Catholics, Friends, Unitarians, Congregationalists, and Jews. I was surprised to hear myself say—"Would you like to hear from a representative of the Mennonites?"

Nervousness followed surprise. I told myself I was ready to go public with my faith. But *that* public? On an issue many Mennonites would leave to Mr. Reagan? And in a manner distasteful to most of them?

I didn't do much to promote the rally. More of my time was used to get ready for my own participation. I told only one of my fellow ministers of the possibility that I would speak for Mennonites at the rally. He encouraged me. And I fasted.

On June 12, I went to the grounds of Sarasota High School, the staging area of the parade. I expected to be the only Mennonite. Imagine how good I felt when four others appeared. ("J.C." later told me how nervous they were about this first-time experience.) I told them of my involvement, and together we marched a mile in the hot sun to the First Congregational Church.

At the church the several hundred marchers settled down for some music and the speeches. The speakers spoke of their personal pilgrimages and read statements adopted by their religious groups. So it was an appropriate setting for me to speak of a Mennonite point of view and of my own perspective on the nuclear freeze. When John Linehan introduced me, this is what I said:

"In my first conversation several months ago with John Linehan, he told me of his experience with Mennonites. He was gathering signatures in a Sarasota mall in support of the nuclear freeze when he saw some Mennonites coming his way. Here are peace-loving people, he thought. Sure signers. But they gave him a cold brush-off. John was puzzled by their behavior.

"I decided that if I had the opportunity to speak today, I would try to explain why the Mennonites of this community are not here en masse, and why I am here. (Four other Mennonites are here this afternoon, and I welcome their company). I do not blame Mennonites for not being here, for my journey here has not been easy.

"The Mennonite Church is known as one of the historic peace churches. It is over 450 years old. It celebrates its martyrs and mourns its soldiers. You might have expected the Mennonite Church to be in the forefront in the activities of this day. But it is not so. Here is the reason why.

"To the Mennonites, a nuclear freeze has several serious flaws. The call for a nuclear freeze is flawed by the condition that it be bilateral. It is the Mennonite understanding that Jesus meant for his followers to lay down their swords unilaterally and unconditionally. So Mennonites are slow to join a movement which is conditioned on the cooperation of the enemy.

"From the Mennonite point of view the call for a nuclear freeze is flawed by its focus on only one kind of weapon. It is our understanding that Jesus meant for his followers to put down all weapons—swords, guns, and bombs of all kinds [applause].

"For us, the war is over, for we will not fight it. So Mennonites are slow to join a movement which focuses on the elimination of only one class of weapons.

"From the Mennonite point of view the nuclear freeze is flawed by its obsession (that may not be a good word to describe it) with survival. We understand that Jesus meant for his followers to seek the welfare of their enemies rather than to be concerned for personal survival.

"Mennonites believe that if enemies are hungry they should be fed, if they are thirsty they should be given drink, that they should be prayed for and blessed, even at the risk of life. So Mennonites are wary of a movement which appears to be motivated by a wish for survival more than by love for one's enemy.

"I have told you as briefly and as directly as I know how, why Mennonites do not rush to the support of a nuclear freeze. I should also say that Mennonites suffer psychological numbness, and apathy, along with the general population. We, too, tend to deny that the horrors of a nuclear war will ever happen.

"So you ask me, if that's the way you Mennonites are, why are you here?

"A few months ago my wife and I came on an accident late at night a few miles south of

Eustis, Florida, on a lonely road. A pickup truck and two cars were involved. In the truck a woman's head was wedged between the end of the front seat and the door on the passenger's side. Beneath the woman's body a little girl with broken limbs was trapped under the dash.

"The door was jammed. I held a light while stronger men struggled with jack handles to try to pry open the door. The officers and medics arrived and they, too, worked with what seemed crude instruments to pry open the door.

"In that emergency we had no prior theological discussion before we began to work together. Lives were in danger and we perceived that their survival depended on our cooperation.

"I don't know whether the man working the jack handle was a Catholic, a Jew, a Protestant, or an unbeliever. He did not know who I was. It was not a time for us to have a theological discussion. It was a time for us to work together.

"I have deep religious convictions. I believe there are times when we should share our different faiths, understandings, and experiences. I also believe that the world is in such danger, that future generations are in such danger, such immediate danger, that I must lend what influence I have in support of a nuclear freeze.

"Yes, the tools with which we go about our work may be flawed. They may be as ineffective as the jack handle used to open the jammed door. But at least the tools are being used. And there is always the possibility that the door may pop open.

"And I work with you in hope. For I believe with the prophet Isaiah that the day will come when the lion will lie down with the lamb, when spears will be turned into pruning hooks, and when the nations will study war no more." (At this point there was a standing ovation.)

I report this incident for two reasons. It is risky for one person to state "the Mennonite point of view." Perhaps it was only my point of view, and it should be corrected. Also, others may need to be encouraged to go public with their faith, and what happened to me may be that encouragement.

To the Old Mennonites from a New One

by Timothy E. Rapson

I'm new to the Mennonite Church. I was raised in the Lutheran Church. I met Christ in an American Baptist church, but I found the family of faith in 1977 at Michigan Avenue Mennonite Church in Pigeon, Mich.

In 1980 my wife and I moved to Dallas, Texas, and joined the Dallas Mennonite Fellowship. The folks here were puzzled by the name Rapson—it is not your typical Mennonite name—but when they discovered that I was from the sovereign state of Michigan, they certainly knew the right question to ask. "Oh, you're an Old Mennonite, then?" To which I replied politely, "Well, actually I'm only 25...."

Two years and several Mennonite history books later, I have been educated concerning the various branches of the Mennonite family tree (the Old Mennonites, the General Conference Mennonites, and the Mennonite Brethren), and I understand there are more to come.

But now I must ask, "Who are we who as adults have chosen the Mennonite way, we who were not born to it?"

Perhaps the most specific name would be the "Non-ethnic Mennonites," but that sounds clinical, rather like a census report. The Quakers call their non-ethnics the "Convicted Quakers," which conjures up an image of tin cups and striped uniforms. (In fact, *all* Mennonites should be Mennonites out of personal conviction, whether they were raised in Mennonite families or not.)

How about calling these "convicts" the "Converted Mennonites"? Personally, I can't buy this one because I didn't convert either to or from anything to become a Mennonite. I merely found that the Mennonites believed just what I'd already learned from a simple reading of the Bible, and from trying to live a Christian life. Since I've found the Mennonites, they have shown me many more truths about the way, in one form or another, but the change has been by growth, not by conversion.

Of course, I didn't write all this without already having thought of a solution. Some of the other good choices that I considered were the "Becoming" Mennonites and the "Young" Mennonites, but I think that I would like most to be called a "New" Mennonite. We are new and strange to you, the "ethnic" Mennonites, and you are equally new and strange to us. Yes, I like that: The New Mennonites.

Now as a New Mennonite I realize that in most of my relationships with other Mennonites I will of necessity be on the receiving end. I've gained a people, a new understanding of God, and a challenging ethic. (I've even learned how to sing "acapulco.") What can possibly repay such gifts as these? Well, the New Mennonites definitely do have something to offer:

•A surprising number of "ethnic" Mennonites are loaded with guilt. They feel like such hypocrites because they can't be perfect Mennonite Christians in today's overwhelmingly consumer-oriented society. To these brothers and sisters we say, "You should have seen the hypocrisy in the churches we've had to come through to find the Mennonites. The Mennonites are at least conscious of the principles of sacrifice and discipleship. We can't say the same for everyone."

•Many "ethnic" Mennonites believe that the church must strive to be relevant to today's world. It must shed all its old-fashioned doctrines of pacifism, separation from the world, and good stewardship in order to emerge into the light of the energetic eighties as a Potent Force for Harmony and Good Feelings. After all, only the backward-looking, prayer-cap-wearing Senior Citizen Resource Personnel Anti-Zipper Brigades take that pacifism stuff seriously anymore. To this we New Mennonites can only say: never, NEVER, *NEVER!*

We did not accept pacifism and simple living because they are traditional, as a convert to the Republican Party would accept an elephant as his new totem. We found them to be integral parts of our devotion to Christ before we ever set foot in a Mennonite Church, yes, long before we ever sang a hymn in German. These same "old-fashioned" doctrines are what have made the Mennonites the most doctrinally sound Christian group in the world for 450 years.

•One great fault of the "ethnic" Mennonites I've known is that for all of their fundamental understanding of the faith, for all their beautiful hymn-singing, and for all their deep concern for the rest of the world, many, if not most of them, have a bad case of dullness. We ought to be a rejoicing people, instead of a sleeping one. We should be a creative people, a buoyant people, but instead we are stubbornly hanging on to everybody else's designs for cast-iron lifeboats, and are in danger of going down with the ship. Let's have some enthusiasm in our singing and sharing. Let's worship God with our hearts.

Thank you for listening.

Timothy E. Rapson: This is not the time for the Mennonite Church to shed its distinctives.

1983

The task of the *Herald* is to encourage both unity and faithfulness. An impossible task, but we still have to do it.

GH—75 in 83
A Reflection on Unity and Faithfulness

Like the Mene, Mene, Tekel ... which faced Belshazzar, the cryptogram above may need interpretation. So it will be provided right away and then we can go on with the discussion.

The *Gospel Herald* is due to become 75 years old in early April 1983. The cryptogram summarizes it. So what shall we do now? Seventy-five years is not very old. We know numbers of people who are older. But the *Herald* has never been 75 before and we want to undertake an appropriate celebration.

Celebrations have their good points, but they have on occasion led to excess. For example, it is reported that the engineer of the first railroad locomotive to have a whistle blew the whistle so continuously that he ran short of steam to pull the train. We do not wish to make too much out of this anniversary.

But we do see it as an occasion to undertake several things which might be done anyway. Two special publications are being planned in honor of this anniversary: an anniversary issue of the magazine to appear on April 5 and a book compiled of selected writing from our past. The special issue will come to all subscribers just as any other issue. The book will be available at a special *Gospel Herald* price....

This special issue is seen as an opportunity to look at where we were as a church, where we are, and where we seem to be going. This kind of glance about is useful occasionally and the special issue provides an opportunity to do it. In the meantime we go on with our regular work as we need to do. As noted above celebrations and holidays are good, but not too often and not too long. This is a mind-set, it may be, inherited from our Hebrew ancestors. As Genesis 1 reminds us, the heavenly bodies are not gods to be worshiped, but merely timepieces to help us keep track of where we are. So with holidays and celebrations. They are good for a change of pace, but our revelry should be of a sort that refreshes, and not something from which we need to recover.

So with our 75th anniversary. It is to be hoped that we can use this as an occasion for renewal, to ask the question, "To what extent is the *Gospel Herald* fulfilling its mandate as a magazine for Mennonites in the U.S. and Canada?" This is not an easy question to answer, for we know from experience that there is a variety of expectations and it is impossible to meet them all.

But this is no excuse. It is our understanding that the *Herald* is a publication for the whole church. It is not intended to serve special interests; it is for all interests. The task of the *Herald* is to encourage unity and faithfulness. Or faithfulness and unity. Put it either way.

Is this too big an order? Of course it is too big an order. But it is what has to be done. For a church is only a church if it is concerned about faithfulness to God as revealed in Christ. A church is only a church if it is concerned about unity. An individualistic Christian is a contradiction in terms. The coming of Jesus is seen in the book of Ephesians as a means to the healing of the rupture between groups with diverse backgrounds. A common solution to a common problem and a common destiny give us a common identity and we need to acknowledge it.

Now it occurs to me as I work my way through this editorial that unity and faithfulness are both abstractions and there can be considerable disagreement over when we have reached either one. And we may find them working at cross-purposes. The doctrine of the remnant is a durable one in our tradition. The

Anabaptists were dissenters. Included in the *Mennonite Yearbook* are lists of Mennonite and related congregations which do not affiliate with Mennonite General Assembly because they do not consider our definition of faithfulness as adequate. They would say there is not unity because there is not faithfulness.

Such groups are commonly written off as legalistic and irrelevant. These are charges they would do well to consider, for as long as they have conversation only with themselves, very little can be learned either way. But their challenge is one that needs at least occasional consideration.

Another anniversary coming up this year is the 300th anniversary of the coming of Mennonites to North America. This celebration is due to climax at Bethlehem 83, a joint meeting of two North American Mennonite groups. Here too the issues of unity and faithfulness are waiting to be discussed. When we get to know Christians—even Mennonites—of other locations or specific traditions two things tend to emerge. One is that we find more concern for faithfulness among the people of the other group than we had expected. On the other hand, they too have biases and blind spots which may be ministered to through tender, loving care.

In spite of the difficulties in definition and the problems of bias, the *Gospel Herald* cannot retreat from a position which holds together *both* a concern for unity and a concern for faithfulness. We may have occasion to give more attention to these issues during this anniversary year.

—*Daniel Hertzler*

To Live by Love, Not Die by Fear

by Lynn A. Miller

The nuclear freeze debate has brought about some interesting thinking within me on the pro and con of this issue. In the heat of this inner battle, and perhaps in some fear of the results of that other battle, my thinking has become the first casualty. For example, sometimes I have allowed myself to be pushed into a position just to make sure that I am not for something that my enemy is for. One of the current heroes of the new pro-family movement recently found himself on nationwide radio opposing a nuclear freeze because some of the people and money in the new European peace movement might have some connection behind the Iron Curtain. (I would be very surprised if the East German peace movement didn't have connections with the Eastern bloc!).

But the point is, the "love your enemy" commandment has been reinterpreted to mean "love your enemy's hates and hate your enemy's loves." The love in the Matthew 5:44 commandment is agape love, the love that has the best interests of the other person at heart. Is the death of my enemy really in his best interest? Or in mine? Is intimidating my enemy with a bigger weapon the best thing for me? Or for him?

And what about the death of Christians and noncombatants living near the enemy's bases? Is it possible that the message of the redeeming love of Christ is what the enemy needs most and that it is the thing what is best for him? Can that be delivered in the nose cone of an ICBM?

Or, take the fear that prevents me from seriously considering a unilateral disarmament (note that the current debate insists that we will partially disarm only if, at the exact same time and in the exact same amount, the enemy does the same). Real unilateral disarmament says, "Okay, I'm going to lay down my arms no matter what you do." And what would the enemy do? What is the worst possible case?

Would the enemy immediately blow me to smithereens? That wouldn't make much sense. I can't or won't, resist, and there would be nothing left to plunder. And where would the enemy get the extra grain that he needs so badly that he buys it from me, his enemy?

Well then. Wouldn't he just invade and occupy? Praise the Lord! What a great opportunity to evangelize these people whom I have called godless all these years. And far cheaper than my going as a missionary to their country. And besides, if the Red army can't manage to keep their own economy afloat, how are they ever going to deal with ours?

And what about the other half of this schizophrenia of mine? What is particularly horrible about nuclear war? Were the atom bombs of Hiroshima and Nagasaki more painful or more horrible for the victims than the firebombs of Dresden or Tokyo? Is immolation by nuclear fireball somehow more evil than immolation by flamethrower? After thinking this through, neither seems to be worse to me, or even the real evil. Rather, isn't the willingness to use either weapon to hurt the enemy the real evil?

And what about my fear that all life on earth will end by nuclear war? Do I really believe that the end of mankind will be determined by mankind itself? Do I really believe that humans have the power to bring about the Eschaton? What happened to my omnipotent God? Have I made him captive to my arrogance and self-interest? Perhaps a more realistic fear for me would be that nuclear war *not* annihilate all life, that we would go on killing each other off, one fireball at a time.

Just what am I afraid of then? I think that mostly I am afraid of what I don't know. I am terrified of the dark, that blank spot in my knowledge of the future. I am frightened because I cannot predict the actions of my enemy. So I take precaution and build high walls in order to force my enemies to do predictable things. *And they do this to me!* I have been trained so well by my enemies that all they have to do is to say something about what they want, and I will oppose it. And, if they can get me to somehow think that they hate something, then I will do anything I can

to make that come about. And vice versa.

It is time for me to do something about this. It is time that I begin telling the rest of the population of North America that the enemies I am pointing these missiles at are mostly just real folks like me. I need to tell my fellow North Americans that the target is good old Uncle Jakob and overweight Aunt Sonja and their five children. And that the youngest of the five just got braces on his teeth (you should see what that cost in rubles), and that the oldest girl got engaged to the boy down the block just when everyone thought that she would never get married.

I could start by showing the family snapshots of my cousins and nephews and nieces who are people first, and Russian citizens only because of where they live, and who are just as much afraid of our government's actions as I am of theirs. I could begin to put faces on the enemy, to turn the unfamiliar into the familiar, and the unknown into the known. I need to put some light on the dark spot in my mind, to illuminate the shadows in my paranoia. Can you really imagine wanting to threaten old Uncle Abram? He may be a doddering old man, but does that deserve a nuclear response?

Or, am I too sensitive to the possibility of being called a traitor to this, my homeland? Am I afraid of being labeled the enemy? And being mistreated because of that label as German-speaking conscientious objectors were in WWII? Is it too costly to be an "enemy-lover," the very thing we are called to be in that Matthew 5:44 commandment of Jesus?

Lord, help me to see that it is my "enemy" who needs my loving, not my pride or my fear. I want to live by love, rather than die by fear.

Afterword

Like a moving train, the work of the *Gospel Herald* goes on. The *Gospel Herald* inherited a 40-year tradition from its predecessor, the *Herald of Truth*. Viewed in this light, its 75 years do not seem so long.

Nevertheless, 75 years is a significant block of time and these last 75 years have been an important era in the history of the North American Mennonite Church. As I implied at the beginning, the selections could not do justice to this creative period in our history, but they provide glimpses of what was happening and what was on people's minds. The final brief article touches on one of the more troubling issues of our time.

If I have called on Zechariah 4:6b at the beginning, what is an appropriate text for an ending? Should it be Romans 8:31b: "If God is for us, who is against us?" Or 1 Corinthians 1:25b: "The weakness of God is stronger than men"? Either of these would do, but I believe I will choose Revelation 5:5, 6: " 'The Lion of the tribe of Judah, the Root of David, has conquered. . . .' And . . . 'I saw a Lamb standing, as though it had been slain.' "

This is the model of leadership which the Lord has provided. Who can follow it?

Paul Erb, second editor of Gospel Herald, *with present editors Daniel Hertzler (left) and David E. Hostetler at grave of Daniel Kauffman in Alverton cemetery, three miles from Scottdale, Pa.*

Partial List of Authors

Alderfer, Helen. Has been an associate editor of *Christian Living* magazine since 1959.

Allen, Anne. Member of the Diamond Street Mennonite Church, Philadelphia, Pa.

Augsburger, David. Teaches pastoral theology at Associated Mennonite Biblical Seminaries, Elkhart, Ind.

Baker, Robert J. Junior high school science teacher and a member of Belmont Mennonite Church, Elkhart, Ind.

Bauman, Alta Yoder. Lives in Lancaster, Pa.

Bender, H.S. (1897-1962). Dean of Goshen College and then of Goshen College Biblical Seminary. He was editor of Mennonite Encyclopedia.

Berg, Ford (1917-1963). Missions editor of *Gospel Herald*, January 6, 1948, to June 26, 1951.

Brackbill, M. T. (1891-1962). Science teacher at Eastern Mennonite College and developed an observatory there.

Brunk, George R. (1871-1938). Moved from Kansas to Denbigh, Va., in 1910 where he became bishop of the Mennonite churches in southern Virginia.

Byers, N. E. (1873-1962). President of Goshen College, 1903-1913.

Derstine, C. F. (1891-1967). Longtime pastor of First Mennonite Church, Kitchener, Ontario, and a Mennonite revivalist.

Drescher, John M. Editor of *Gospel Herald*, 1962-1973.

Durr, J. N. (1853-1934). Served as a bishop in the Southwestern Pennsylvania Conference (now Allegheny) for 61 years.

Erb, Alta. Home life editor of *Christian Living* magazine, 1954-1959.

Erb, Paul. Editor of *Gospel Herald*, 1944-1962.

Fly, Harold M. Pastor of the Towamencin Mennonite Church, Kulpsville, Pa.

Funk, John F. (1835-1930). Editor and publisher of *Herald of Truth*, 1864-1908.

Gooding, Lorie C. Mennonite poet from Killbuck, Ohio.

Graber, J. D. (1900-1978). Missionary to India and served later as executive secretary of the Mennonite Board of Missions and Charities, Elkhart, Ind.

Hartzler, J. E. (1879-1963). President of Goshen College, 1913-1918.

Hartzler, J. S. (1857-1953). Member of Mennonite Board of Education, 1895-1917.

Hartzler, Robert. Pastor of the Washington (Iowa) Mennonite Church.

Hershberger, Guy F. Taught history and sociology at Goshen College. He is the author of *War, Peace, and Nonresistance*, *The Way of the Cross in Human Relations*, and many other publications. He lives in Glendale, Ariz.

Hertzler, Daniel. Editor of *Gospel Herald* since 1973.

Hertzler, Milford R. For many years a music leader among Mennonite congregations of eastern Pennsylvania. He is retired and living near Jessup, Md.

Horsch, John (1867-1941). Mennonite historian and editor who served at Mennonite Publishing House, 1908-1941.

Hostetler, David E. News editor of *Gospel Herald* since 1971.

Hostetler, John A. Sociologist and authority on Amish, Hutterites, and Mennonites.

Hostetler, Rosanna Yoder. Manager of the Provident Bookstore in Scottdale, Pa. She and her husband, David, were missionaries in Brazil, 1955-1969.

Kauffman, Daniel (1865-1944). Editor of *Gospel Herald*, 1908-1943.

King, Cena. Lives in Eaglesham, Alta.

Kniss, Paul G. Mennonite missionary in Bihar, India.

Lapp, George J. (1879-1951). Served as a Mennonite missionary in India, 1905-1945.

Lapp, James M. Pastor of students at Goshen College. He was formerly pastor of the Albany (Ore.) Mennonite Church.

Lederach, Willis K. (1896-1983). Superintendent of the First Mennonite Church in Norristown, Pa., 1921-1928.

Lehman, C. K. (1895-1980). Dean and Bible teacher at Eastern Mennonite College. He served as a member of the advisory music committee for the *Church Hymnal* and of the joint hymnal committee for *The Mennonite Hymnal*.

Lehman, Martin W. General secretary of the

Southeast Mennonite Convention.

Longenecker, Charles B. Teaches at Lancaster Mennonite High School.

Loucks, Aaron (1864-1945). General manager of Mennonite Publishing House, 1908-1935.

Miller, Lynn A. Recent student at Associated Mennonite Biblical Seminaries, Elkhart, Ind.

Minnich, R. Herbert. Pastor of Pleasant View Mennonite Church near Goshen, Ind.

Nelson, Boyd. Pastor of Bonneyville Mennonite Church, Bristol, Ind.

Ortiz, Jose. Teaches in the Hispanic Ministries Program at Goshen College, Goshen, Ind.

Rapson, Timothy E. From Carrollton, Tex.

Ressler, J. A. (1867-1936). Came to Mennonite Publishing House in 1911 and was for many years associate editor of the *Gospel Herald*.

Ressler, Lina Z. (1869-1948). Editor of *Beams of Light*, 1937-1946.

Sauder, J. Paul. Many services included being a Mennonite pastor in Tampa, Fla., and principal of Kraybill Mennonite School, Mt. Joy, Pa. He is retired and living at Landis Homes, Lititz, Pa.

Schrock, Simon. Pastor of Faith Christian Fellowship, Catlett, Va.

Sell, Glen M. Minister in Lancaster Mennonite Conference.

Shank, J. W. (1881-1970). Missionary to Argentina, 1917-1949.

Shetler, Sanford G. Author of *Preacher of the People*, Herald Press, 1982.

Showalter, Elizabeth. Editor of *Words of Cheer* at Mennonite Publishing House, 1949-1959.

Smoker, George R. Office editor of *Gospel Herald*, July 4, 1940, to March 18, 1945. He later went to Africa as a missionary with the Eastern Mennonite Board of Missions and Charities.

Steiner, Clara Eby (1873-1929). Wrote a history of the Mennonite Women's Missionary Society in 1926.

Wentland, Theodore. Retired Mennonite minister who served in the Illinois Mennonite Conference.

Yake, C. F. (1889-1974). Editor of *Youth's Christian Companion*, 1920-1954, and editor of the Herald Summer Bible School Series which appeared first in 1948.

Yoder, John Howard. Author of *The Politics of Jesus* and various other books on war and peace.

Yoder, Jonathan G. Mennonite physician in Goshen, Ind.

Yordy, Richard J. Pastor of St. Jacobs (Ont.) Mennonite Church.

Zook, Ellrose. Formerly executive editor at Mennonite Publishing House.

The Editor

Daniel Hertzler was born on a farm near Elverson, Pa., dropped out of high school after the sophomore year, and spent the next five years farming. He went to Eastern Mennonite College, 1947-52, where he majored in Bible. He was married to Mary Yoder of Streetsboro, Ohio, in July 1952, and came to Mennonite Publishing House at Scottdale in September 1952. The Hertzlers have four children: Dennis, Ronald, Gerald, and Dan Mark.

Some of his assignments at Mennonite Publishing House have included: office editor, *Mennonite Community Magazine*, 1952-53; assistant editor, *Christian Living*, 1954-1960; editor, *Christian Living*, 1960-73; editor, *Children's Uniform Lessons*, 1957-59; editor, *Adult Uniform Lessons*, 1956-71; editor, *Builder*, 1964-71; and editor, *Gospel Herald*, 1973-.

From 1954-55, he studied at Goshen College Biblical Seminary on leave from Mennonite Publishing House and received the BD degree; from 1960-66, he studied religious education at University of Pittsburgh and received the PhD. In 1978-79, he was a special student at Pittsburgh Theological Seminary.

From 1952-54, Hertzler was assistant pastor at Kingview Mennonite Church. He has been a member there throughout his time in Scottdale. He has served as secretary of Allegheny Mennonite Conference Mission Board, a member of the Goshen College Board of Overseers, and acting president of the Mennonite Board of Education. Since 1980, he has been moderator of Allegheny Mennonite Conference.